THE CATHOLIC UNIVERSITY OF AMERICA
CANON LAW STUDIES
Number 45

MATRIMONIAL DISPENSATIONS, POWERS OF BISHOPS, PRIESTS, AND CONFESSORS

A DISSERTATION

Submitted to the Faculty of Canon Law of the Catholic University of America in partial fulfillment of the requirements for the Degree of

DOCTOR OF CANON LAW

BY THE

REV. GERALD MICHAEL O'KEEFFE, J. C. L.
Of the Diocese of Los Angeles and San Diego

THE CATHOLIC UNIVERSITY OF AMERICA
WASHINGTON, D. C.
1927

Nihil Obstat:

✠ THOMAS J. SHAHAN,

Censor Deputatus.

Washingtonii, D. C., die 10 Maii, 1927.

Imprimatur:

✠ MICHAEL J. CURLEY,

Archiepiscopus Baltimorensis.

Baltimorae, die 10 Maii, 1927.

WASHINGTON MONOTYPE COMPOSITION COMPANY
WASHINGTON, D. C.

To The

Right Rev. John J. Cantwell, D.D.

Bishop of the Diocese of Los Angeles and San Diego,

This Work

As a Token of Gratitude,

Is Most Respectfully

Dedicated by the

Author

TABLE OF CONTENTS

PAGE

FOREWORD vii

PART I

HISTORICAL INTRODUCTION

CHAPTER

I. The Reasonableness of the Existence and the Exercise of Dispensatory Power within the Church 1

II. Dispensation, definition and notion 3

III. Historical Survey of the Development, previous to the year 1888, of the Dispensatory Power of Bishops regarding:

Art. I. Public Diriment Impediments 8

Art. II. Occult Diriment Impediments 14

I. Post Matrimonium Contractum 15

II. Ante Matrimonium Contractum 28

Art. III. Impedient Impediments 32

Art. IV. Doubtful Impediments 39

IV. The Church's Legislation from 1888 to 1918 45

PART II

THE NEW LEGISLATION

FOREWORD 53

CHAPTER

V. The Power of Dispensing Granted by the Code to Local Ordinaries in Case of Danger of Death 55

VI. Power of Dispensing Granted by the Code to Priests in Case of Danger of Death 102

Art. I. Powers Granted to Parish Priests 103

Art. II. Powers Granted to Priests 110

Art. III. Powers Granted to Confessors 117

VII. The Obligation of Reporting and Recording Dispensations granted in Cases of Danger of Death 125

VIII. Power of Dispensing conferred by the Code on Local Ordinaries in Case of Urgency 129

IX. The Powers of Priests and Confessors in Cases of Urgency 153

X. Impedient Impediments, the Power of Dispensing 187

XI. Doubtful Impediments, the Power of Dispensing 211

BIBLIOGRAPHY 223

TITULI 229

VITA 233

FOREWORD

The authority and jurisdiction of the Church, centered in the Holy See as its fount and origin, is shared to a greater or less extent by the different degrees of the hierarchy. Many cases are beyond the normal competency of priests and must be referred to the Ordinary; others must be referred by the Ordinary to the Holy See.

Matrimonial impediments constitute part of the general legislation of the Church, with the result that no one, save the Roman Pontiff himself, can dispense from them "jure proprio et nativo." Since he possesses the plenitude of dispensatory power, and can, consequently, dispense in so far as the Church herself can dispense, it seems unnecessary to include a treatment of his powers within the scope of this work, which takes for granted this claim to the plenitude of power: "secundum plenitudinem potestatis de jure possumus super jus dispensare."[1]

The New Code has given very definite teaching on the powers of Bishops and Priests over matrimonial impediments, and it will be of help to every one engaged in the sacred ministry to have at hand a small work in English dealing expressly with this important aspect of their ministerial labors. This dissertation is the result of an attempt to supply this help. It confines its attention to those powers possessed by Bishops and Priests in virtue of the common law, as the time at disposal would not permit any treatment of delegated faculties. The interpretation of the common law is the greater need of the day, and, because of this, it has been chosen as the subject matter of this work.

When death is imminent, and when cases of urgency unexpectedly present themselves, the Church, whose chief concern is the spiritual welfare of her children, suspends her ordinary regulations, and grants the widest powers

[1] Innocent III, C, 4, X, *De concessione praebendae*, III, 8.

over all sorts of cases. The commonest and most familiar example is, of course, the supplied jurisdiction given to every priest to absolve from all sins and censures in the hour of death. Similar provisions are made regarding the matrimonial legislation of the Church. But as these laws are somewhat of an intricate character, and not entirely free from obscurity, it will be necessary for many, and useful for all, to have them arranged and explained. The opportunity of applying them will not arise every day, but when it does occur the circumstances are generally so pressing that an accurate knowledge of one's faculties is clearly desirable if they are to be of any use. Miracula non sunt speranda, and hence it is all important that every priest should be thoroughly cognizant of the laws of the Church which regulate his action in such pressing circumstances, for it is only through a realization of their terms that he can hope to discharge an intelligent ministry. Realizing this necessity, the author has devoted the greater part of this work to a treatment of the faculties bestowed by the Code in danger of death and cases of urgency. Two small chapters on impedient and doubtful impediments have been added, in order to complete the Church's common law on matrimonial dispensations.

When called on a sick call, or when confronted with unexpected perplex cases of urgency, a priest should, under no condition, become perturbed. Let him first endeavor to recall his canon law, and, above all, let him invoke the aid of the Holy Spirit, that, with His Help, he may speak and act correctly; otherwise he may easily blunder so awkwardly that his mistakes are irreparable: "*magna hic prudentia ac circumspectione opus est: unde merito executor hic non tantum humana, sed vel maxime Divina consilia, et auxilia adhibebit, recurrendo ad Patrem luminum, ut eum lumine suo illuminet, quid in casu adeo perplexo agere debeat.*" [2]

---

[2] Benedict XIV, *Institutiones Ecclesiasticae,* II, Inst. Eccles. LXXXVII, n. 66.

PART I

HISTORICAL INTRODUCTION

CHAPTER I

The Reasonableness of the Existence and the Exercise of Dispensatory Power

It is natural that a society, spread over the whole globe and comprising members of the most diverse types living in different climes and under various conditions, cannot apply the law with equal vigor at all times and in all circumstances. In the administration of law prudence demands that particular circumstances be taken into account, burdens apportioned according to individual strength, and general legislation adapted to special needs. For the sake of the common good, or to avoid greater evils, illegal actions may be legitimized afterwards so that they have all their juridical effects; or exemption may have to be granted from a law which it would not be wise to enforce in a particular case. Hence from the earliest times the Church was compelled to mitigate the strictness of her laws. This is appropriately expressed by Abbo of Fleury when he says that one must take into consideration the situation of countries, the character of the times, the frailty of men, and other reasons which of necessity change the laws of different provinces; that the same is true concerning Papal decrees which are of such authority that many judges expect the verdict of the Roman Pontiff; and that in these things utility and equity must prevail, but not the enticing enjoyment of desires.[1]

This is especially true of the Church's marriage laws: "*Ecclesia nihil unquam de matrimoniis statuit, quin respectum habuerit ad statum communitatis, ad conditiones populorum; nec semel suarum ipsa legum praescripta quoad pot-*

[1] *Collectio Canonum*, c. VIII, *M.P.L.*, CXXXIX, 481.

uit, mitigavit, quando ut mitigaret causae justae et graves impulerunt."[2]

The preservation of the sanctity of marriage life, the good of the offspring, and the protection of Catholic parents and offspring against dangers to the faith, necessitated the institution of matrimonial impediments. But the frailty of men, and other varying circumstances, made it impossible for the Church so to frame these laws that their application would not offer serious difficulties calling for exceptions, and, therefore, for the exercise of her dispensatory power. The justification of the Church's action in thus relaxing her marriage laws may well be stated in the following words of St. Thomas: "Contingit autem quandoque quod aliquod praeceptum quod est ad commodum multitudinis ut in pluribus, non est conveniens huic personae vel in hoc casu; quia vel per hoc impediretur aliquid melius, vel etiam induceretur aliquod malum, sicut ex supra dictis patet. Periculosum autem esset ut hoc judicio cujuslibet committeretur nisi forte propter evidens et subitum periculum, ut supra dictum est. Et ideo ille qui habet regere multitudinem, habet potestatem dispensandi in lege humana, quae suae auctoritati innititur, ut scilicet in personis vel in casibus in quibus lex deficit, licentiam tribuat ut praeceptum legis non servetur."[3]

Hence the *raison d'être* for dispensation lies in the nature of prudent administration, which often counsels the adapting of general legislation to the needs of a particular case by way of exception. The divine purpose of the Church, the welfare of souls, obliges her to reconcile, as far as possible, the general interests of the community with the spiritual needs, or even weaknesses, of its individual members.

---

[2] Leo XIII, ep. encycl. *Arcanum,* 10 February 1880, par. 21. *Fontes,* 580.
[3] *Summa Theologica,* I-II, q. XCVII, a. IV.

CHAPTER II

Definition and Notion of Dispensation

Dispensation, in general, may be defined as "an act whereby in a particular case a lawful superior grants relaxation from an existing law." [1]

A *matrimonial dispensation* may be defined as: "a legitimate act of a superior by which the obligation prohibiting marriage, with or without the nullity of the contract, is relaxed in a particular case." [2]

For a better understanding of the term, a more detailed definition may be given: "actus potestatis legitimae quo in casu particulari, aut quoad personam particularem, relaxatur lex in sua vi irritante vel prohibente matrimonium, manente illa vi legis quoad reliqua membra communitatis aut alios casus." [3]

A dispensation, therefore, is the relaxation of a law in a particular case. The law remains in force for the community in general, but its obligation is withdrawn in a particular case, that is, in favor of an individual person, physical or moral, or of a whole community, but for one act only, or for a fixed definite time. The nature of this relaxation is such that a person who is subject to a special marriage regulation made by law and who, as a result, was incapable of contracting marriage, whether lawfully or lawfully and validly at the same time, is freed from this obligation of law so completely that once the dispensation is effectively granted the obligation, which first existed, never revives.[3a]

---

[1] Cf. Canon 80.

[2] Vermeersch-Creusen, *Epitome Juris Canonici,* II, n. 301.

[3] De Smet, *De Sponsalibus et Matrimonio,* II (ed. IV), n. 732.

[3a] Vlaming, *Praelectiones Juris Matrimonii* (ed. III), I, n. 382.

Dispensation differs from *abrogation* and *derogation* inasmuch as these suppress the law totally or in part, whereas a dispensation leaves it still in vigor for all other members of the community; and from *epikeia,* or a favorable interpretation of the purpose of the legislator, which supposes that he did not intend to include a particular case within the scope of his law, whereas by dispensation a superior withdraws from the power of the law a case which otherwise would fall under it.

In order that a dispensation be valid it is necessary that it be given by a competent authority. From the very nature of things it is evident that only the legislator, his successor, and superior can, of their own inherent right, dispense from a law, and that any faculties possessed by others are simply the result of their concession.[4]

The position of the legislator himself, his superior, or his successor, calls for no remark: "ubi sola voluntaria constitutio est causa quare aliquid prohibetur, per consequens sola voluntas contraria causa erit quare prohibitio relaxetur..... Ejus enim est destruere et interpretari jus, qui illud condidit." [5]

Since matrimonial impediments and the form of marriage are established by general laws of the Church, no one except the Roman Pontiff can dispense from them *jure proprio et nativo.* His subordinates can do so only in the measure that he permits: "lex superioris per inferiorem tolli non potest."[6] This communication of power by the superior to his subordinates can be made either by personal act or through the medium of the law. The concession too may be explicit or implicit, general or for a particular case or cases. If the communication of the power of dispensing is made to an inferior by reason of an office which he holds, his

---

[4] Canons 80, 1041.

[5] Innocent IV, apud Brys, *De Dispensatione in Jure Canonico,* p. 191.

[6] C. 2, *de electione et electi potestate,* I, 3, in Clem. Cf. canon 81.

power, though derived, is ordinary; if it is only given by way of personal communication, it is known as delegated power.[7]

A just cause is required before a dispensation can be granted lawfully and, at times, validly. The legislator himself is not bound, under pain of invalidity, to the existence of a just cause: "obligationis vinculum pendet a legislatoris voluntate; quare cessante voluntate, cessat ipsa obligatio, utpote effectus ejusdem; nam voluntas legislatoris est causa obligationis, haec vero effectus ex ea profluens. Proinde si cessat causa, cessat eo ipso etiam effectus." [8]

But a just cause is always required for the lawful granting of a dispensation, even on the part of the legislator.[9] A dispensation is a *vulnus legis,* and some justifying reason is necessary to compensate for the infliction of such a wound: "si pro sua voluntate licentiam tribuit, non est fidelis in dispensatione." [10] An inferior, however, is bound to the existence of a just cause, not only for the liceity of the dispensation, but also for its validity.[11]

From this it follows that the Roman Pontiff alone can validly dispense without a just cause from matrimonial impediments of the ecclesiastical law, and from the form to be observed in marriage. Regarding the impedient impediments arising from the five simple vows of virginity, celibacy, of receiving sacred orders, of embracing the religious state, and of perfect chastity,[12] if he dispenses from the vows themselves, even the Roman Pontiff is subject, under pain of the invalidity of the dispensation, to the existence of a just cause. The same is to be said of a dis-

[7] Canon 197, par. 1.

[8] Cappello, *De Sacramentis,* III, n. 217; Cf. canon 84.

[9] "Ad liceitatem requiri justam causam, etiam apud R. Pontificem, omnes admittunt," Brys, *De Dispensatione in Jure Canonico,* p. 192.

[10] St. Thomas, *Summa Theologica,* I–II, q. 97, a. 4, in corp.

[11] Canon 84, par. 1; Cf. *Conc Trid.* sess. XXV, de Ref., c. 18.

[12] Canon 1058, par. 1.

pensation granted from a matrimonium ratum sed non consummatum.[13] These belong to the divine law, and, therefore, to the law of a superior from which he cannot validly dispense,—or rather *declare* the cessation of the vow, or the breaking of the bond, for his action is not strictly speaking a dispensation—without a just cause.[14]

Bishops, priests, and confessors cannot, however, validly exercise the faculties committed to them by common law or by personal commission unless a just cause for dispensing is present,[15] for the impediments and form of marriage are part of the Church's general legislation, and, consequently, belong to the law of their superior. Hence these three classes of persons, in exercising the faculties conferred on them by common law, are bound, under pain of an invalid exercise of their power, to the existence of the causes demanded by that law, as in canons 1043 and 1045. If they dispense by virtue of delegated powers, the valid exercise of these faculties will depend on the existence of one of the canonical causes recognized generally by canonists as sufficient.

Lastly it is required that the law, from which the dispensation is to be granted, be dispensable. There is a twofold class of indispensable impediments. The first class comprises those from which the Church cannot dispense because they belong to the divine law, either natural or positive. These are 1°, the bond arising from a consummated marriage between faithful;[16] 2°, certain impotency;[17] 3°, consanguinity in the first degree of the direct line.[18] The second class is comprised of those impediments which *doubtfully* belong to the natural or divine law, and from which, consequently, the Church cannot dispense because

[13] Canon 1119.
[14] Cf. Brys, *o. c.*, pp. 191, 192.
[15] Canon 84, par. 1.
[16] Canons 1069, 1118.
[17] Canon 1068, pars. 1, 2.
[18] Canon 1076, par. 3.

of the certain danger which would be otherwise incurred. Such are 1°, all grades of consanguinity in the direct line exceeding the first; 2°, the first degree in the collateral line.[19]

The form of marriage and all impediments of the ecclesiastical law are, absolutely speaking, dispensable, but the Church de facto does not dispense from all of them. From some she never dispenses, from others she is not wont to dispense, and from still others she dispenses for just and reasonable causes. This latter aspect of the dispensability of impediments, and other obstacles to marriage, will be dealt with in their proper place in the following pages of this work, as the necessity for such a treatment will arise.

---

[19] Canon 1076, par. 3; Cf. Cappello, *De Sacramentis,* III, n. 224; Vlaming, *Praelectiones Juris Matrimonii* (ed. III), I, n. 392, 2a.

CHAPTER III

Historical Survey of the Development of the Dispensatory Power of Bishops

It has always been the constant and universal teaching of the Church that Bishops, and all others inferior to the Roman Pontiff, cannot dispense *"jure ordinario et nativo"* from matrimonial impediments, diriment or impedient, because they constitute part of the general law of the Church, and an inferior cannot dispense from the law of a superior:[1] "cum episcopi debent servare canones, non debent facere contra, nisi expresse concedatur." [2] Any powers acquired by Bishops, in the course of time, obtained their legal force from the will of the Supreme Pontiff, either express, tacit, or presumed.

ARTICLE I

Public Diriment Impediments

Until the year 1888 Bishops possessed no power, by common law, to dispense from public diriment impediments. Any attempt to arrogate to themselves such power was

[1] Rigantius, *Commentaria in Regulas, Constitutiones, et Ordinationes Cancellariae Apostolicae*, Reg. XLIX, can. 1; Sanchez, *De Sancto Matrimonii Sacramento*, lib. VIII, dis. VI, n. 14; Reiffenstuel, *Jus Canonicum Universum*, IV, Appendix, *De Dispensatione super Impedimentis Matrimonii*, n. 14; Benedict XIV, *De Synodo Diocesana*, lib. IX, cap. II; Gasparri, *De Matrimonio* (ed. III), I, n. 432; Aichner, *Compendium Juris Ecclesiastici* (ed. VI), p. 621; Van de Burgt, *De Dispensationibus Matrimonialibus* (ed. 1885), p. 132.

[2] Innocent IV, Commentarius, C. 15, X, *de temporibus ordinationum*, I, 11; Cf. Benedict XIV, ep. encycl. *Magnae Nobis*, 29 June 1748, par. 9: "quilibet Episcopus eo jure inferior est, proindeque illius [Romani Pontificis] legibus derogare nequit,"—*Fontes*, 387.

quickly frowned upon, and promptly condemned, by the Church. In the reign of Alexander VIII, the Bishop of Syracuse wrote to Cardinal Corradus that in some dioceses, conterminous with his, certain Bishops were acting on the opinion that, in case of urgent necessity, a Bishop could dispense from public diriment impediments with a view to the contraction of marriage. The writer wished to be informed if it were lawful for him to use this faculty. The Cardinal presented the matter to the Pope, at whose mandate the question was deferred to the Sacred Congregation of the Council.[3] On May 13, 1660, the following doubt was proposed to this Congregation: "An Episcopus in casu urgentissimae necessitatis possit ante contractum matrimonium in impedimento publico dispensare?," and the Sacred Congregation of Cardinals for the Interpretation of the Council of Trent responded "negative."[4] Then the opinion which attributed this power to Bishops was examined, and the censors of the Sacred Congregation of the Inquisition, to whom this examination was committed, issued the following condemnatory decision: "Proposito asserens Episcopum posse dispensare in publico impedimento matrimonii dirimente consanguinitatis pro matrimonio contrahendo, sive in articulo mortis, sive in alia urgentissima necessitate, in qua contrahentes non possint expectare dispensationem sedis apostolicae, est falsa, temeraria, scandalosa, perniciosa, et seditiosa."[5] This decision was confirmed and approved by the Sacred Congregation of the Council on 19 January, 1661.[6a]

These two decisions indeed expressly denied to Bishops the power of dispensing from public diriment impediments before marriage is contracted, and cannot be interpreted as equally denying this power for the convalidation of marriages already invalidly contracted. But an instruc-

[3] Rigantius *o. c.*, reg. XLIX, can. 11.
[4] *Coll. de Prop. Fide*, 399.
[5] *Coll. de Prop. Fide*, 399.
[6a] *Ibid.*

tion of the Holy Office, 8 June, 1756, reconfirms the same doctrine without any limitation whatever: "Quapropter nullam particularis Episcopus adjudicare sibi potest auctoritatem in hujusmodi dirimentibus publicis impedimentis, quaevis urgeat necessitas, valide ac licite dispensandi." [6b]

Particular Councils can also be cited to demonstrate how sternly the Church refused ever to recognize the power of Bishops to dispense from public diriment impediments. An abuse existing in Gaul of certain Bishops usurping such dispensatory power was promptly condemned by local councils. The Council of Tours in 1583 expressly declared the incompetency of Bishops concerning dispensations from the public diriment impediments of consanguinity, affinity, and spiritual relationship: "in quarto consanguinitatis et affinitatis, necnon cognationis spiritualis, prohibitis gradibus supra expressis episcopis non licere declaramus."[7] This declaration was confirmed, at least implicitly, by the Council of Toulouse in 1590.[8] In Germany, the Council of Cologne, in 1536, also insisted on the necessity of obtaining from the Supreme Pontiff faculties to dispense from public impediments; otherwise any dispensation granted by a Bishop would be invalid.[9a]

When Joseph II of Austria and Napoleon I of France prohibited recourse to Rome for dispensations, the Holy See refused to recognize, even in such a difficult situation, the legal capacity of Bishops to dispense.[9b]

In a general meeting of the Bishops and clergy of France it was previously declared that not only did all matrimonial dispensations pertain to the Pope only, but that any attempt by the Government to arrogate to Bishops such power must be opposed.[10] Hence no abuse or custom militated against

[6b] *Coll. de Prop. Fide,* 399.

[7] Tit. IX; *Mansi,* XXXIV, A, p. 819.

[8] Cap. VIII, n. 3; *Mansi,* XXXIV, B, p. 1290.

[9a] Part VII, cap. 46; *Mansi,* XXXII, p. 1268.

[9b] Gasparri, *De Matrimonio* (ed. III), I, n. 434, nota 2.

[10] Benedict XIV, *De Synodo Dioecesana,* lib. IX, cap. II, n. 5.

the constant and insistent teaching of the Church, that Bishops were bereft of all ordinary dispensatory power over public diriment impediments, and the words of Innocent III on a similar matter may well be quoted here to demonstrate the mind of the Church on this matter: "ex tali consuetudine, si qua foret, disrumperetur nervus ecclesiasticae disciplinae, ipsam de consensu fratrum nostrorum duximus irritandam."[11]

During subsequent centuries the Church remained inflexible in her attitude, so much so that as late as 1872 she issued a decision which corroborated her earlier declarations. This decision is embodied in an answer to the following doubt proposed to the Sacred Penitentiary: "utrum Episcopi possint valide dispensare ab impedimentis matrimonium dirimentibus jure ecclesiastico suos subditos junctos matrimonio civili tantum, quando aliquis eorum ita graviter infirmatur, ut in mortis periculo sit et petat matrimonii sacramentum." The answer given was: "quoad impedimenta publica Episcopum nullatenus dispensare posse."[12]

Notwithstanding this stern attitude, however, the Holy See was not oblivious of the spiritual welfare of her children, and often delegated generous faculties to Bishops when the necessities of their respective dioceses called for such additional powers. The rather extensive powers conferred on the Bishops of Freising, in Germany, may be cited as an example of this. On 14 June 1696, Innocent XII granted the following faculties to this Bishop:

1. Dispensandi in tertio et quarto simplici, et mixto tantum cum pauperibus in contrahendis ex uno stipite, in contractis vero cum haereticis conversis, etiam in secundo simplici, et mixto, dummodo nullo modo attingat primum gradum, et in his casibus prolem susceptam declarandi legitimam.

---

[11] C. 5, X, *de consuetudine,* I, 4.

[12] *N. R. T.,* IV, p. 582.

2. Dispensandi super impedimento publicae Honestatis et justitiae ex sponsalibus proveniente.

3. Dispensandi super impedimento criminis neutro tamen conjugum machinante, ac resituendi jus petendi debitum amissum.

4. Dispensandi in impedimentis cognationis spiritualis praeter levantem et levatum.[13]

The concession expressly declared that these faculties were bestowed on him as a delegate of the Holy See, and that the dispensations were not to be granted except with the clause "dummodo mulier rapta non fuerit, et si rapta fuerit in potestate raptoris non existat." The faculty of subdelegating these powers, either totally or partially, to suitable priests laboring in his diocese, was also conceded. These faculties were conferred "ad quadriennium," and were to be exercised only in the city and diocese of Freising. On 24 March 1706, these faculties were renewed "ad quinquennium." Reiffenstuel attributed these powers to all the Bishops of Germany by virtue of the concession of 14 June 1696, which is difficult to reconcile seeing that it is expressly mentioned in the concession itself that these faculties were valid for the city and diocese of Freising only.[14]

The Council of Trent constituted Bishops the executors of all dispensations to be granted outside the Roman Curia.[15]

After the Council of Trent ample faculties of dispensing were conferred on Bishops and apostolic missionaries in remote regions. As instances of this may be cited the faculty received from Pius V, 4 August 1571, by the Bishops of India, and also from Gregory XIII, 25 June 1576;[16] those generally received by the Papal Nuntios of Spain;[17] those

---

[13] Reiffenstuel, *Jus Canonicum Universum,* IV, Appendix, *De Dispensatione super Impedimentis Matrimonii,* n. 22.

[14] *O. c.,* n. 145.

[15] Sess. XXII, c. 5, de Refor: *Mansi,* XXXIII, p. 135.

[16] Rigantius, *Commentaria in Regulas, Constitutiones, et Ordinationes Cancellariae Apostolicae,* reg. XIV, n. 51.

[17] De Justis, *De Dispensationibus Matrimonialibus,* lib. II, cap. II, n. 172.

generally received from the Congregation of the Inquisition by the Archbishops, Bishops, and Vicars Apostolic of Ireland;[18] those powers conferred on missionaries in Germany, Poland, Flanders, and other places occupied by heretics, and where there were no resident Bishops.[19]

Many special faculties of this kind were conferred on Bishops and missionaries in all parts of the world during the sixteenth and seventeenth centuries, when, to provide for the growing necessities of the times, still more extensive powers were communicated through the "*quinquennial*" and "*triennial*" faculties for the external and internal forums respectively.[20] As the treatment of delegated faculties does not enter directly into the scope of this work, suffice it to say here that standardized formulas of these "quinquennial" and "triennial" faculties appeared before the time of Urban VIII (1623–1644), for a special Commission of Cardinals was set up by this Pontiff for the purpose of reformulating these faculties.[21] It took almost three years to complete the work of revising the old formulas and of adopting new ones. The Commission decided to adopt certain general regulations to be followed in the granting of faculties; new general faculties were composed which, according to these general regulations, could be expedited easily for the various parts of the world.[22]

Mention of the various instances of delegated powers, and of the permanent standardized formulas of faculties, has been made only to show the mind of the Church regarding the claims of Bishops, from various parts of the world, of ordinary power over public diriment impediments. She sternly and promptly condemned any abuse whereby such ordinary power was claimed on the plea of urgent necessity,

[18] Rigantius, *o. c.*, n. 78

[19] Pignatelli, *Consultationes Canonicae*, IV. Consult. XXXIV, n. 59.

[20] Wernz, *Jus Decretalium* (ed. 1904), IV, n. 610.

[21] *Praefatio Emi. D. Card. de Cremona in For. Fac.*, 1637, *Coll. de Prop. Fide*, 88; Cf. Benedict XIV, *Apostolicum Ministerium*, n. 11, *Fontes*. 425.

[22] *Praefatio R. D. Francisi Ingoli in For. Fac., Coll. de Prop. Fide,* 89.

and supplied the needs of the times by recourse to delegation. The Congregation of the Council, 19 April 1692, reiterated the past condemnatory declarations of the Holy See on any attempt made by Bishops to arrogate to themselves such powers.[23] As late as 1872 and 1873 the Sacred Penitentiary[24] and Holy Office[25] reaffirmed the incompetency of Bishops to dispense from public diriment impediments, even in urgent necessity, without special delegation. It was not until 20 February 1888, as will be shown in a subsequent chapter, that Bishops were endowed by a general concession with such powers for the danger of death.[26] Previous to that year, notwithstanding the delegation of such extensive powers, those inferior to the Roman Pontiff possessed no power, by common law, over public diriment impediments.

ARTICLE II

Occult Diriment Impediments

It has been established in the preceding article that ordinarily, or by common law, Bishops or any others inferior to the Roman Pontiff could not dispense from diriment impediments, whether public or occult, since they were introduced by a decree of the Supreme Pontiff or General Council, from which a Bishop, or any other inferior, could not *ordinarily* dispense. However a Bishop possessed this power *extraordinarily,* that is, in cases of great and urgent necessity. Given certain conditions, Doctors taught, *as certain doctrine,* that Bishops could dispense from occult diriment impediments, not only *"ad matrimonium contra-*

---

[23] Ad. III, Pallottini, *Collectio omnium Conclusionum et Resolutionum quae in Causis propositis apud Sacram Congregationem Cardinalium S. Concilii Tridentini Interpretum,* VII, p. 471.

[24] *N. R. T.,* XIV, p. 582.

[25] *N. R. T.,* XIV, p. 528.

[26] *Coll. de Prop. Fide,* 1685.

hendum," but also "*ad matrimonium convalidandum,*" but only for the internal forum.

Post Matrimonium Contractum

It has been the common and certain teaching of Theologians and Canonists that if six conditions were present simultaneously, Bishops could dispense from diriment impediments.[1] These conditions may be given as enumerated by Benedict XIV: 1. That the marriage was already contracted "*in facie ecclesiae*" with all the requisite solemnities; 2. That it was contracted in "*good faith,*" in ignorance whether of law or of fact; 3. That the marriage was consummated; 4. That the impediment was occult; 5. That the Holy See could not easily be approached, or that a dispensation could not be obtained from the Pope without great difficulty, because of the poverty of the parties, of distance from Rome, or other similar reasons; 6. That a separation of the parties could not be effected without scandal to others.[2] If any of these necessary conditions were not verified, Canonists refused to recognize the Bishop's competency to dispense. It must be noted that even in the concurrent presence of these six conditions the Bishop's power was restricted to the forum of conscience, and by no means extended to the external form.[3]

It is indeed true that no legal document actually conferring this power is available. The Doctors, however, did not seek the origin of this power in the expressed will of

---

[1] Reiffenstuel, *Jus Canonicum Universum,* IV, Appendix, *De Dispensatione super Impedimentis Matrimonii,* n. 15; Pyrrhus Corradus, *Praxis Dispensationum Apostolicarum,* lib. VIII, cap. IV, n. 35; Van de Burgt, *De Dispensationibus Matrimonialibus,* p. 132; De Becker, *De Sponsalibus et Matrimonio* (ed. 11), p. 304; Aichner, *Compendium Juris Ecclesiasticae* (ed. VI), p. 623; Dens, *De Sponsalibus et Matrimonio,* p. 385; Wernz, *Jus Decretalium,* IV (ed. 1904), n. 618; Gasparri, *De Matrimonio* (ed. III), 1, n. 440; Feije, *De Impedimentis et Dispensationibus Matrimonialibus* (ed. III), n. 633.

[2] *De Synodo Diocesana,* lib. IX, cap. II, n. 1.

[3] Cf. Van de Burgt, *l. c.*

the Supreme Pontiff or any General Council, but taught unanimously that the legal source of this faculty was to be found in the tacit, and not merely interpretative, consent of the Pope. It was maintained that Bishops had exercised these powers, within the delineated limits, for a very long time, and that this immemorial custom, *"optima legum interpres,"* prescribed against the law, and conferred the necessary jurisdiction. That custom was a true source of power cannot be doubted. In Roman Law custom was recognized as a source of law.[4] Canon Law also recognized custom, from early times, as a source of power: "Innocentius IV et Hostiensis, et alii post eos, alium adhuc fontem potestatis dispensandi in certis legibus generalibus ecclesiae agnoscunt, *consuetudinem* nempe *legitime praescriptam.*"[5]

As to the existence of the custom there can be no doubt, for all the Doctors testified to it: "constat autem, Doctores talem potestatem passim Episcopis tribuisse, et istos illam ab immemorabili exercuisse sciente et non contradicente Pontifice."[6]

Canonists, however, were not content to rely merely on custom as a justification for their common and certain teaching, but gave, as the ultimate legal source, the tacit consent of the Supreme Pontiff who, knowing that these powers were being exercised, did not condemn their use but rather tacitly approved of it.[7]

The main reason for the attribution of these powers to Bishops was founded on the pastoral care of souls. The pastoral office of a Bishop seemed to demand this power if he were to help fully souls constituted in such grave and

---

[4] I, i, 2, 9; "ex non scripto, jus venit quod usus comprobavit. Nam diuturni mores consensu utentium comprobati legem imitantur." Cf. D. 1, 3, 33.

[5] Brys, *De Dispensatione in Jure Canonico,* p. 250, who quotes Innocent IV, *Commentarius* ad c. 15, X, *de temporibus ordinationum,* 1, 11, and Hostiensis, *Lectura,* ad c. 28, X, *de praebendis,* III, 5; Cf. Holy Office, 8 June 1756, *Coll. de Prop. Fide,* 399.

[6] Giovine, *De Dispensationibus Matrimonialibus,* I, consult. CCCXXXIV, n. 1; Cf. Ojetti, *Synopsis Rerum Moralium et Juris Pontificii,* n. 2372, d.

[7] Reiffenstuel, *o. c.,* n. 16, "qui tacet consentire videtur."

urgent necessity. If he could not dispense there was no other remedy in such extraordinary circumstances, and thus the sheep committed to his care would remain exposed to very grave danger of scandal, sin, and defamation, which is repugnant to a pastoral government of the Church, whose concern is, not for the destruction, but for the sanctification of souls.[8] Realizing this truth, authors commonly attributed dispensatory power to Bishops for urgent necessity; nay some authors openly and freely ascribed this power to Bishops as tacitly conceded by the Pope for the common good of souls. If this doctrine were wrong it could have been easily contradicted and condemned; nay it should have been condemned since it involved the validity of a sacrament.

Research has failed to discover the author who first attributed these powers to Bishops, or the exact time at which the custom of so dispensing began. Villien[9] falsely upholds Sanchez as the first Canonist to propound this doctrine. He inverts the order of that author's writing by claiming that Sanchez first propounded the theory attributing dispensatory power to Bishops for the revalidation of invalid marriages, and then extended his doctrine to its logical limits by defending the same opinion regarding marriages to be contracted. This is not so, as will be shown in the following article. Sanchez was indeed the first Canonist to vindicate to Bishops power over occult diriment impediments in urgent necessity, when there was question of marriages to be contracted, but Sanchez himself testifies that, regarding the convalidation of marriages, both opinions were held at the time of his writing, but that to him the doctrine attributing such power to Bishops appeared the better teaching ("multo verior").[10] All other authors are satisfied with the statement that Bishops exercised this

---

[8] Reiffenstuel, *o. c.*, n. 15.

[9] *Le Canoniste Contemporain,* XXVI, pp. 544, 545.

[10] *De Sancto Matrimonii Sacramento,* lib. II, dis. XL, n. 3; Cf. lib. II, dis. XL, n. 8.

power for a long time. Giovine[11] tells us that at one time the question was greatly discussed, but that in the course of time the affirmative opinion obtained the unanimous consent of the Doctors. Pyrrhus Corradus[12] quoted the affirmative opinion as the common teaching of his time. Even Fagnanus[13] put aside his cloak of strictness in this instance, and willingly subscribed to the common opinion, and added, moreover, additional justification to his contention by quoting a decision of the Sacred Rota which expressly ratified the doctrine that a Bishop, in case of great utility and necessity, could dispense from the canons: "Episcopus ex magna causa utilitatis et necessitatis dispensare possit contra canones, etiam concilii, salvis octo infracriptis declarationibus." The eight declarations, to which the decision referred, are given by Fagnanus in the subsequent numbers: 1. That the urgent necessity be new, and one unforeseen by the Council; 2. That the Superior could not be approached; 3. That there be danger in delay; 4. That the Bishop should proceed as one dispensing in a particular case, and not as one abrogating a statute; 5. That the marriage was publicly contracted; that the impediment was occult, and that separation of the parties could not be effected without grave scandal; 6. That the dispensation be granted for the forum of conscience only; 7. That the parties had contracted marriage in good faith, with probable ignorance of the impediment; otherwise they were unworthy of a dispensation; 8. That recourse should be made to Rome by those dispensed for a new dispensation as soon as they conveniently could.[14] Fagnanus concluded that when all these conditions concurred, a Bishop could dispense, for "non est credendum

[11] *O. c.*, consult. CCCXXXIV, n. 1: "gravissima olim hac in re agitata est controversia."

[12] *Praxis Dispensationum Apostolicarum*, lib. VIII, cap. IV, n. 35.

[13] Lib. 1, Decret. cap. *"Nimis" De Filiis Presby.*, n. 24; cap. *"Canonum Statuta," de Constit.*, n. 122.

[14] *Ibid.*

canonis conditorem fuisse crudelem, et salutem omnium despicere voluisse."[15]

Hence there can be no doubt that the teaching of the older Canonists attributing the power of dispensing to Bishops, under the given conditions, was a common and certain doctrine, and that the custom, to which this teaching appealed as the source of this power, actually existed. It can be said with certainty that this custom did not date back beyond the twelfth century. It is practically the unanimous teaching of authors that the Church did not begin to exercise her power of dispensing from matrimonial impediments until the first half of the eleventh century.[16] Hence it is scarcely conceivable that the custom, under discussion, could have already existed so universally as to constitute a source of power before the beginning of the twelfth century. Villien[17] tells us that the custom existed towards the end of the sixteenth century, less than fifty years after the Council of Trent. He maintains that the existence of this custom was one of the practical consequences of the distinction drawn between public and occult impediments, which became gradually more prominent after the teaching of the Council of Trent.[18]

This opinion of Villien is clearly borne out by a decision of the Congregation of the Council, 19 April 1692, which recognized the power of a Bishop to dispense, for the forum of conscience, from impediments that were not publicly known.[19] But the explicit and official confirmation of this

---

[15] Lib. 1, Decret, cap. "*Nimis,*" *de Filiis Presby.*, n. 42.

[16] Rigantius, *o. c.*, IV, reg. XLIX, n. 5; Lupus, *Synodorum Generalium ac Provincialium Decreta et Canones*, IV, p. 189; Gasparri, *De Matrimonio* (ed. III), I, n. 321; Wernz, *Jus Decretalium* (ed. 1904), IV, n. 610; De Becker, *De Sponsalibus et Matrimonio* (ed. II), p. 290; Thomassinus, *Vetus et Nova Ecclesiae Disciplina*, lib. III, part II, c. XXIX, n. 10; Stiegler, *Dispensation Dispensationswesen und Dispensationsrecht im Kirshenrecht*, I, p. 287; Brys, *o. c.*, p. 16; Heiss, *o. c.*, p. 187.

[17] *L'Empechement de Marriage. Sa Notion Juridique dans L'Histoire*, in *Le Canoniste Contemporain*, XXVI, pp. 544, 545.

[18] Cf. Sess. XXIV, de Refor. Mat., cc. 4, 5, 6.

[19] Ad nn. 3, 4, 5, 6, *Pallottini*, VII, p. 471.

opinion came on 3 August 1873, when the Holy Office put its official seal on the teaching of Canonists on this matter: "Caeterum, relate ad facultatem Ordinariorum dispensandi super impedimentis dirimentibus certo existentibus in vim praesumptae voluntatis S. Sedis, res est multis implexa difficultatibus, quibus obviandis omnino adhaerendum est doctrinae traditae a S. M. Benedicto XIV, in suo opere *'De Synodo Dioecesana,'* lib IX, cap. VIII, quam etiam Sacra haec Congregatio tenet, citra quam facile nimis abusus, ideoque etiam nullitas dispensationis evenire potest."[20] As has already been shown, Benedict XIV taught, as unanimous and certain doctrine, that Bishops had power to dispense when the six conditions, enumerated by him, concurred, adding, however, that if one of these conditions were not verified, a Bishop could not claim power on the presumed will of the Pontiff. The Holy Office not only sanctioned this doctrine of Canonists, as propounded by Benedict XIV, but gave it its official seal, so that it can be said to be the teaching of the Church from 1873 on. There is, however, a little discrepancy in the decision as given above, evidently due to a misprint or some other slight error, as it is in the second chapter, and not in the eighth, that Benedict XIV set forth the teaching in question.

In verifying the concurrence of the six necessary conditions the first most necessary investigation was that of determining whether the impediment in the case were occult or not: "ante omnia distinguatur impedimentum publicum ab occulto."[21] As to the extension of the term *occult impediment,* there was not unanimity among the Canonists. All admitted that it embraced impediments that were occult in nature and in fact, as the faculty of the Major Penitentiarius extended to these.[22] But there was not, however,

[20] Apud Planchard, *Dispenses Matrimoniales,* n. 94, and *N. R. T.*, XIV, p. 528; Cf. S. Poenitentiaria, 30 July 1873, *Coll. de Prop. Fide,* 1405.

[21] Feije, *De Impedimentis et Dispensationibus Matrimonialibus* (ed. III), n. 633, a; Cf. Ojetti, *o. c.*, n. 2372.

[22] Benedict XIV, *o. c.*, lib. IX, cap. 11, nn. 1 ff.

absolute agreement as to how many an impediment could be known before it would cease to be occult in fact. Benedict XIV, summing up the opinions of those who were intimately connected with the Sacred Penitentiary, and who, consequently, were in a position to know how far an impediment should be considered occult, embraced the view that an impediment was still occult when it was not known to more than five or six prudent and discreet persons in a town, or to more than eight or nine in a city, so that there was no danger of immediate divulgation: "res adhuc est occulta, si in oppido est nota quinque, aut sex personis, in civitate vero septem, aut octo, adhuc occulta censeri debet, modo scilicet ab aliis non fuerit divulgata."[23a]

When, however, the impediment was of its nature public but *per accidens* occult, or, in other words, when it was public in nature but occult in fact, there was not agreement among the authors as to whether it fell within the ambit of a Bishop's power to dispense or not. Many of the authors did not treat with this particular aspect of the question. Some denied that the Bishops' power extended to these impediments, on the ground that greater power was not to be attributed to Bishops than to the Major Poenitentiarius.[23b] But the affirmative opinion was defended by many noted Canonists, and grew in authority as time went on, and was undoubtedly a solidly probable opinion during the period immediately preceding the New Code. Sanchez[24] and Reiffenstuel[25] taught, at least indirectly, that such an impediment came within the scope of the Bishop's power.

[23a] *Institutiones Ecclesiasticae*, Inst. Eccles., LXXXVII, n. 45. He summed up the opinions of Fagnanus, Marcus Paulus Leo, P. Thesaurus, Tiburtius Navarrus, and Syrus, of the Franciscan Order.

[23b] Cf. Benedict XIV, *l. c.*; Santi, *Praelectiones Juris Canonici*, lib. IV, Appendix, *de Dispensatione in Impedimentis Matrimonii*, n. 18; Feije, *o. c.*, n. 634, 7.

[24] *O. c.*, lib. 11, dis. XL, n. 11.

[25] *O. c.*, IV, appendix, n. 44; Cf. Giovine, *De Dispensationibus Matrimonialibus*, 1, consult. CCCXXXIV, n. 4.

Pignatelli[26] and De Becker[27] seem to have upheld the same opinion. Gasparri[28] and Wernz[29] expressly embraced it. Feije[30] discussed the question *ex professo,* and, while inclining to the opposite opinion, would not dare to deny the affirmative doctrine, and his conclusion may be taken as voicing the feeling of the time: "non obstantibus gravibus hisce rationibus, non audemus pro praxi negare episcopi potestatem in impedimentis natura sua publicis, sed per accidens occultis, dummodo non extendatur ultra facultates ordinarias Majori Poenitentiario pro iis concessas. . . ." This conclusion was undoubtedly well warranted in the light of a decision of the Sacred Congregation of the Council, 19 April 1696. In a doubt proposed to it as to the dispensatory power of a Bishop in cases of urgency, this Congregation answered: "non posse secluso scandalo . . .; posse autem quatenus impedimentum non sit publice detectum."[31]

Another aspect of "occult impediment" also caused a divergence of opinion among the older Canonists. The question arose as to whether an impediment which was *materialiter* public but *formaliter* occult could be considered an occult impediment, and consequently, as falling under the dispensatory power of Bishops. An impediment was considered materially public but formally occult when the fact from which the impediment arose was publicly known, but it was not known, except to a few discreet persons at most, that an impediment resulted from that fact, as, for instance, if the inhabitants of a town or city knew generally that one of its citizens lived in concubinage with a certain woman, but did not know that from those relations resulted an impediment of affinity opposing marriage with that

[26] *Consultationes Canonicae,* consult. XXXIII, n. 8.

[27] *De Sponsalibus et Matrimonio* (ed. 11), p. 304.

[28] *O. c.,* 1, n. 440; Cf. Marc, *Institutiones Morales Alphonsianae,* 11, n. 2046.

[29] *Jus Decretalium,* IV (1904), p. 890, nota 79.

[30] *O. c.,* n. 634, 7; Cf. Wernz, *l. c.*

[31] Pollottini, *o. c.,* VII, p. 471.

woman's sister.[32] Benedict XIV[33] declared, and was prepared to confirm his statement by oath, that the Sacred Penitentiary, during all those years in which he was connected with it, always regarded such an impediment as public, always taking cognizance only of the fact whether it was materially public or not, and never even considered its formal occultness. Many authors, however, maintained that such an impediment could be considered occult, at least when considered in its relation to the faculty of the Bishop to dispense in urgent cases.[34] This teaching was undoubtedly confirmed by a decision of the Sacred Congregation of the Council, 29 January 1881.[35] The case decided was one in which the impediment was affinity that was materially public but formally occult. The vota of the two "consultores" and the "animadversiones" of the "defensor vinculi" were in agreement, on the ground that Bishops possessed the faculty of dispensing, by extraordinary power (jure extraordinario, by reason of the tacit concession of the Pope), from such an impediment. The Congregation decided that the marriage, contracted after a dispensation had been given from such an impediment, in case of urgency, was not proven to be invalid: "non constare de matrimonii nullitate." Of course this decision was not an official approbation of the teaching of Canonists, but since the decision did not establish the nullity of the marriage in the case, it added a little weight to this teaching, especially since the consultores appealed, in their vota, to the above opinion as taught by various Canonists.

The defenders of the view that occult impediments included those public by nature, and those materially public, provided they were de facto occult in both cases, were not in agreement as to whether a new dispensation was neces-

---

[32] Van de Burgt, *De Dispensationibus Matrimonialibus*, p. 8, c.

[33] *Institutiones Ecclesiasticae*, Inst. Eccles. LXXXVII, n. 48.

[34] Gasparri, *o. c.*, I, n. 442; Van de Burgt, *o. c.*, p. 8, c; Cf. Feije, *l. c.*; Wernz, *l. c.*

[35] *A. S. S.*, XIV, pp. 155–165.

sary for the external forum should the impediment afterwards become public. Reiffenstuel,[36] Benedict XIV,[37] and Wernz[38] maintained the affirmative opinion, while Gasparri[39] inclined to the opposite opinion and maintained that such a dispensation should be obtained for the external forum "potius ob convenientiam vel majorem firmitatem, quam ob strictam necessitatem." Pontius[40] and Ojetti[41] taught, without reservation, what Gasparri suggested.

The second very important condition insisted on by Canonists was that the marriage should have been contracted *in good faith.* Reiffenstuel[42] interpreted "good faith" as "probable ignorance of the existence of the impediment." Sanchez[43] gave a somewhat wider interpretation: that *bona fides* was not absent even though it proceeded from culpable ignorance. He had recourse to the teaching of the Council of Trent as a proof of his contention: "si quis inter gradus prohibitos *scienter* matrimonium contrahere praesumpserit, separetur, et spe dispensationis consequendae careat."[44] Sanchez argued that when a decree demanded that anything should be done *knowingly* (*scienter*), any ignorance whatever, even *"ignorantia crassa,"* excused, *deceit* (dolus) being necessary to constitute non-compliance with the behest; that the word *"praesumpserit"* also implied *"deceit"* or "temerity." Sanchez concluded that "good faith" was absent only when the ignorance was so crass as to amount to excessive temerity (*"ingens temeritas"*), for then it was equivalent to *deceit.*

If both parties had contracted marriage in bad faith a Bishop could not dispense without special delegated power,

[36] *O. c.*, n. 45; Cf. Van de Burgt, *o. c.*, p. 135.
[37] *De Synodo Dioecesana,* lib. IX, cap. 11, n. 1.
[38] *Jus Decretalium,* IV, p. 890, nota 79.
[39] *O. c.*, 1, n. 441.
[40] *De Sacramento Matrimonii,* lib. VIII, dis. XIII, n. 5.
[41] *Synopsis Rerum Moralium et Juris Pontificii,* n. 2373.
[42] *O. c.*, n. 57; "cum probabili ignorantia obsistentis impedimenti."
[43] *O. c.*, lib. 11, dis. XL, n. 4.
[44] Sess. XXIV, *De Ref. Mat.*, cap. V; *Mansi, XXXIII,* p. 154.

for whatever power he possessed was derived from the tacit or presumed consent of the Supreme Pontiff, whose benign consent could not be presumed against the express will of the Council of Trent, as manifested in the above quotation.[45]

Hence "bona fides" on the part of one of the parties at least was required. But was it necessary that both parties should have been in good faith when they contracted marriage? It was the certain teaching of Canonists that good faith on the part of one of the contracting parties alone sufficed: "certum est non requiri bonam fidem ex parte utriusque."[46] De Justis maintained that this teaching was doubtful, and accepted the other opinion as more probable. He argued from the words of the Council of Trent, already quoted, and contended that the word "quis" is a generic term comprehending all men and women, and demands that both parties should have been in good faith, otherwise they were to be deprived of even the hope of a dispensation.[47] But against him can be arrayed such men as Sanchez,[48] Reiffenstuel,[49] De Becker,[50] Feije,[51] Van de Burgt,[52] Heiss,[53] Dens,[54] and practically all other authors. Against him can also be quoted a decision of the Sacred Congregation of the Council, 19 April 1692; the question: "an possit [Episcopus dispensare] quando ignorantia impedimenti concurrit in uno tantum contrahentium"? received the answer: "posse autem quatenus impedimentum non sit publice detectum."[55] Nay some authors went so far as to claim that if both

---

[45] Dens, *De Sponsalibus et Matrimonio* (1861), p. 385: "si uterque mala fide contraxerit, *communissime* et *verius* negant auctores Episcopum dispensare posse"; Cf. St. Alphonsus, *Theologia Moralis,* lib. VI, n. 1124.

[46] St. Alphonsus, *o. c.,* lib. VI, n. 1124.

[47] *De Dispensationibus Matrimonialibus,* lib. 11, cap. 11, nn. 137, 138, 139.

[48] *O. c.,* lib. 11, dis. XL, n. 4.

[49] *O. c.,* n. 59.

[50] *O. c.,* p. 304.

[51] *O. c.,* n. 634, 1.

[52] *O. c.,* p. 131.

[53] *De Matrimonio,* p. 196.

[54] *O. c.,* p. 385.

[55] Ad IV; Pallottini, *o. c.,* VII, p. 471.

parties were in good faith a Bishop had no power to dispense, as the parties were to be left in their good faith while a dispensation was being procured from Rome.[56]

The common teaching also demanded, as a very essential condition, that urgent necessity should have been present. They acknowledged that such *was* present when recourse to Rome was difficult, and the parties could not be separated without causing grave scandal, and yet there was danger of incontinency while the Holy See, or one having delegated faculties to dispense, was being approached.[57] The necessity should have been so grave that if the parties could have continued cohabitation without danger of incontinency, or could have been separated without grave scandal, a Bishop was bereft of power to dispense.[58]

Reiffenstuel refused to subscribe to one aspect of the common teaching, namely, that poverty of the parties, when it rendered recourse to the proper authority impossible, or difficult, constituted urgent necessity. From poverty alone, he contended, urgent necessity rarely resulted, since the Sacred Penitentiary, which was the competent authority to grant dispensations for the internal forum, could ask nothing on the occasion of granting such a dispensation, nay, should not accept what was freely offered. It was not necessary, moreover, that a journey should be made to Rome for the dispensation, which could be procured by letter.[59] Fagnanus had already held this opinion defended by Reiffenstuel, and he tells us that Navarrus gloried in being the first to propound the opposite theory, namely, the sufficiency of poverty to constitute urgent necessity, and that some Bishops actually dispensed on that title.[60] Sanchez also defended the affirmative opinion which, on the admission

[56] Feije, *l. c.*

[57] Reiffenstuel, *o. c.*, n. 49; Sanchez, *o. c.*, lib. 11, dis. XL, n. 3; De Becker, *o. c.*, p. 304; Van de Burgt, *De Dispensationibus Matrimonialibus*, p. 132.

[58] Reiffenstuel, *o. c.*, n. 46.

[59] *O. c.*, n. 51.

[60] *Com. in Lib. I, Decret.*, cap. "*Nimis,*" *de Filiis Presbyt.*, n. 27.

of Reiffenstuel himself, one of its great opponents, was the common teaching at his time.[61] Benedict XIV expressly numbered poverty among the causes of urgent necessity.[62]

Another very necessary condition was that the marriage should have been contracted "in facie ecclesiae" with all the requisite solemnities. The reason why the presence of this condition was demanded was founded on the teaching of the Council of Trent: "quod si ignoranter id fecerit, siquidem solemnitates requisitas in contrahendo matrimonio neglexerit, eis subjiciatur poenis [i. e. separetur, et spe dispensationis consequendae careat]."[63] Hence a Bishop could not dispense, where "Tametsi" was in force, if the solemnities had been omitted in the contraction of marriage, because the consent of the Supreme Pontiff could not be presumed if the solemnities had been omitted without a dispensation, or with a dispensation fraudulently obtained, because of the teaching of the Council of Trent and the necessity of good faith as a condition. Moreover, the Roman Pontiffs were not accustomed to dispense, except very rarely, from clandestinity, and hence the consent of the supreme Pontiff could not be presumed if the solemnities had been omitted.[64] If, however, the solemnities had been omitted with the permission of, or after having obtained a dispensation from, the Ordinary, the parties were not subject to the penalties imposed by the Council of Trent, and, therefore, a Bishop could dispense if the other necessary conditions were present.[65]

Benedict XIV and other Canonists demanded that the marriage should have been consummated.[66] Many other Canonists, however, made no mention of this condition, either because they did not regard it as necessary, or, pre-

---

[61] *O. c.*, lib. 11, dis. XL, n. 3.
[62] *De Synodo Dioecesana*, lib. IX, cap. 11, n. 1.
[63] Sess. XXIV, *de Refor. Mat.*, cap. V, *Mansi*, XXXIII, p. 154.
[64] Giovine, *De Dispensationibus Matrimonialibus*, 1, consult. CCCXXXIV, n. 4.
[65] Sanchez, *o. c.*, lib. 11, dis. XL, n. 4.
[66] *O. c.*, lib. IX, cap. 11, n. 1 ff; Cf. Heiss, *De Matrimonio*, p. 196.

sumably, because, in practice, consummation of marriage was to be presumed.[67] It seems certain that in later years, especially in the days immediately preceding the new codification, the presence of this condition was not required: "quibus conditionibus aliqui addunt (sed hodie minus recte), debere matrimonium esse consummatum."[68]

It was absolutely necessary that the six conditions, which have been treated above, should have been present simultaneously in every particular case before a Bishop was empowered to dispense in virtue of custom. In the absence of any one of them he could not dispense without delegated faculties, not even in very urgent necessity.

It must also be noted that the power of dispensing was valid only for the internal forum,[69] and only for those impediments from which the Holy See was accustomed to dispense.[70]

Lastly the power was regarded as ordinary or quasi-ordinary and, consequently, as capable of being delegated to the Vicar General and other suitable priests.[71]

So far this work has considered the dispensatory power of Bishops, in urgent necessity, only in reference to the revalidation of invalid marriages.

Ante Matrimonium Contractum

It was also the common teaching of Theologians and Canonists that Bishops could dispense, "ad contrahendum," in urgent necessity, from diriment impediments of the ecclesiastical law, provided the following conditions were concurrently present:

[67] Cf. Giovine, *o. c.*, I, CCCXXXIV, n. 4; Feije, *o. c.*, n. 634, 5.

[68] De Becker, *De Sponsalibus et Matrimonio* (ed. 11), pp. 304, 305; Cf. Feije, *l. c.*: "hanc conditionem (hodie) non esse necessariam, patet ex doctrina jamdiu vere communi de matrimonio contrahendo."

[69] Van de Burgt, *De Dispensationibus Matrimonialibus*, p. 132.

[70] Feije, *o. c.*, n. 634, 6, who, for this reason, excluded clandestinity from this power.

[71] Reiffenstuel, *o. c.*, n. 32; Wernz, *Jus Decretalium*, IV, n. 618; Sanchez, *o. c.*, lib. 11, dis. XL, n. 14; Gasparri, *o. c.*, I, n. 435.

1. That the impediment was occult, and one from which the Pope was accustomed to dispense;

2. That there was urgent necessity;

3. That a dispensation could not be received from the Holy See, or one with the requisite delegated power, without difficulty.

This doctrine, in the course of time, became the common and morally certain teaching of Canonists, who founded their contention on the presumed, or, at least, interpretative, consent of the Supreme Pontiff,[1] but it never received the explicit approbation of the Holy See.[2]

All authors agreed in maintaining that this power of dispensing was valid only for the internal forum.

The authors enunciated two *principal* cases of urgency: 1. If a person were in danger of death and wished to contract marriage with his or her concubine, in order to legitimate offspring or to repair injury, and recourse to Rome for a dispensation was difficult; 2. If all preparations had been made for the marriage which could not be postponed, until such time as the necessary dispensation was procured, without grave danger of scandal or defamation.[3]

The first very important condition demanded was that the impediment should have been occult. As has already been shown in Article I, Bishops were bereft of all dispensatory power over public impediments, even in very urgent necessity. All that has already been said regarding the various questions arising from the term "occult impedi-

---

[1] Reiffenstuel, *Jus Canonicum Universum,* IV, Appendix, *De Dispensatione super Impedimentis Matrimonii,* n. 63; Benedict XIV, *De Synodo Dioecesana,* lib. IX, cap. 11, n. 2; Gasparri, *De Matrimonio* (ed. 111), 1, n. 442; Santi, *Praelectiones Juris Matrimonii,* IV, Appendix, *De Dispensatione in Impedimentis Matrimonii,* n. 11, Wernz, *Jus Decretalium,* IV, n. 619; Aichner, *Compendium Juris Ecclesiastici* (ed. VI), p. 623; Van de Burgt, *De Dispensationibus Matrimonialibus,* p. 132; Dens, *De Sponsalibus et Matrimonio,* p. 387; Scavini, *Theologia Moralis,* 111, lib. 111, tract XII, dis. 3, cap. 2.

[2] De Becker, *De Sponsalibus et Matrimonio* (ed. 11), p. 305.

[3] Sanchez, *l. c.;* Reiffenstuel, *l. c.;* Gasparri, *l. c.;* Feije, *De Impedimentis et Dispensationibus Matrimonialibus* (ed. 111), n. 635.

ment," when dealing with the dispensatory power in its relation to the convalidation of marriages, is to be applied here also. The same application is to be made in the interpretation of the remaining two conditions.

The first to propound the doctrine attributing dispensatory power to Bishops, in these extraordinary circumstances, was Sanchez, who wrote about the year 1592: "et ausim dicere nullius auctoris patrocinio fretus, posse Episcopum dispensare aliquando in impedimento matrimonio dirimenti, antequam matrimonium contrahatur, quando urgentissima necessitas postularet."[4] Having enumerated the most cogent cases of urgent necessity, Sanchez gave as the fundamental reason for his theory the argument that the same reasons were valid for cases of necessity before marriage, as for those occurring after marriage had been contracted. This teaching of Sanchez was accepted as probable by Pignatelli.[5] Pontius accepted it without reservation, and gave as the very evident reason for his view the argument that in such cases of necessity reservation ceased just as for marriages already contracted: "ea necessitate urgente potest inferior in legibus superiorum dispensare."[6] Pontius added, against authors generally, that this doctrine was *taught* before the time of Sanchez by Gabriel Vasquez.

Pyrrhus Corradus,[7] fully endorsing the theory of Sanchez for the same reasons, testified that this teaching was confirmed by Pope Sixtus V. Corradus claimed to have heard of the following incident, on which rests his proof of Sixtus' confirmation, from Lambertus Ursinus, abbreviator of the Major Presidency. The Bishop of Alessandria, having dispensed before marriage in a case of necessity, wrote to the Cardinal who was then Prodatarius of Sixtus V, informing him of his action. The Cardinal, having first consulted the

---

[4] *De Sancto Matrimonii Sacramento,* lib. 11, dix. XL, n. 8.

[5] *Consultationes Canonicae,* IV, consult. LIII, n. 6.

[6] *De Sacramento Matrimonii,* lib. VIII, cap. XIII, n. 6.

[7] *Praxis Dispensationum Apostolicarum,* lib. VIII, cap. IV, n. 40: "qui habet verisimilitudinem pro se habet pro se similitudinem legis."

Pope, informed the Bishop in return that it was lawful to dispense in such a case, and that he acted prudently in such necessity. Corradus, after describing this incident, adds: "ac plures per pluries Episcopos ita practicatum extitisse non ignoramus."[8]

Fagnanus, however, refused to subscribe to this doctrine, going so far as to state that Bishops could not act on this opinion without danger of incurring the excommunication inflicted (Bulla Coenae) for the usurpation of jurisdiction and rights reserved to the Pope.[9] Busembaum also joined in the rejection of the doctrine under discussion.[10] Benedict XIV, strictly speaking, gave no juridical judgment on the theory propounded by Sanchez. On the one hand, from the theological considerations and answers of its adversaries, he seems to have inclined to the opinion of Fagnanus, while, on the other hand, it seems that he did not dare to reject the other opinion. At any rate he testifies that the opinion of Sanchez was the common teaching of his time.[11]

Notwithstanding the opposition of some authors the teaching of Sanchez gradually gained in authority. The opinion prevailed, the practice of dispensing continued, and no Bishop scrupled to dispense in case of urgency and necessity from an occult diriment impediment. As time approached the eventful year of 1918 the doctrine of Sanchez was gaining ground, so much so that Feije[12] termed it the "communis auctorum doctrina," De Becker,[13] "opinio hodie vere communis," Wernz,[14] the "communis sententia doctorum," while Santi[15] gave it the strongest appellation when he said: "ita fert communissima inter Doctores sententia, necnon experientia et longaeva consuetudo Epis-

---

[8] *O. c.*, n. 41.
[9] *Com. in Lib. I*, Decret., cap. "Nimis, *de Filiis Presbyt.*," nn. 34, 35.
[10] *Medulla Theologiae Moralis*, I, p. 635.
[11] *De Synodo Dioecesana*, lib. IX, cap. 11, n. 2.
[12] *O. c.*, n. 636.
[13] *O. c.*, p. 305.
[14] *O. c.*, *IV*, n. 619.
[15] *O. c.*, IV, Appendix, n. 11.

coporum." A decision of the Sacred Penitentiary, 30 July 1873, certainly and, at least, implicitly approved of this doctrine regarding the occult impediment of affinity "ex copula licita."[16]

While it can be said that this doctrine of Sanchez and other authors generally was less certain than the doctrine attributing the power to Bishops for the convalidation of marriages, nevertheless it can be said also that it was the common teaching, and was sufficiently certain to act upon. The juridical status of this doctrine, in so far as it pertained to urgency in danger of death, from 1888 on, will be shown in a subsequent chapter. The doctrine, as a whole, did not, however, become absolutely certain until the promulgation of the New Code.[17]

ARTICLE III

Impedient Impediments

It was just as certain under the old law as it is today that Bishops cannot dispense *"jure proprio et nativo"* from impedient matrimonial impediments, as these also constitute part of the Church's general law. Without the consent of the Roman Pontiff, either expressly or tacitly received, Bishops, and all others inferior to the Roman Pontiff, were bereft of all power to dispense from impedient impediments. Long custom, however, approved by many Popes, amply conferred this power on Bishops.[18] This custom was approved by the Supreme Pontiffs in a manner which recognized the power to dispense as joined to the episcopal office,

---

[16] *Coll. de Prop. Fide,* 1405.

[17] Cf. Wernz, *o. c.,* IV, p. 891, nota 83.

[18] Feije, *De Impedimentis et Dispensationibus Matrimonialibus* (ed. 111), n. 613; Van de Burgt, *De Dispensationibus Matrimonialibus,* p. 134; Aichner, *Compendium Juris Ecclesiastici* (ed. VI), p. 621; De Becker, *De Sponsalibus et Matrimonio* (ed. 11), p. 301.

so that the power was not delegated, but ordinary [1] or quasi-ordinary.[2]

The tacit consent of the Pope extended to those impedient impediments that were not expressly reserved to the Holy See. Because of this reservation it was certain that Bishops could not dispense, in ordinary cases, from the impediment of mixed religion.[3] It was also the practically certain teaching of Canonists that Bishops could not dispense from this impediment even in very urgent necessity: "neque de jure, neque ex consuetudine . . . et ne in casibus quidem extraordinariae necessitatis competere unquam potest Episcopis, aliisque Pontifici inferioribus, auctoritas dispensandi super impedimento mixtae religionis."[4]

Planchard[5] and De Becker[6] maintained that while a

certainly in a timid manner.

Bishop could not dispense from the impediment of mixed religion in ordinary circumstances, nevertheless this power was not to be denied him in cases of urgent necessity. They argued that this opinion was never condemned by the Holy See and that, otherwise, it would be difficult to see how the Church, who is ever solicitous for the welfare of her children, should have excluded this impediment from the very ample faculties of 20 February 1888. But against these two can be arrayed, in full armor, all other authors,[7] who founded their view on two facts, namely, that this impediment could not be considered occult, and, secondly, because the consent of the Supreme Pontiff could not be presumed in such a case, since the Popes themselves frequently refused to grant a dispensation from this impediment.[8] Moreover

---

1 Cf. De Becker, *l. c.*

2 Feije, *l. c.*

3 *Instr. S. C. S. Officii*, 3 Jan. 1871, ad 3, *Coll. de Prop. Fide*, 1362; Cf. De Becker, *o. c.*, p. 280.

4 Giovine, *De Dispensationibus Matrimonialibus*, 1, const. CLXXI.

5 Apud *N. R. T.*, XV, p. 519 ff.

6 *O. c.*, p. 280; but he puts forth this opinion somewhat vaguely and

7 Benedict XIV, *De Synodo Dioecesana*, lib. IX, cap. 111, n. 2; Feije, *o. c.*, n. 613; Giovine, *o. c.*, 1, consult. CLXXI, n. 5; Van de Burgt, *o. c.*, p. 135; Dens, *o. c.*, p. 383; Gasparri, *o. c.*, 1, n. 495.

8 Giovine, *l. c.*

an Instruction of the Holy Office to the Archbishop of Corfu, 3 January 1871, can also be invoked against them.[9] Among other things this Instruction laid down, in clear terms, that no mixed marriage could be contracted without a dispensation from the Holy See, clearly implying that a Bishop could not dispense. The Holy Office certainly intended to include cases of urgent necessity within the limits of this prohibition, for it immediately added that the Pope, Pius IX, to remove any difficulty which may arise, conferred on the Archbishop the faculty of dispensing, *"in forma rescripti,"* for thirty urgent cases.

Moreover no custom could be invoked as a justification for the exercise of such power by any Bishop. The authors rejected the plea of custom,[10] and the Instruction of the Holy Office just quoted brushed aside any recourse to custom: *"qualibet non obstante consuetudine."*

Neither could a Bishop dispense, in ordinary cases, from the impedient impediments resulting from the simple vow of perfect chastity, and the vow of entering a religion with solemn vows, because these vows were reserved to the Holy See. This was the common and certain teaching of Theologians and Canonists.[11] But the power of dispensing was not denied Bishops in cases of urgent necessity. When there was danger of grave scandal, or any other serious evil, and the Holy See could not be approached in time to avert this evil, Canonists generally maintained that a Bishop could dispense from these two impediments, but only for the internal forum. In such circumstances the Bishop exercised quasi-ordinary power, as the consent of the Roman Pontiff could be lawfully presumed in such extraordinary cases.[12] But here too the impediment should have been occult, and hence the doctrine propounded was valid only

---

[9] *Coll. de Prop. Fide,* 1362.

[10] Cf. Benedict XIV, *l. c.;* Giovine, *l. c.*

[11] Reiffenstuel, *o. c.,* IV, Appendix, n. 12; Feije, *o. c.,* n. 613; Dens, *o. c.,* p. 383; Aichner, *o. c.,* p. 621; Giovine, *l. c.*

[12] Reiffenstuel, *o. c.,* n. 13; Feije, *o. c.,* n. 613.

when these two vows were taken privately, and not in any religious Congregation.[13] Moreover the dispensation was valid only for the marriage then contracted, so that the vows continued to bind outside the lawful use of that marriage, and constituted an impediment to any future marriage should the first become dissolved for any reason, as, for instance, by the death of the other spouse.[14]

There can be no doubt that these two simple vows, and no others, were reserved to the Holy See, as Benedict XIV expressly taught this in his encyclical *"Inter Praeteritos,"* 3 December 1749.[15]

Authors likewise excluded from the dispensatory power of Bishops, *in ordinary cases,* the impediment that resulted from sponsalia.[16]

Having established that Bishops could dispense from those impedient impediments that were not reserved, and having enumerated those that were reserved, and shown how far they were dispensable in urgent cases, we deduce at once that they *could* dispense, not merely in urgent cases, but also *in ordinary cases,* from the impediments resulting from the simple vows of celibacy (not-to-marry), of receiving sacred orders, from an imperfect vow of chastity, and the vow not to seek the debitum conjugale. Those vows were not reserved to the supreme authority, because they were not regarded as perfect vows: "vota quae non sunt in suo esse perfecta, non sunt reservata."[17]

It was also the common and certain teaching of Theologians and Canonists that Bishops could dispense *in ordinary cases* from the impediment prohibiting the petitioning or rendering of the debitum conjugale, when this impediment arose from affinity or spiritual relationship contracted

---

[13] Feije, *l. c.*

[14] Feije, *o. c.*, n. 613.

[15] *Fontes,* 404.

[16] Zitelli, *De Dispensationibus Matrimonialibus,* p. 46; Van de Burgt, *o. c.*, p. 134; Feije, *o. c.*, n. 612.

[17] Giovine, *o. c.*, consult. CLV, n. 7; Cf. Aichner, *o. c.*, p. 62.

by one of the parties with the other after marriage.[18] No author questioned this power regarding the impediment of spiritual relationship. Nay Reiffenstuel[19] maintained that the right of seeking the debt was not lost through this impediment. Pyrrhus Corradus[20] expressly questioned the Bishop's power to dispense, in ordine ad debitum conjugale, when the prohibition had resulted from the contraction of affinity after marriage. Mostly all other authors did not place this limitation.[21] Corradus maintained his opinion for the one reason that the prohibition resulted from an impediment (of affinity) from which a Bishop could not ordinarily dispense. He did not, however, deny the title of custom, as put forward by other canonists, to confer on Bishops power to dispense, and admitted that his teaching was opposed to the commonly received doctrine of Canonists: "sequitur nullam habere Episcopum super hoc facultatem, nisi forsan ratione jam praescriptae consuetudinis, quamvis D. D. communiter contrarium tenent."[22]

It was, moreover, the common and certain teaching of Canonists and Theologians that Bishops could dispense, even outside cases of urgency, from the impediment to seeking the conjugal debt when this impediment arose from a vow from which he could dispense. The vow, it was maintained, was the sole cause and source of this impediment, so that when the vow ceased to bind, the consequent prohibition of seeking the debitum conjugale was eo ipso removed: "cessante causa cessat effectus."[23]

---

[18] Sanchez, *o. c.*, lib. VIII, dis. XII, n. 13; Pontius, *De Sacramento Matrimonii,* lib. VIII, cap. XIII, n. 9; Van de Burgt, *o. c.*, p. 135; Reiffenstuel, *o. c.*, n. 565.

[19] *O. c.*, n. 558.

[20] *Praxis Dispensationum Apostolicarum,* lib. VIII, cap. 11, n. 55.

[21] Reiffenstuel, *o. c.*, IV, Appendix, n. 565; Sanchez, *o. c.*, lib. VIII, dis. XII, n. 13; Van de Burgt, *o. c.*, p. 135; Aichner, *o. c.*, p. 621; Benedict XIV, *Institutiones Ecclesiasticae*, Inst. Eccles. LXXXVII, n. 22; Pontius, *o. c.*, lib. VIII, cap. XIII, n. 9: "verius est, inspecta consuetudine, posse Episcopum in ejusmodi impedimentis dispensare."

[22] *O. c.*, n. 60.

[23] Reiffenstuel, *o. c.*, n. 559: "conclusio caret controversia ob evidentem rationem"; Cf. Van de Burgt, *o. c.*, p. 135.

A Bishop could also dispense from all vows of chastity taken after the contraction of marriage, even from those taken unconditionally, provided they had not been elicited with the intention of entering religion, or by mutual consent. This power was not restricted to urgent cases.[24]

Although all vows of perfect chastity taken before marriage were reserved to the Pope, they were not accompanied with such reservation when taken after marriage had been contracted, because they could not then be called perfect vows of chastity, even though elicited perfectly and unconditionally, from the very fact that the party under vow, although forbidden to seek the debt, was nevertheless bound to render it.[25] A Bishop could dispense from the impediment to the seeking of the debt, but he could not dispense from the vows themselves, so that if the marriage was dissolved by the death of the free party, the obligation of observing the vow revived.[26]

If, however, a vow of chastity had been taken unconditionally after marriage had been contracted, but before its consummation, with the intention of entering religion, a Bishop could not dispense, not even in ordine ad debitum petendum vel reddendum, within the first two months after the contraction of marriage.[27] The Bishop's power was here restricted because within the first two months after marriage, if not consummated, the parties were free to enter religion, nay were bound to fulfill the vow, and, consequently, could neither seek or render the debitum conjugale during that period, since the vow still continued to run. The vow remained reserved during that period, but once marriage was consummated, even though this occurred within the first two months, the obligation of the vow ceased, at least during that marriage, and the marriage

---

[24] Reiffenstuel, *o. c.*, IV, Appendix, nn. 559–561; Van de Burgt, *o. c.*, p. 135; Sanchez, *o. c.*, lib. VIII, dis. XI, n. 9 ff.

[25] Reiffenstuel, *l. c.*

[26] Sanchez, *o. c.*, lib. VIII, cap. XII, n. 9.

[27] Reiffenstuel, *o. c.*, n. 560; Sanchez, *o. c.*, lib. VIII, dis. XI, n. 4.

debt could freely and lawfully be asked and rendered.[28] It was the opinion of Reiffenstuel[29] that once marriage had been consummated there was no need of a dispensation, as the parties were at once free to seek and render the debt. Sanchez, however, implied that a dispensation was necessary, but expressly attributed power of dispensing to Bishops, even in circumstances in which the Holy See was within easy approach.[30]

Again, if the parties, after marriage, had mutually agreed or contracted ("per modum mutui contractus aut reciprocae conventionis") to vow abstention from seeking and rendering the marriage debt, a Bishop could not dispense, outside cases of urgency, from this self-imposed obligation. The mutual agreement liberated each party from the obligation of rendering the debt, and, consequently, the vow could and should be observed,[31] as it was a perfect and absolute vow, and thus reserved to the Pope: "quod Deo pari consensu voveratis perseveranter usque in finem reddere debuistis, a quo proposito, si ille lapsus est, tu saltem instantissime persevera."[32] This was the common and practically certain teaching of Theologians and Canonists.[33] A Bishop, however, could dispense from the vow, in so far as it prohibited the licit use of marriage, in urgent necessity, when there was danger of incontinency to either party, and the Holy See could not easily be approached.[34] But even in cases of urgency a Bishop could not dispense from the vow itself absolutely, but only from the impediment to the lawful use of marriage which resulted therefrom, so that the vow

[28] Reiffenstuel, *o. c.*, n. 560; Sanchez, *o. c.*, lib. VIII, dis. 11, n. 4; lib. IX, dis. XXXV, n. 23.

[29] *L. c.*

[30] *O. c.*, lib. VIII, dis. XI, n. 4.

[31] Reiffenstuel, *o. c.*, n. 561; Sanchez, *o. c.*, lib. VIII, dis. XI, n. 10.

[32] C. 4, C, XXXIII, q. 5.

[33] Sanchez, *o. c.*, lib. VIII, dis. XI, n. 10: "quia ex natura rei est quoque reservatum Pontifici in eo ad petendum debitum"; Cf. Reiffenstuel, *l. c.;* Van de Burgt, *l. c.*

[34] Reiffenstuel, *o. c.*, n. 563; Sanchez, *o. c.*, lib. VIII, dis. XI, n. 10; Feije, *o .c.*, n. 613.

revived, and continued to bind, after that marriage had been dissolved.[35]

The more common teaching of Canonists also attributed to Bishops power to dispense, after marriage had been contracted, from the impediment to the lawful use of marriage resulting from a perpetual vow of chastity taken by one of the parties before marriage was contracted. This power was not restricted to cases of urgency.[36] The authors had recourse to custom as the source of this power: "consuetudine, quae jurisdictionem praebet, obtentum est hanc dispensationem Episcoporum esse."[37] Reiffenstuel opined that a Bishop did not possess this power of dispensing if the custom did not run in his diocese.[38] If this custom existed he could dispense.

ARTICLE IV

Doubtful Impediments

The three preceding articles have considered the dispensatory power of Bishops over impediments when they were known with certainty to exist. The whole treatment in these various articles has presupposed this note of certainty. But what if any one of these impediments, diriment or impedient, public or occult, was not known with certainty to exist? Did Bishops or any others possess any power of dispensing?

Authors were not in absolute agreement on the question of the power of a Bishop to dispense from doubtful dispensable matrimonial impediments. This disagreement, it seems, was due to the fact that a different species of cases

[35] Reiffenstuel, *o. c.*, IV, Appendix, n. 560; Sanchez, *o. c.*, lib. VIII, dis. XI, n. 4; lib. IX, dis. XXXV, n. 23.

[36] Reiffenstuel, *o. c.*, n. 564; Sanchez, *o. c.*, lib. VIII, dis. XII, n. 4; Van de Burgt, *o. c.*, n. 134; Feije, *o. c.*, n. 613, who added that the vow continued to bind outside the lawful use of marriage and regarding future marriages.

[37] Sanchez, *o. c.*, lib. VII, dis. XII, n. 4.

[38] *O. c.*, n. 567.

was treated by each division of the disputants. Besides the usual distinction of doubts into those of law and those of fact, some authors seem to have subdistinguished doubts of fact into those in which a strong presumption urged in favor of the existence of the impediment, and those in which no such presumption urged, but the existence of the impediment was simply doubtful in fact. This distinction seems to have been made by Sanchez.[1] He admitted, in the first place, that when the doubt was one of law, provided the opinion in favor of the non-existence of the impediment was truly probable, no dispensation was necessary: "quando res non est vere dubia, sed essent opiniones, quibusdam asserentibus id esse impedimentum, aliis vero negantibus, si opinio negans esset vere probabilis, quamvis affirmans esset probabilior, posset ille sequens opinionem probabilem inire id matrimonium absque ulla dispensatione." In dealing, however, with doubtful impediments, when the doubt was one of fact, he had recourse to the distinction of doubt to which was superadded presumption in favor of the existence of the impediment. He concluded that when it was really doubtful, with a doubt of fact, whether the impediment existed or not, and no presumption urged in favor of its existence, there was no need of a dispensation; a Bishop could declare that no dispensation was necessary, or he could dispense *"ad cautelam,"* but such would not be a real dispensation, so much so that if the existence of the impediment afterwards became certain, a Papal dispensation was necessary, even though the marriage may have been already contracted, "quia nullibi invenio posse Episcopum *vere* dispensare in hoc dubio in impedimentis dirimentibus; sed est quaedam prudentialis declaratio, quam etiam vir prudentialis posset facere." When, however, it was not altogether doubtful whether the impediment existed or not, but there was a strong presump-

---

[1] *De Sancto Matrimonii Sacramento,* lib. VIII, dis. VI, n. 18.

tion in favor of its existence, a dispensation was necessary, and a Bishop could not dispense, at least in ordinary cases.[2]

This distinction made by Sanchez regarding doubts of fact was accepted by many subsequent canonists. Bangen[3] renewed this distinction, and expressly allied himself with Sanchez regarding the distinction and its application to the dispensatory power of Bishops. Other followers of Sanchez may be enumerated in the persons of Giovine,[4] Heiss,[5] Feije,[6] and Aichner.[7]

The other division of Canonists did not so subdistinguish doubts of fact. They simply considered doubtful impediments under two categories, namely, when the doubt was one of law, and when it was one of fact. The more modern authors preceding the New Code especially adhered to this simple distinction.[8]

Both schools admitted that if the doubt was one of law, no dispensation was, strictly speaking, necessary, but that if time permitted the Holy See should be consulted. When the doubt was one of fact, those of the second school of canonists commonly admitted that a dispensation was necessary at least "ad cautelam," but recognized in Bishops the power to dispense, even in cases in which recourse to the Holy See was possible, provided the impediment, about which the doubt existed, was one from which the Holy See was accustomed to dispense: "quod si impedimentum esset dubium, communissima est sententia posse etiam episcopum dispensare."[9] The Church was cognizant of this teaching of

---

[2] *L. c.*

[3] *Instructio Practica de Sponsalibus et Matrimonio*, tit. XX, p. 156.

[4] *De Dispensationibus Matrimonialibus*, consult. CCCXXXVI, n. 1.

[5] *De Matrimonio*, p. 197.

[6] *De Impedimentis et Dispensationibus Matrimonialibus* (ed. III), n. 636.

[7] *Compendium Juris Ecclesiastici* (ed. VI), p. 620.

[8] Dens, *De Sponsalibus et Matrimonio*, p. 390; Van de Burgt, *De Dispensationibus Matrimonialibus*, n. 131; De Becker, *De Sponsalibus et Matrimonio* (ed. II), p. 305, 4°; Gasparri, *De Matrimonio* (ed. III), I, n. 438; Wernz, *Jus Decretalium* (ed. 1904), n. 620.

[9] St. Alphonsus, *Theologia Moralis*, 1, Appendix 2, cap. III, n. 57; Cf. De Becker, *l. c.*; Dens, *l. c.*

Canonists and did not condemn it, and, hence, authors claimed that a Bishop dispensed, in the circumstances, *"cum potestate ordinaria,"* with the tacit consent of the Supreme Pontiff.[10]

As to the exact limits of this dispensatory power of Bishops there was not unanimity among these canonists themselves. It can be stated with certainty that, according to the common teaching, this power extended at least to occult impediments and the internal forum.[11] Some authors restricted the power to these limits and maintained that if the impediment afterwards became certain a new dispensation from the competent authority was necessary.[12] Many other authors, however, made no such restriction, but simply attributed, without qualification, dispensatory power to Bishops.[13] Some canonists went still further and expressly extended the power of Bishops, over doubtful impediments, to the external forum and public impediments, and defended the view that no new dispensation was necessary if the impediment afterwards became certain: "nam potestas illa dispensandi Episcopis tanquam ordinaria communiter ab auctoribus tribuitur in omnibus casibus sive occultis sive publicis."[14] This opinion was defended also by St. Alphonsus[15] and Gasparri.[16]

The Holy Office, being interrogated as to the power of Bishops to dispense from doubtful impediments, gave the following answer, 18 September 1852: "Consulat auctores probatos et in casibus gravioris dubii recurrat ad Sanctam

---

[10] Cf. Dens, *o. c.*, p. 390; Pyrrhus Corradus, *Praxis Dispensationum Apostolicarum*, lib. VIII, cap. IV, n. 66.

[11] Cf. Wernz, *l. c.;* De Smet, *De Sponsalibus et Matrimonio* (ed. 1909), n. 355, 3.

[12] Giovine, *o. c.*, consult. CCCXXXVII, n. 2; Heiss, *o. c.*, p. 197.

[13] Cf. De Becker, *o. c.*, p. 305, 4°; Dens, *o. c.*, p. 390; Van de Burgt, *o. c.*, p. 131; Feije, *o. c.*, n. 636.

[14] Wernz, *o. c.*, IV, n. 620, nota 93.

[15] *Theologia Moralis*, lib. VI, n. 902: "cum reservatio sit odiosa, stricte est interpretanda, et restringenda tantum ad casus certos"; Ojetti, *o. c.*, 11, n. 2372.

[16] *O. c.*, 1, n. 438.

Sedem";[17] but the approved authors recognized the power of Bishops to dispense "ex consuetudine," at least for occult impediments and the internal forum. The response, it will be noted, continues that in the more serious doubts recourse should be made to the Holy See. Perhaps this addition was made in deference to the teaching of the earlier Canonists, and could be interpreted as referring to those doubts in which a strong presumption urged in favor of the existence of the impediment. It is probably from this reasoning that Gasparri[18] wrote that in case such a presumption should exist, the Bishop should abstain from dispensing.

A Canadian Bishop, because of the many difficulties encountered in dealing with doubtful impediments, wrote to the Holy See for faculties to dispense. The Holy Office, 9 December 1874, conferred the desired faculties: "sive impedimentum sit certum, et dubitetur tantum de gradu cognationis, sive dubium versetur circa ipsam impedimenti existentiam. . . . Notandum tamen, in secundo casu, hoc est cum ambigitur de ipsamet impedimenti existentia, dispensationem esse ad cautelam."[19] This response may be taken as an argument against the common teaching of canonists, for if the Bishop had already possessed *ex consuetudine* ordinary power to dispense, why should the Holy See confer delegated power? The authors met this difficulty by maintaining that these faculties were conferred *"ad abundantiam."*[20]

To conclude, it was certain that Bishops possessed power to dispense from doubtful impediments. The very common teaching of theologians and canonists established this power on the ground of custom and the tacit consent of the Supreme Pontiff. All admitted that no dispensation, in the strict sense, was necessary when the doubt was one of law.

[17] Pallottini, *o. c.*, VII, p. 528.

[18] *L. c.*

[19] *Coll. de Prop. Fide,* 1427.

[20] Gasparri, *o. c.*, I, n. 438; Wernz, *o. c.*, IV, n. 620, nota 92; De Becker, *o. c.*, p. 306.

When the doubt was one of fact the earlier authors upheld the view that a Bishop could not dispense when a strong presumption urged in favor of the existence of the impediment; but that if no such presumption existed, a Bishop could dispense, or rather permit the marriage to be celebrated, but a real dispensation would be required if the impediment afterwards became certain.[21] The authors, however, who wrote during the last half century before the New Code, made no such distinction regarding doubts of fact, but simply recognized the power of Bishops to dispense "ad cautelam" in all doubts of fact, without there being any necessity of a new dispensation if the impediment afterwards became certain. But at no time was it fully certain that Bishops could exercise this power over public impediments and in the external forum. Yet the authors who immediately preceded the new codification had little hesitation in maintaining the affirmative opinion, and their opinion was certainly safe in practice. As will be shown later, the New Code settled all difficulties, giving a radical solution in favor of these more modern authors.

---

[21] Cf. Sanchez, *o. c.*, lib. VII, dis. VI, n. 18.

CHAPTER IV

THE CHURCH'S LEGISLATION FROM 1888 TO 1918

The previous chapter, throughout its various articles, has shown that Bishops possessed no ordinary dispensatory power over public impediments when such certainly existed. It has also been shown that their power over occult diriment impediments was circumscribed by many restrictive conditions. The power of Bishops over impedient and doubtful impediments has been shown to have been somewhat more extensive.

The growing increase in the spread of the true Gospel, the gradual diffusion of heresy as a result of the so-called Reformation, the increasing decrease of faith and piety, all pointed to the fact that somewhat extensive powers should be conferred on Bishops, especially over public impediments and for cases of urgency. Hence the Vatican Council (1869–1870) was grasped as an opportunity for requesting the fulfillment of these desires. Petitions were made by Bishops from various parts of the world both for a decrease in the number of impediments and an increase in the Bishop's power to dispense. The Bishops of Germany asked that all Bishops be invested with power to dispense from the impediments of consanguinity and affinity in the third degree.[1] The Archbishops and Bishops of Quebec and Halifax requested for a decrease in the number of matrimonial impediments in the prospective codification of Church Law, or, at least, an extension of the Bishop's power to dispense.[2] The Bishop of Concordia explained how the

[1] Martin, *Omnium Concilii Vaticani Documentorum Collectio,* p. 176.
[2] Martin, *o. c.,* p. 186.

great necessities of the times called for such a concession: "cum enim, praesertim in oppidis, nullum fere contrahi possit matrimonium quin opus sit ejusmodi dispensationibus, timendum est ne quis hisce miserrimis temporibus, in quibus fides et pietas refrigescunt, civile matrimonium contrahere malit, quam a S. Sede praedictas dispensationes petere, atque, ut obtineat, pecuniam solvere."[3]

Not many years were to pass before the Bishops of the world were to receive, at least in part, the fulfillment of their desires. In accordance with the wishes, and by virtue of the mandate, of Leo XIII, the question was proposed to the Holy Office as to the advisability of increasing the power of the Ordinaries of places to enable them to dispense from public diriment impediments for the benefit of those who were joined in civil marriage, or otherwise lived in concubinage, and who, being in danger of death, wished to contract a valid marriage "in facie ecclesiae," and thus obtain peace of conscience. After diligent and careful examination of the question, the Sacred Congregation, with the approbation and confirmation of the Cardinals, on 20 February 1888, conferred the power on local Ordinaries to dispense, in these circumstances, either personally or through another recommendable ecclesiastic, from all public diriment impediments with the exception of those resulting from the order of the Priesthood, and affinity in the direct line "ex copula licita": "Sanctitas sua benigne annuit pro gratia, qua locorum Ordinarii dispensare valeant sive per se, sive per ecclesiasticam personam sibi benevisam, aegrotos in gravissimo mortis periculo constitutos, quando non suppetit tempus recurrendi ad S. Sedem, super impedimentis quantumvis publicis matrimonium jure ecclesiastico dirimentibus, excepto sacro Presbyteratus Ordine, et affinitate lineae rectae ex copula licita proveniente."[4] The Congregation, however, wished that if it were ever necessary to dispense,

---

[3] Martin, *o. c.*, p. 191.

[4] *Coll. de Prop. Fide*, 1685; *Fontes*, 1109.

in these circumstances, a sub-deacon or deacon, or those who had made solemn religious profession, and who, after being dispensed, became well, the Ordinary should notify the Holy Office, and, in the meantime, use every means in his power to remove any scandal which may be given, either by inducing the parties to betake themselves to some place where their ecclesiastical or religious condition was unknown, or, if this were not possible, by imposing salutary penances and a mode of life calculated to repair past excesses.[5]

The Holy Office declared, 17 September 1890, that this faculty of 20 February 1888 was valid only for those who were in very grave danger of death, and who, moreover, had contracted a civil marriage or had otherwise lived in concubinage.[6] On 1 July 1891 it declared that the faculty could be used not only when the impediment directly affected the sick person, but also when the impediment affected the healthy party directly and the sick party only indirectly.[7] The Holy Office further declared that the faculty included also power over occult impediments,[8] and did not exclude clandestinity;[9] but it expressly excluded the impedient impediments, especially that of mixed religion.[10] It was later declared that the faculty included also the power of legitimating offspring, excepting, however, adulterous progeny and the children born of a sacrilegious union, that is, of those who had received major Orders, or had made solemn religious profession.[11]

As has already been shown, local Ordinaries were enabled to dispense, within the prescribed limits, either personally or through another recommendable ecclesiastic. On 9 July 1889, the Holy Office decided that this faculty could be

[5] *L. c.*
[6] *Coll. de Prop. Fide,* 1741.
[7] *Coll. de Prop. Fide,* 1758; *Fontes,* 1139.
[8] 23 April 1890, *Coll. de Prop. Fide,* 1728.
[9] 13 Dec. 1899, *Coll. de Prop. Fide,* 2072.
[10] 18 March 1891, *Coll. de Prop. Fide,* 1750.
[11] 8 July 1903, *Coll. de Prop. Fide,* 2071.

subdelegated for all cases ("habitualiter") to parish priests (but not to confessors), but only for cases in which time did not permit recourse to the Ordinary, and there was danger in delay.[12] It was later declared that the term "parish priest" ("parochus") comprehended all who exercised the care of souls, with the exception of "vice-parochi" and "chaplains"; that missionaries who exercised the office of the care of souls, even though not parish-priests in the strict sense of the word, were also included under the term "parochus," provided they actually exercised pastoral offices.[13]

Neither parish priests or simple priests possessed any power, by common law, of dispensing from matrimonial impediments until the year 1909. Parish priests, of course, could be subdelegated by Bishops to dispense in danger of death. The Decree "Ne Temere," of 2 August 1907, empowered simple priests to assist at marriage validly and lawfully when, in danger of death, the local Ordinary, parish priest, or a priest who had been delegated by either to assist at marriages, could not be present: "imminente mortis periculo ubi parochus, vel loci Ordinarius, vel sacerdos ab alterutro delegatus, haberi nequeat, ad consulendum conscientiae et, si casus ferat, legitimationi prolis, matrimonium contrahi valide et licite potest coram quilibet sacerdote et duobus testibus."[14]

Subsequent to the granting of these powers to priests, the Bishop of Parma, with many other Bishops, petitioned the Sacred Congregation of the Sacraments to grant to priests power to dispense from marriage impediments when assisting at marriage in circumstances permitted by the decree "Ne Temere." Having carefully considered the matter, and referred the question to the Pope, Pius X, the Sacred Congregation, 14 May 1909, granted to priests the

---

[12] *Coll. de Prop. Fide,* 1698; *Fontes,* 1113.
[13] 23 Avril 1890, ad nn. 2, 3, 4, *Coll. de Prop. Fide,* 1728; *Fontes,* 1121.
[14] Art. VII; *A. A. S.,* I, 468.

faculty of dispensing from all diriment impediments of the ecclesiastical law, with the exception of the two reserved by the decree of 20 February 1888, when assisting at marriages in accordance with the provisions of the decree "Ne Temere," Art. VII.[15] The same Congregation declared, 16 August 1909, that this faculty was valid even for those who have not lived in concubinage, provided the condition "ad consulendum conscientiae et, si casus ferat, legitimationi prolis" was present.[16] Any doubt which may have remained as to the inclusion of parish priests under the above faculty of 14 May 1909 was removed by the Congregation of the Sacraments, 29 July 1910, when it declared that parish priests, even those who were not delegated "habitualiter" by Bishops in virtue of the Leonine Decree of 20 February 1888, also enjoyed this faculty.[17]

It will be noted, on a close reading, that the decree of 14 May, 1909, did not include clandestinity within the ambit of the power it conferred, but apparently required that the presence of some priest was necessary for validity.[18] Whatever doubt there may have been on this point was certainly removed by the Congregation of the Sacraments when it declared, 31 January, 1916, that in danger of death any priest could dispense from clandestinity, and permit marriage to take place validly and lawfully before witnesses alone, in circumstances in which the priest himself could not assist without grave incommodum, because of the civil law of anteriority, that is, in cases where the civil law, requiring, under grave penalty, that a civil marriage should precede the religious service, could not be complied with.[19]

Such is a resume of the final legislation of the Church, previous to the New Code, on the matter of marriage dispensations. So far this work has delineated the historical

---

[15] *A. A. S.*, I, 468, 469.
[16] *A. A. S.*, I, 656.
[17] *A. A. S.*, 11, 650.
[18] Cf. De Smet, *De Sponsalibus et Matrimonio* (ed. IV), I, p. 117, nota 1.
[19] *A. A. S.*, VIII, 36, 37.

development of the various powers of dispensing from matrimonial impediments enjoyed by Bishops, and others inferior to the Supreme Pontiff, up to the time of the codification of Church law. The various titles or sources of these powers have received some consideration. The express, tacit, and presumed will of the Roman Pontiff, custom, and the concessions of common law, have been shown to be the various sources of the various dispensatory powers. The years 1888 and 1909 stand out as the two great landmarks of the Church's positive legislation on this matter. But yet the powers conferred were incomplete and insufficient for all contingent necessities. The culminating point was reached in the promulgation of the New Code. This introduced a somewhat radical change in the whole matter of matrimonial dispensations, notably by the change it effected regarding the number and nature of impediments, and by the amplification of the powers to dispense. Now all cases of urgency are sufficiently provided for, and the dreams of the Fathers of the Vatican Council were fully realized in the eventful year of 1918.

PART II

The New Legislation

FOREWORD

"Praeter Romanum Pontificem, nemo potest impedimenta juris ecclesiastici sive impedientia sive dirimentia abrogare, aut illis derogare; item nec in eisdem dispensare, nisi jure communi vel speciali indulto a Sede Apostolica haec potestas concessa fuerit." (*Canon 1040.*)

No one except the Roman Pontiff can abrogate impediments of the ecclesiastical law, whether impedient or diriment, or derogate from them; neither can anyone dispense from them unless this power has been granted him by the common law or by special Indult of the Apostolic See.

This canon introduces no change in principle. Matrimonial impediments are imposed by general law, and with general laws no one but the supreme legislator himself, or his delegates, can interfere whether wholly ("abrogation"), or partially ("derogation"), or even by relaxation in particular cases ("dispensation").

It has already been shown, in Part I of this work, that in the past this faculty was often exercised even when no special text of law could be quoted in its favor: custom and common opinion were held to justify the policy, but the tacit or, at least, presumed consent of the Supreme Pontiff was always invoked as the ultimate *fons et radix* of the power claimed under these two titles. Hence those powers too were conferred by common law (*lex non-scripta*), and the principle enunciated in Canon 1040 was as true and as certain then as it is today under the New Code.

The New Code has expressly conferred certain powers of dispensing from marriage impediments on Bishops, Priests, and Confessors. As has already been shown, in

Part I of this work, in pre-Code days Bishops had powers by common law in (I) urgent cases, (II) over certain impedient impediments, and (III) in case of doubtful impediments. The powers of priests were more circumscribed. So far as the Code went, each and every one of these faculties was left intact or extended considerably.

For the sake of uniformity and more intelligent interpretation, in dealing with the legislation of the New Code on the subject under discussion, the same order will be adopted as in Part I. Hence, (I) cases of urgency (Canons 1043-1045), (II) impedient impediments (Canons 1309, 1313), and (III) doubtful impediments (Canon 15), will come up for treatment.

CHAPTER V

Danger of Death

Powers of Local Ordinaries

"Urgente mortis periculo, locorum Ordinarii, ad consulendum conscientiae et, si casus ferat, legitimationi prolis, possunt tum super forma in matrimonii celebratione servanda, tum super omnibus et singulis impedimentis juris ecclesiastici, sive publicis sive occultis, etiam multiplicibus, exceptis impedimentis provenientibus ex sacro presbyteratus ordine et ex affinitate in linea recta, consummato matrimonio, dispensare proprios subditos ubique commorantes et omnes in proprio territorio actu degentes, remoto scandalo, et, si dispensatio concedatur super cultus disparitate aut mixta religione, praestitis consuetis cautionibus." (*Canon 1043.*)

This is the most extensive faculty ever given to Ordinaries in case of urgent danger of death. The historical development and the juridical basis of the powers conferred by this canon have already been discussed, and the reader is referred to Part I, Chapter III, arts. I, II, and chap. IV, of this work, as the old legislation must be kept in view for a better and more satisfactory idea of the new regulations. The present law is but the final development of the former. Its extensiveness is due to the fact that it eliminates many restrictions found in the former decrees.

The conditions under which this extraordinary faculty may be used are clearly specified, namely, if urgent danger of death necessitates the adjustment of matters of conscience, and, should the case call for it, the legitimation of offspring.

Danger of Death:

As to how imminent the danger of death must be, to justify the use of the faculty, is not stated in the Code, nor is it possible to define this danger more closely, for it is a matter which varies in every case.[1] The New Law no longer requires *"gravissimum periculum mortis,"* as did the Leonine Decree of the 20 February, 1888,[2] nor *"imminent danger of death,"* as did the decree of the Sacred Congregation of the Sacraments, 14 May, 1909,[3] but simply *"urgent danger of death."* There is "urgent danger of death" when a person is constituted in circumstances in which it is truly and solidly probable that he may survive or die, each alternative being probable in the case.[4] The danger is to be morally estimated;[5] a reasonably prudent judgment as to the proximity of the danger is all that can be commanded under the circumstances. The Ordinary may rely on the opinion of the parties themselves or of those present, and on the physician's verdict. Their judgment may be mistaken, but it can be safely said that the Code requires no more than an ordinary reasonable fear that such danger actually exists.[6]

One need not be scrupulous regarding the validity of the dispensation if the sick person becomes well after a few days. The fact that he gets well so soon does not affect it, provided at the time of dispensing it was prudently estimated that death would probably follow.[7] Some

---

[1] Woywod, *A Practical Commentary on the New Code of Canon Law,* n. 1011; Ferreres, *Compendium Theologiae Moralis* (ed. 13), II, n. 1082.

[2] *Coll. de Prop. Fide,* 1685.

[3] *A. A. S.,* I, 468, 469.

[4] Cappello, *De Sacramentis,* III, n. 232, a; Vermeersch-Creusen, *Epitome Juris Canonici,* II, n. 306; Farrugia, *De Matrimonio et Causis Matrimonialibus* (ed. 10), n. 83, d.

[5] Wernz-Vidal, *Jus Canonicum,* V, n. 413.

[6] Augustine, *A Commentary on the New Code of Canon Law* (ed. 3), V, p. 97; Woywod, *H. P. R.,* XXIV, p. 1168.

[7] Genicot-Salsmans, *Casus Conscientiae* (ed. IV), casus 1078; Blat, *Commentarium Textus Codicis Juris Canonici,* lib. III—P. I, De Rebus, n. 435.

authors [8] maintain, because of the use of the word "urgente," that there is not "urgens mortis periculum" if it is morally possible to approach the Holy See for faculties to dispense. There is nothing in the law to justify this restriction, for the qualification, *"quando tempus non suppetit recurrendi ad S. Sedem,"* expressly made in the Leonine Decree, is not repeated in the New Law.[9]

The Law fails to specify any particular cause from which the danger must result in order that the faculty may become operative. The Leonine Decree demanded that the danger of death should have arisen from sickness ("aegroti in gravissimo mortis periculo constituti"), but all authors since the Code are agreed that any cause whatsoever will suffice, provided it may be qualified as "urgens mortis periculum."[10] Hence the danger required in this context is not equivalent to that which is required for the Sacrament of Extreme Unction, as danger from an external cause suffices. "A soldier in the first line of trenches, a person aboard a submerging ship, are as much in urgent danger of death, in the sense of this Canon, as one who is critically ill owing to grave sickness, or as the result of an unsuccessful minor operation involving the patient in a critical condition."[11]

The decree of the Holy Office, 20 February, 1888, corroborated by another decree of the same Congregation, 17 September, 1890,[12] demanded for the validity of the dis-

---

[8] Blat, *o. c.*, n. 435; Linneborn, *Grundriss des Eherechts* (ed. II and III), p. 113, nota 1; Sebastiani, *Summarium Theologiae Moralis* (ed. VI), n. 561, 1.

[9] Cf. De Smet, *De Sponsalibus et Matrimonio* (ed. IV), n. 760, c; Vlaming, *Praelectiones Juris Matrimonii* (ed. III), II, n. 401, d; Wernz-Vidal, *o. c.*, V, n. 413, b; Vermeersch, *Theologia Moralis*, III, n. 758.

[10] Petrovits, *The New Church Law on Matrimony* (ed. 11), n. 152; Vlaming, *Praelectiones Juris Matrimonii*, II, n. 401; De Smet, *De Sponsalibus et Matrimonio*, II (ed. IV), n. 758; Chelodi, *Jus Matrimoniale*, n. 41; Ayrinhac, *Marriage Legislation in the New Code of Canon Law*, p. 87; Motry, *Diocesan Faculties According to the Code of Canon Law*, p. 129.

[11] Petrovits, *o. c.*, n. 152; Cf. De Smet, *o. c.*, II, n. 758.

[12] *Coll. de Prop. Fide*, nn. 1685, 1741.

pensation that the persons dispensed should have lived in concubinage, or have been joined in civil marriage. Pighi [13] is still imbued with the old law when he maintains that an Ordinary cannot dispense those who have lived in concubinage, but do not now live in it, at least equivalently. This condition is no longer required, not even for liceity; nay, it had already been abrogated by the S. Congregation of the Sacraments, 16 August, 1909,[14] which demanded only that marriage be necessary, in a general way, for the relief of conscience, or, if it were necessary, for the legitimation of offspring. The New Law does not reinstate this condition, and hence its presence is not necessary either for the validity or lawfulness of the dispensation.[15] However, while this is true, those not living in concubinage, or in civil marriage, will more rarely have a just cause to contract marriage "in periculo mortis."[16]

It matters not whether the danger of death threatens the party who is directly bound by the impediment or not; all that is necessary is that there is a dispensable impediment between the parties who desire marriage, and that either one of them is in danger of death.[17] If both parties are laboring under a dispensable impediment the Ordinary can a fortiori dispense.

"Ad consulendum conscientiae et, si casus ferat, legitimationi prolis."

The second condition in the absence of which the Ordinary may not avail himself of this faculty is the very condition which occasioned its granting, namely, the necessity of adjusting matters of conscience, and, should the case need it, the legitimatization of offspring.

[13] *De Sacramento Matrimonii* (ed. 11), n. 90, 2, a.

[14] *A. A. S.*, I, 656.

[15] Cf. Ayrinhac, *Marriage Legislation in the New Code of Canon Law*, p. 87; Cappello, *o. c.*, III, n. 232, p. 253, nota 5; Vlaming, *o. c.*, II, n. 401, a; Chelodi, *Jus Matrimoniale* (ed. III), n. 41; Wernz-Vidal, *Jus Canonicum*, V, n. 413; De Smet, *o. c.*, II, n. 758.

[16] Genicot-Salsmans, *Institutiones Theologiae Moralis* (ed. X), II, n. 523.

[17] Holy Office, 1 July 1891, *Coll. de Prop. Fide*, 1758; Cf. Vlaming, *o. c.*, II, n. 401, b; Chelodi, *l. c.;* Wernz-Vidal, *l. c.;* De Smet, *o. c.*, n. 759.

There can be no doubt that this condition is necessary for the validity of the dispensation. It is the "justa et rationabilis causa" required by Canon 84, par. 1, for the validity of a dispensation.[18] All authors, with the possible exception of Fanfani,[19] imply, and many state expressly, that this condition is absolutely necessary for validity.[20]

It is not, however, necessary that both these reasons be present; either suffices separately, as is demonstrated by the very hypothesis that a dispensation can be granted even though there is no offspring to be legitimated ("et, si casus ferat, legitimationi prolis").[21] Hence the word *"et"* in this context is to be taken as disjunctive, and not as copulative. One of these conditions can easily be present without the other. Previous to the New Code it was the common interpretation that either of these two reasons sufficed for validity.[22]

"Ad consulendum conscientiae:"

As to the extension of this condition there is not agreement among canonists. All admit that the demands of this condition are fulfilled when the vice of luxury has been the source of the disturbance of conscience which now calls for adjustment by means of marriage. When sin, or the proximate occasion of sin, some strong temptation, or scandal, which has arisen from illicit relations, can be removed by the marriage of the parties, then there is no

---

[18] Simon, *Faculties of Pastors and Confessors for Absolution and Dispensation,* p. 86, nota 4; Genicot-Salsmans, *Institutiones Theologiae Moralis* (ed. X), II, n. 523.

[19] *De Jure Parochorum* (1924), n. 306, B: "Non *liceret* igitur praedictis facultatibus uti, si nulla ratio conscientiae vel legitimationis prolis exstaret."

[20] Cf. Genicot-Salsmans, *l. c.;* Motry, *Diocesan Faculties according to the Code of Canon Law,* p. 130; Cappello, *De Sacramentis,* III, n. 232, d.

[21] Augustine, *A Commentary on the New Code of Canon Law* (ed. III), V, p. 97; Vlaming, *o. c.,* II, n. 401, c.

[22] Vermeersch-Creusen, *Epitome Juris Canonici,* II, n. 306, b; Vermeersch, *De Forma Sponsalium ac Matrimonii post Decretum "Ne Temere,"* p. 40; Wouters, *Commentarius in Decretum "Ne Temere,"* p. 51.

doubt that the Ordinary has sufficient ground to act, and avail himself of the faculty bestowed by this canon.[23]

But what if the peace of conscience, now to be restored, was disturbed by some sin other than one contrary to the sixth or ninth commandments? Can the Ordinary dispense when, for instance, the necessity of settling matters of conscience arises from the desire of the dying party to restore the good name of another, to repair, by means of the "jus viduae acquisitum," material damage done to the intended spouse, to bring an end, by marriage, to standing enmities and disagreement between families, or any other serious reason? Authors generally maintain that no matter from what cause the necessity arises, provided there is necessity to soothe the conscience of one or both of the parties, the condition "ad consulendum conscientiae" is adequately fulfilled.[24] The sentiments of these canonists may well be summed up in the words of Vermeersch: "Conscientiae consulit, non is tantum qui ejus praeceptis paret, sed etiam qui ejus suasionibus obtemperat. Quare, praeter strictam obligationem, aliud etiam serium conscientiae motivum sufficere nobis videtur ut facultate praesentis dispositionis frui possis. Non haec itaque tantum afferri possunt exempla: si aliter ac contracto matrimonio removeri nequeat proxima peccandi occasio ob tentationes quas aegrotus patiatur, vel cessare scandalum ex publico concubinatu aut matrimonio civili, vel prospici securitati et honestae sustentationi personae superstitis;—sed etiam haec et similia sunt addenda; si per matrimon-

---

[23] Cappello, *o. c.*, III, n. 232, d; Petrovits, *o. c.*, n. 155; Vlaming, *Praelectiones Juris Matrimonii,* II, n. 401, c; Woywod, *A Practical Commentary on the Code of Canon Law,* n. 1011; Chelodi, *Jus Matrimoniale,* n. 41; Wernz-Vidal, *o. c.*, V, n. 413.

[24] Cappello, *l. c.;* Petrovits, *l. c.;* Woywod, *l. c.;* Vlaming, *l. c.;* Chelodi, *l. c.;* Wernz-Vidal, *l. c.;* Ferreres, *Compendium Theologiae Moralis* (ed. XIII), II, n. 952, IV; Augustine, *A Commentary on the New Code of Canon Law,* V, p. 97; Vermeersch, *Theologia Moralis,* III (1923), n. 758.

ium fama melius restituatur, damnum magis plene sarciatur."[25]

This doctrine of Vermeersch, however, was not left go unchallenged by Wouters. This author maintains[26] that Vermeersch's extension beyond matters of the sixth and ninth commandment is unwarranted for the following reasons: (a) The words, "ad consulendum conscientiae," should be thus interpreted—"that the eternal salvation of one or both parties be placed in safety—." This end can be accomplished, without marriage, in the circumstances and cases contemplated by Vermeersch; (b) because of the addition: "et, si casus ferat, legitimationi prolis;" the very conjunction of the two clauses seems to insinuate that by the words, "ad consulendum conscientiae," should be understood a cause which, as a rule, concurs with the second cause, and, therefore, implies that the source of the upsetting of conscience should have arisen from some sin against the sixth or ninth commandment. Since the promulgation of the New Code De Smet[27] has espoused the teaching of Wouters.

The view of authors generally is undoubtedly the better opinion, and is, of course, absolutely safe in practice. However, theoretically, the more restrictive interpretation appears to have more intrinsic probability. Wouters, no doubt, seems to be too strict in his paraphrase of the clause "ad consulendum conscientiae," but, nevertheless, putting aside the strictness of his view in this particular aspect of his contention, his second argument has much weight and significance. Both the "Ne Temere" (Art. VII) and the Code connect the two reasons by the particle "*et,*" and there must be some reason for its use, seeing that the particle "vel" or "aut" would be quite in place if the two phrases were intended to connote two causes of a com-

[25] *De Forma Sponsalium ac Matrimonii post Decretum "Ne Temere"* (1908), n. 73.

[26] *Commentarius in Decretum "Ne Temere"* (1909), p. 53.

[27] *De Sponsalibus et Matrimonio* (ed. IV), p. 215, nota 2.

pletely distinct species. It seems, then, that the legislator, by the insertion of this word *"et,"* intended to imply a parity in species between the two causes, and then added the qualification, "si casus ferat," to show that the conception or actual birth of offspring, from their sinful relations, is not a necessary condition for the obtaining of a dispensation. In this connection then the particle *"et,"* while it is indeed disjunctive "simpliciter," can be said to be copulative "secundum quid." However, the milder opinion has far greater extrinsic probability in its favor, and is the one to be followed in practice, and, above all, it is to be remembered that neither concubinage or civil marriage is demanded as a prerequisite condition for dispensing.[28]

The phrase *"ad consulendum conscientiae"* gives rise to another important question: Is this condition fulfilled only when it is the conscience of the dying party which needs soothing, or is the use of the faculty to dispense justifiable when only the healthy party seeks for adjustment of matters of his or her conscience, while that of the dying party is quite at ease and undisturbed. This question has perhaps little application in practice when the parties concerned are both Catholics, for it is hard to conceive how the conscience of the dying Catholic could remain undisturbed while that of the other party is ill at ease. But the question assumes practical importance when one of the parties, especially the dying party, is a non-Catholic, and suffers no remorse of conscience even in such extremities.

De Smet,[29] Gearin,[30] and Augustine[31] maintain that a dispensation can be validly and lawfully granted even when the condition "ad consulendum conscientiae" is verified only in the case of the non-dying party. "As marriage is an in-

---

[28] That concubinage is not necessary was expressly decided by the S. Congregation of the Sacraments on 16 August 1909, *A. A. S.*, I, 656.

[29] *De Sponsalibus et Matrimonio,* II, n. 759.

[30] *The New Canon Law in its Practical Aspects,* p. 151.

[31] *A Commentary on the New Code of Canon Law* (ed. III), V, p. 97.

dividual contract," argues Augustine, "and the troubled conscience of the party who is not sick may, at least indirectly, affect the party who is, it would seem that the legislator means also to grant a dispensation in that case." The same author maintains that his interpretation is corroborated by a declaration of the Holy Office of 1 July, 1891,[32] but wrongly so, since this decision of the Holy Office did not deal with the point at issue, but declared that a dispensation can be granted even when the healthy party only is affected by the *impediment* to be dispensed from, and the other party at least only indirectly.

Petrovits[33] defends the other opinion. Should the dying non-Catholic, he argues, refuse to become a convert, the Ordinary could go no further unless he possessed the faculty of granting a "sanatio in radice." This reasoning is, however, dubious. There is nothing either in the canon itself or in the old law to justify the demand that the conversion of the non-Catholic, if he is the dying party, is a necessary condition for the use of the faculty to dispense bestowed by this canon. Nay, the law itself points to the contrary conclusion. It enables the Ordinary, given all the other conditions, to dispense from the impediments of mixed religion and disparity of cult, which presupposes that this faculty is operative even when one of the parties is still a non-Catholic at the time of dispensing. Neither is there anything in the phrase "as consulendum conscientiae" to justify the conclusion of Petrovits, as the phrase is quite general and does not exclude from its ken the non-Catholic party.

Woywod[34a] also espouses the stricter view when he states expressly that the words of the Code are verified only when the marriage is necessary as a means to afford relief to the conscience of the dying party. The other commentators do not discuss this particular point expressly, but are sat-

[32] *Coll. de Prop. Fide*, 1758.

[33] *The New Church Law on Matrimony* (ed. II), n. 154.

[34a] *A Practical Commentary on the Code of Canon Law*, n. 1011.

isfied with simply explaining the meaning of the condition, "ad consulendum conscientiae," without reference to the particular party whom this condition must affect.

In the legislation preceding the Code the more restrictive interpretation would seem to have been the better opinion. The whole Preface to the decree of the Holy Office, 20 February, 1888, insinuates that the purpose of the extraordinary faculty, which it conferred, was to benefit the dying party *directly*, and the healthy party only indirectly: "ut morituri in tanta temporis angustia in facie Ecclesiae rite copulari, et propriae conscientiae consulere valeant."[34b] However, no apodictic argument can be drawn from the Leonine Decree as it uses the plural gender throughout, and, therefore, can be interpreted as referring to either party. Moreover, as concubinage or civil marriage was required by that Decree for validity, it was scarcely conceivable how the conscience of either party could remain undisturbed at the point of death.

While it is true that Canon 1043 intends to benefit the dying party directly and the healthy party only indirectly, nevertheless there is nothing in the law itself to establish the view that the faculty is not applicable when only the healthy person seeks marriage as a means to obtain peace of conscience. It uses the very general unqualified phrase "ad consulendum conscientiae" which can, and ought to, be regarded as verified where only the healthy person in question needs pacification of conscience. Moreover, the divergency of views among the authors who have discussed this point renders each opinion probable, so that there is at least a dubium juris, and by virtue of Canon 15 the milder opinion can safely be followed in practice.

To recapitulate, it is certain that the Ordinary has power to dispense when the dying party needs rectification of conscience. It is equally certain that he can do likewise when both parties are in such need; and it *is* safe in prac-

[34b] *Coll. de Prop. Fide,* 1685.

tice to act on the opinion that he can also dispense when the non-dying party only seeks, by marriage, relief of conscience.

"Legitimatio Prolis:"

First of all it must be noted that the presence of this circumstance is not per se necessary for the validity of the dispensation, as is clear from the fact that even if there is no offspring to be legitimated the dispensation can still be granted.

The interpretation of the word *"prolis,"* in this context, is of supreme importance for two reasons; first, to determine how far the legitimation of offspring extends as an effect of the dispensation granted in danger of death; and, secondly, to establish how far this cause can be invoked as a sufficient cause to dispense, when the first condition "ad consulendum conscientiae" is not present in a particular case.

There are various classes of "filii illegitimi": (a) Naturales, those who are born of parents between whom, either at the time of conception, during the period of gestation, or at time of birth, a valid marriage could exist.[35] (b) Spurii, those born of parents between whom at no time a valid marriage could exist because of the presence of some diriment impediment. These latter can be either, (α) adulterous, if born of parents one or other of whom was actually wedded to another; (β) sacrilegious, if born of a union in which one (or both) of the parties was bound by solemn religious vows, or the father was a cleric in Major Orders; (γ) incestuous, if born of a union in which the parents are related either in consanguinity or affinity; (δ) nefarious, if born of parents related in the direct line, that is, of any direct ascendent and descendent.[36]

Prohibitive impediments can never render a child ille-

---

[35] Canons 1114, 1116: Cf. Augustine, *o. c.*, V, p. 333; Petrovits, *o. c.*, n. 173; Wernz, *Jus Decretalium* (1904), IV, n. 679.

[36] Augustine, *l. c.*; Petrovits, *l. c.*; Wernz, *l. c.*

gitimate.[37] Simple vows (except those of the Jesuits) do not affect the legitimacy of the children.[38]

It is certain that Canon 1043 legislates for natural children; these are eo ipso legitimated by the granting of the dispensation.[39] To what extent does it affect spurious offspring? It is equally certain that spurious children, who are not adulterous or sacrilegious, are intended, for, although these are not eo ipso legitimated by a future valid marriage of the parents,[40] they are legitimated by the very granting of a dispensation enabling a valid marriage.[41] Nefarious offspring are certainly to be excluded from Canon 1043, since their parents can entertain no hope of being dispensed, not even in danger of death.

But the question arises regarding adulterous and sacrilegious offspring. Should the validation of marriage take place, would such children be legitimated? All authors, with the possible exception of Cappello,[42] answer in the negative to this question.[43] These authors insist that Canon 1043 is to be interpreted in the light of Canon 1051 which excludes adulterous and sacrilegious offspring from the legitimating effect of a dispensation. Moreover, the Holy

---

[37] Wernz, *Jus Decretalium* (ed. 1904), n. 679.

[38] Wernz, *l. c.*

[39] Canons 1051, 1116; De Smet, *o. c.*, II, n. 759.

[40] Canon 1116.

[41] Canon 1051. This canon is more extensive than canon 1116, and includes spurious children who are not adulterous or sacrilegious. Cf. De Smet, *o. c.*, n. 759: "Spurious children, with the two exceptions, are indirectly intended by canon 1043." Before the Code it was not certain that such offspring were thus legitimated. Cf. Wouters, *o. c.*, p. 40.

[42] *De Sacramentis,* III, n. 232 (d), whose opinion, in this matter, will be considered at a later period.

[43] Woywod, *A Practical Commentary on the Code of Canon Law,* n. 1011; Vlaming, *Praelectiones Juris Matrimonii,* II, n. 401; Petrovits, *The New Church Law on Matrimony,* n. 156; Wernz-Vidal, *Jus Canonicum,* V, n. 413; Wouters, *Commentarius in Decretum "Ne Temere,"* p. 156; Farrugia, *De Matrimonio et causis Matrimonialibus,* n. 83; Vermeersch, *Theologia Moralis* (1923), III, n. 758, and, *Epitome Juris Canonici,* II, n. 306, b; Leitner, *Lehrbuch des katholischen Eherechts* (ed. 3), p. 324; Blat, *Commentarium Textus Codicis Juris Canonici,* lib. III—P. 1, De Rebus, n. 435; Noldin, *De Jure Matrimoniali,* n. 123, b.

Office, 8 July, 1903,[44] declared that the Leonine Faculty of 1888 did not contain this power, but that a special rescript of legitimation from the Holy See itself is necessary. However, it is consoling to note that, given the other conditions, the marriage can be validated by a grant of the necessary dispensation, even though this would not benefit the children already born of such a union (that is, adulterous or sacrilegious).

But a second and more important question now presents itself. In some instances it may, perchance, happen that the legitimation of children may be the only reason which can be invoked as a cause for dispensing, as the condition "ad consulendum conscientiae" may be absent in certain cases. Such a case will seldom, if ever, be encountered in practice because, as a rule, the second condition will be accompanied by the first. If marriage is desired for the sake of children born out of lawful wedlock, then generally the condition "ad consulendum conscientiae" will be also present, as it is difficult to see how the second condition could be verified without offering some relief of conscience to the parties concerned. Nay, the grammatical construction of the canon itself seems to imply this, for seeing that it is certain that the two conditions need not be present in one and the same case for the giving of a dispensation, and yet the conjunction "et" is used to connect both causes, it would seem that "et" in this respect is to be regarded as copulative ("secundum quid"), as connecting two things existing in the same case, namely, the adjustment of matters of conscience and the legitimation of offspring. Hence if marriage is desired, in some instances, for the sake of legitimating children, this would be the primary intention, but a secondary one, namely, the settling of matters of conscience, would be implicitly included in it.

But supposing that such a case would come up for

[44] *Coll. de Prop. Fide,* 2171.

treatment in practice could an Ordinary dispense when the legitimation of adulterous or sacrilegious offspring is the only reason or cause for the dispensation,[45] the condition "ad consulendum conscientiae" being, in no way, present?

Most of the authors give an unqualified negative response to this question.[46] They maintain that since such offspring cannot be legitimated by a dispensation, of this kind, the dispensation itself cannot be granted for that sole purpose; that this teaching is in conformity with the decision of the Holy Office, 8 July, 1903: "Utrum intelligatur concessa etiam facultas declarandi ac nunciandi legitimam prolem spuriam, forsitan . . . susceptam, . . . an contra pro susceptae prolis legitimatione necesse sit novam gratiam a S. Sede postea impetrare?" Response: "Affirmative quoad primam partem, excepta prole adulterina et prole proveniente a personis Ordine sacro aut solemni professione religiosa ligatis.—Quoad secundam partem, provisum in prima."[47]

Some Canonists, however, respond by drawing a distinction.[48] While admitting, at least implicitly, that the direct intention of legitimating adulterous or sacrilegious children is not of itself a justifying cause for dispensing, they nevertheless maintain that the legitimation of such offspring can be indirectly a sufficient ground to justify the use of the faculty. They do not deny that a

---

[45] It is certain that he is invested with power to dispense if the legitimation of natural or spurious (excepting adulterous and sacrilegious) offspring would be the only cause present.

[46] Vlaming, *o. c.*, II, n. 401; Woywod, *o. c.*, n. 1011; Wernz-Vidal, *o. c.*, V, n. 413; Augustine, *o. c.*, V, n. 97; Noldin, *De Jure Matrimoniali*, n. 123, b; Leitner, *o. c.*, p. 324; Wouters, *o. c.*, p. 54; Simon, *Faculties of Pastors and Confessors for Absolution and Dispensation*, p. 86; Farrugia, *o. c.*, n. 83, d; Blat, *o. c.*, n. 435; Genicot-Salsmans, *Institutiones Theologiae Moralis* (ed. X), II, n. 523, and, *fusius*, in *Casus Conscientiae* (ed. IV), Casus 1077, where he solves, in accordance with this opinion, a very clear case on this particular point.

[47] *Coll. de Prop. Fide*, 2171.

[48] Vermeersch, *De Forma Sponsalium ac Matrimonii post Decretum "Ne Temere,"* p. 40; Chelodi, *Jus Matrimoniale*, n. 41; Ferreres, *Compendium Theologiae Moralis* (ed. XIII), II, n. 952, IV; Cappello, *o. c.*, III, n. 232, d.

special rescript of legitimation from the Holy See is necessary for the actual legitimatization of such offspring, but they maintain that such a rescript can be more easily obtained when the parents are already married than when they are unmarried. They build on this fact and conclude that the intention of creating a spes probabilis of obtaining such a rescript of legitimation is a sufficient cause to justify the Ordinary to dispense. There can be no doubt that this opinion enjoys internal and external probability, and is quite safe in practice. At first sight it may appear that the greater part of external authority opposes it, so great as almost to destroy its probability. But this is not so. As a matter of fact, mostly all other authors do not discuss this particular aspect of the question at all. They are satisfied with simply stating that an Ordinary cannot dispense to legitimate adulterous or sacrilegious offspring, if this condition is unaided by the cause "ad consulendum conscientiae." No one, with the possible exception of Cappello, as will be seen later, will deny this. But they do not discuss the point (and therefore cannot be invoked on either the affirmative or negative side), whether this intention can indirectly and mediately constitute a cause to dispense, the intention of obtaining a rescript of legitimation constituting the immediate and direct intention.[49] Some, however, do consider this point of the question and deny that the faculty of Canon 1043 can be extended so far.[50] The greatest difficulty which can be urged against the more benign opinion is the decision of the Holy Office, 8 July, 1903, already quoted. But on close examination it will be seen that this response does not cover the point in question. All it establishes is that a dispensation granted

[49] This point is evidenced by a study of the two works of Vermeersch, *De Forma Sponsalium ac Matrimonii post Decretum "Ne Temere,"* p. 40, and *Theologia Moralis,* III, n. 758.

[50] Wouters, *Commentarius in Decretum "Ne Temere,"* p. 54; Ojetti, *In Jus Antepianum et Pianum ex Decreto "Ne Temere,"* n. 116; Wernz-Vidal, *Jus Canonicum,* V, n. 413, refers to it, but neither accepts or rejects it.

in danger of death does not legitimate adulterous and sacrilegious offspring; that a special rescript from the Holy See is necessary to obtain this desired effect; and, at most, that the direct intention of legitimating such offspring by the dispensation itself is not a sufficient cause to justify the use of the faculty to dispense.

Seeing, therefore, that no conclusive argument against the milder opinion can be deduced either from external authority or internal reasoning, and that some canonists of no mean juridical weight espouse it, it is safe in practice to follow this opinion if the case should arise. At the very least the law restricting the power of the Ordinary in such circumstances is doubtful, and "lex dubia non obligat."[51] Hence Ordinaries may dispense if such a case should arise, until such time as the Holy See shall give an official decision, or the teaching of canonists render the opinion improbable. At any rate, as has already been said, such an unique case will scarcely ever present itself in practice, as the condition "ad consulendum conscientiae" will, as a rule, accompany the desire to legitimate offspring.

In dealing with this whole question of the legitimation of offspring Cappello[52] uses language which is, to say the least, dangerous. It would seem to follow from the words he uses that he embraces the opinion that an Ordinary could dispense with the direct intention of legitimating adulterous or sacrilegious offspring; he does not qualify his statement. If he means this he is isolated in his contention. However, he quotes Chelodi, Ferreres, and some others on behalf of his opinion which, more than anything, goes to show that he is simply embracing their opinion (that an Ordinary can dispense with the sole intention of rendering it more easy for the parties to obtain a rescript of legitimation for adulterous or sacrilegious children),

---

[51] Canon 15.

[52] *De Sacramentis,* III, n. 232, d.

rather than propounding a doctrine so adverse to the teaching of the Holy Office and the views of canonists.

Who can dispense?

The faculty contained in this canon is granted to the Ordinaries of places ("locorum Ordinarii"). Besides the Roman Pontiff, who is the Ordinary of Ordinaries, under the name of local Ordinary the present legislation includes,[53] all Residential Bishops, Abbots and Prelates nullius, as well as their Vicars Generals; also Apostolic Administrators, Apostolic Vicars, Prefects, and their Vicarii Delegati,[54] the Vicars Capitular, or Administrators, during the vacancy of a See. The Higher Superiors of exempt Clerical Orders of religious, except in cases where they are at the same time Prelates nullius,[55] are not local Ordinaries, but simply Ordinaries, and, therefore, are not included. Hence the Vicar General possesses this faculty by common law, but not the diocesan Chancellor.

Ambitus Potestatis:

The Code says that in these circumstances local Ordinaries can dispense from the form of marriage, and from all impediments of ecclesiastical origin, whether public or occult, diriment or impedient, or even multiple, with the sole exception of the impediments arising from the Priesthood, and affinity in the direct line arising from a consummated marriage.

The first dispensation which the canon empowers the Ordinary to grant regards the Form, that is, from certain formalities to be observed in the celebration of marriage, according to Lib. III, Tit. VII, Cap. VI of the Code. First it should be noted, against De Smet,[56] that the Code mentions the Form separately from the impediments. The Form is likewise treated in its own separate chapter of

---

[53] Canon 198, pargs. 1, 2.

[54] *A. A. S.*, XII, 120.

[55] Augustine, *o. c.*, II, p. 174; Maroto, *Institutiones Juris Canonici* (ed. III), I, n. 701.

[56] *De Sponsalibus et Matrimonio* (ed. IV), II, n. 463.

the Code, and, in that part of the Code dealing with the convalidation of marriage, a consistent and sharp distinction is drawn between impediments and Form. It is, therefore, now apparently a settled matter that the Form does not constitute a canonical impediment in the present strict terminology of the Code.[57] The Form of marriage connotes that the marriage must be celebrated before the Ordinary or Parish-Priest of the place, or a delegate of either, and at least two witnesses.[58] The Ordinary, being enabled to dispense from the Form, can, therefore, dispense from the presence of the priest, or from the presence of the witnesses, or even from both, if such be necessary, which necessity scarcely ever occurs in practice.[59] The presence of witnesses, therefore, is not, strictly speaking, necessary for marriage "urgente mortis periculo." If one witness only were to be had, there would be no obligation to ask him or her to be present for the marriage, since the presence of one witness would not satisfy the requirements of the Church on Form.

But if two witnesses can be procured, the question at once arises as to the obligation of observing the prescribed form. Could the Ordinary, then, for any reason whatever, validly dispense from the presence of the witnesses? Authors generally do not discuss this question expressly; they simply state that a dispensation from the presence of the witnesses can be given when these cannot be conveniently procured.[60] Motry[61] discusses this precise point at some length. He admits, in the first place, that if the presence of the witnesses were a seriously disagreeable matter, in

---

[57] Cf. Vlaming, *Praelectiones Juris Matrimonii,* I (ed. III), n. 183 ff; Motry, *Diocesan Faculties According to the Code of Canon Law,* p. 130.

[58] Canons 1094–1098.

[59] Vermeersch-Creusen, *Epitome Juris Canonici,* II, n. 307; Farrugia, *De Matrimonio et Causis Matrimonialibus,* n. 83, d; Vlaming, *o. c.,* n. 401, b.

[60] Cf. Genicot-Salsmans, *Institutiones Theologiae Moralis* (ed. X), II, n. 525; Farrugia, *o. c.,* n. 83, d; Cerato, *Matrimonium* (ed. III), n. 35.

[61] *Diocesan Faculties According to the Code of Canon Law,* p. 131 ff.

such a case the law concerning the observance of the prescribed form should not be considered binding. But in the case in which the witnesses could be called in without "grave incommodum" to the persons affected by the dispensation,—including the offspring to be legitimatized—the legislation of the Code concerning the convalidation of marriage would have to be followed, provided, of course, it were a question of simple convalidation. In the supposition that the persons concerned had not attempted marriage, and "urgente periculo mortis" desired to enter upon marriage, the law concerning form should be observed if it can be done "sine grave incommodo." The danger of death which would permit the observance of form does not seem to be a sufficiently just and reasonable cause for dispensing from the observance of form. He concludes, however, with the remark that since the lawgiver has made no distinction, the necessity of a distinction is not evident.

This opinion of Motry seems to be confirmed, at least implicitly, by many authors who state that the Ordinary can dispense from the presence of the witnesses where these cannot be conveniently ("congruenter") had.[62]

From a consideration of the canon itself it would seem that there is nothing to restrict the power of the Ordinary to dispense even in cases where the witnesses can be had without "grave incommodum" to the parties or offspring, if there were such. The causes necessary for the valid exercise of the power are enumerated "taxative," namely, urgent danger of death, the necessity to adjust matters of conscience, or to legitimate offspring. Even when all these are present there seems to be no reason for demanding an extra cause for exercising the faculty of dispensing regarding the form. However, a declaration of the Holy Office, 13 December, 1899, would seem to point to the con-

[62] Genicot-Salsmans, *l. c.;* Farrugia, *l. c.;* Cerato, *l. c.;* Blat, *Commentarium Textus Codicis Juris Canonici* (ed. II), Lib. III—P. 1, De Rebus, n. 435.

trary conclusion. This Congregation answered in the affirmative to the following question: "Utrum in citatis decretis (20 Februarii, 1888, et 1 Martii, 1889) vere comprehendatur etiam facultas dispensandi ab impedimento clandestinitatis; adeo ut ex. gr. parochus, ab Episcopo habitualiter delegatus, possit in sua paroecia vel conjungere non suos sed extraneos inibi casu existentes, dispensando a praesentia parochi proprii, ad quem nullimode valeat haberi recursus; vel etiam conjungere suos, sed sine testibus, pariter dispensando ab eorum praesentia, cum omnino non sint qui testium munere fungi possint."[63] This response seems to restrict the power to dispense from the presence of the witnesses to cases where witnesses cannot be had.

The question is, at any rate, more theoretical than practical. If it is physically impossible to procure two witnesses then the Ordinary can certainly dispense, as the decision of the Holy Office just quoted clearly establishes. When it is morally impossible to have them present, that is, only with grave incommodum to the witnesses themselves, or the parties concerned, including the offspring to be legitimated, it is equally certain that he can likewise dispense. A collation of Canon 1044 with Canon 1098 places this beyond doubt. If two witnesses can be present without grave incommodum to any of the persons concerned there is no reason in the world why the marriage should not be celebrated in the prescribed form. Of course, if death, or unconsciousness, or any other evil, is prudently feared from delay in obtaining the necessary witnesses, then, undoubtedly, he can dispense from this part of the form, as grave incommodum to the parties themselves would then be present.

Impediments: As far as the impediments are concerned, all those that have been introduced by the Church Law fall within the scope of this faculty, be they diriment or impedient, public or occult, or even multiple. Two are,

---

[63] *Coll. de Prop. Fide*, 2072.

however, exempted, namely, the impediments which arise from the order of the priesthood, and from affinity in the direct line, provided in the latter instance the marriage, which was the source of the affinity in the case, had been consummated. The original faculty, 20 February, 1888, did not include prohibitive impediments,[64] but it is now certain that all these, even mixed religion, fall within the ambit of the present faculty—"super omnibus et singulis impedimentis—." The Ordinary can also dispense even if the impediment is multiple. Consanguinity, affinity, and crime can be multiple impediments, but it is not certain whether public honesty and spiritual relationship can be multiple.[65] Before the New Code the "potestas cumulandi," that is, the power to dispense when many dispensable impediments of a different kind occur in one and the same case, was not included in the faculty of dispensing.[66] Under the present legislation the "potestas cumulandi" is certainly conferred, as is evident from the end of the law and especially from the very ample words "super omnibus et singulis impedimentis etiam multiplicibus."[67]

Since the impedient impediments are now dispensable in danger of death, the Ordinary can dispense from the impediments resulting from the five simple vows enumerated in Canon 1058, namely, the simple vow of virginity, of perfect chastity, of celibacy, of receiving Sacred Orders, and of embracing the religious state. The question now naturally suggests itself, is the Ordinary here empowered to dispense, not only from the impediments arising out of these vows, but also from the vows themselves, or, in other words, can the Ordinary dispense from the vow only in so

---

[64] Holy Office, 18 March 1891, *Coll. de Prop. Fide*, 1750.

[65] Canons 1075, 1076, par. 2; 1077, par. 2; Cf. Chelodi, *Jus Matrimoniale* (ed. III), n. 104, n. 106; De Smet, *De Sponsalibus et Matrimonio*, II, p. 134, nota 3, and n. 637; Vlaming, *o. c.*, I, nn. 104, 106.

[66] Wernz, *Jus Decretalium* (ed. 1904), IV, n. 617, nota 67; Blat, *Commentarium Textus Codicis Juris Canonici*, Lib. III—P. 1, De Rebus, n. 435.

[67] Chelodi, *o. c.*, n. 41; De Smet, *o. c.*, n. 761, d; Farrugia, *o. c.*, n. 83; Blat, *l. c.* One could also argue by analogy from canon 1049, par. 2.

far as it impedes this particular marriage, so that the vow, even after dispensation, would continue to bind *outside* the lawful use of this marriage, and regarding all future marriages, should the party recover? Commentators on the New Code do not discuss this question, being satisfied with the statement that impedient impediments are now dispensable. It is certain that the Ordinary can dispense not only from the impediments, but also from the vows themselves, when the vows in question are not reserved to the Holy See, and the strict right of another is not violated by the relaxation of the obligation of the vow.[68] Hence he can dispense from the vows enumerated above with the exception of the simple vow of perfect and perpetual chastity, and the vow of entering a religion with solemn vows, provided they are taken *absolute* and after the completion of the eighteenth year of age, for these two are reserved to the Holy See.[69]

But regarding these two reserved vows, the vow taken in the reception of Major Orders, and Solemn Vows, can the Ordinary likewise dispense? It is certain that he can dispense from the impediments, diriment or impedient, arising out of these vows (with the exception of the Priesthood) for this particular marriage "urgente mortis periculo" ("super omnibus et singulis impedimentis"). But the question remains, do these vows, after such a dispensation has been granted, continue to bind outside the lawful use of marriage, and still constitute a canonical impediment regarding future marriages, if the occasion of such should ever arise? The canon itself perhaps can found no apodictic argument, but, nevertheless, it would point to an affirmative response, for it authorizes the Ordinary to dispense only from the *impediments,* and mentions nothing of the vows themselves. Moreover, a consideration of the old law would seem to render this interpretation certain.

---

[68] Canon 1313: for he can dispense from these in ordinary cases.
[69] Canon 1309.

Although the Leonine Faculty of 20 February, 1888, did not include the simple vows, the powers attributed to Bishops, previous to 1888, on the plea of custom and the common teaching of Theologians (which is really the original *fons et radix* of the powers conferred by Canon 1043), included these simple vows, even the two reserved in those days which were practically the same as those reserved today.[70] However, the power over the reserved vows was restricted to the particular marriage in question, and they continued to bind outside the lawful use of that marriage, and regarding all future marriages.[71] It is quite justifiable to apply this teaching of the old law to the present legislation since the two laws are practically in agreement regarding this particular aspect of vows. In practice the most prudent and advisable action would be to keep silent, regarding this particular point, if the parties themselves know nothing of this distinction in the matter of vows, which, as a rule, will be the case in practice.

Exempted Impediments:

Three classes of impediments are exempted from the dispensatory power of the Ordinary "urgente mortis periculo." The canon speaks of impediments of ecclesiastical origin, thereby implicitly excluding those of the natural or divine law. The first class of exempted impediments comprises those which certainly belong to the natural or divine law, and from which the Church cannot dispense, namely, *Ligamen,*[72] and consanguinity in the first degree of the direct line.[73] If impotency is certain, likewise he cannot dispense, or, rather, cannot permit the celebration of marriage. If, however, the impotency is doubtful, either with a doubt of fact or doubt of law, he can, and ought to, permit marriage,[74]

[70] See Part I, Chap. III, Art. III, of this work.

[71] Reiffenstuel, *Jus Canonicum,* IV, Appendix, *De Dispensatione super Impedimentis Matrimonii,* nn. 12, 13; Feije, *De Impedimentis et Dispensationibus Matrimonialibus* (ed. III), n. 614.

[72] Canon 1069.

[73] Canon 1076, par. 3; Cf. Cappello, *o. c.,* III, n. 224.

[74] Canon 1068, par 2.

but this latter point is not practical because in danger of death a case of doubtful impotency will scarcely ever occur.

By the second class are excluded those impediments which *doubtfully* belong to the natural or divine law and from which the Church does not dispense, namely, all grades of consanguinity in the direct line exceeding the first, and the first grade in the oblique line.[75]

The third class excludes those impediments which are certainly of ecclesiastical origin, but which the canon expressly withdraws from the ambit of the Ordinary's power, namely, those arising from the sacred order of the Priesthood, and from Affinity in the direct line arising out of a consummated marriage.

Priesthood: This exception was likewise contained in the Leonine Faculty of 1888. Neither this decree nor the present legislation excludes the order of subdeaconship or deaconship from the dispensatory power of Ordinaries. It is no longer obligatory to notify the Holy Office of a dispensation granted to one in major orders or to one solemnly professed, if such should afterwards become well, for the Code does not repeat this obligation which was imposed by the Leonine Decree.[76]

Affinity: The impediment of affinity is excluded only when the affinity has arisen from a consummated marriage. Kubelbeck [77] wrongly applies the phrase "consummato matrimonio" to the whole canon, remarking, however, that, as a condition, it is necessary only for liceity. This clause refers only to affinity; otherwise it should have found its place either at the beginning of the canon or immediately before "remoto scandalo."[78] The clause could not refer to

---

[75] Canon 1076, par. 3; Cappello, *De Sacramentis,* III, n. 224; Vlaming, *Praelectiones Juris Matrimonii* (ed. III), n. 393, 1, b.; Augustine, *o. c.,* V, p. 100.

[76] Cf. Augustine, *o. c.,* V, p. 100.

[77] *The Sacred Penitentiaria and its Relations to Faculties of Ordinaries and Priests,* p. 62.

[78] Augustine, *A Commentary on the New Code of Canon Law,* V (ed. III), p. 100.

the impediment of the priesthood, else the consequence should be that, provided the illegitimate union be not consummated, the Ordinary could dispense. This certainly cannot be the intention of the lawgiver, for the Church does not dispense from the impediment arising out of the Priesthood for the private good of any individual.[79] Moreover, the clause "consummato matrimonio" is a substitute for the form "ex copula licita" (the phrase used in the Leonine Faculty). This substitution was necessitated by the change in the nature of affinity introduced by the Code, for the origin of affinity is no longer "copula licita vel illicita," but any valid marriage, be it consummated or not.[80] Hence if the marriage giving rise to the affinity in the case has been consummated—and consummation is always presumed—the impediment arising from such in the direct line is indispensable, even in danger of death. Since the law fails to discriminate as regards the degree, it is lawful to infer that the expression *"ex affinitate in linea recta"* comprehends every degree in the direct line. Thus, for instance, if the marriage occasioning the affinity has been consummated, an Ordinary could not grant a dispensation by virtue of which one could marry one's daughter-in-law, or mother-in-law, or step-daughter, or step-mother.[81] The reason for this prohibition seems to be based on the fact that this impediment results from consanguinity, and the Church will not dispense for the same reasons that she will not dispense from consanguinity; that there is the possibility that reputed affinity in the direct line from a consummated marriage may really be occult consanguinity.[82]

If the marriage occasioning the affinity has not been consummated, the impediment arising from that affinity is dispensable in danger of death. It may happen, how-

[79] Mahoney, *E. R.*, LXXII, p. 509.

[80] Canon 97, par. 1.

[81] Petrovits, *The New Church Law on Matrimony*, n. 158.

[82] De Smet, *De Sponsalibus et Matrimonio*, II, p. 216, nota 5; Cerato, *Matrimonium* (ed. III), n. 352; canon 1076, par. 3.

ever, though very very rarely, that, even though the marriage had not been consummated, a prohibition to marry may arise, but from another source. It may happen that a man may wish to marry the daughter of a woman with whom he had illicit intercourse before marriage, even though the marriage itself was not consummated. In such a case it may at times be doubtful as to whether there is relationship in consanguinity in the direct line between the man and the daughter of his former wife; if so, provided the doubt is a prudent and solid one, marriage could not be permitted.[83] The following doubt was proposed to the *Pontifical Commission for the Authentic Interpretation of the Code*: "Quid si copula illicita et occulta praecesserit nativitatem nubendae, de qua dubitari possit an sit filia vel soror alterius partis;" and the answer given was: "Provisum per can. 1076 par. 3."[84] The response presupposes that the copula was had in such circumstances as to create a prudent fear of relationship in consanguinity. Not every copula had before marriage would constitute the case considered by the Commission, as there should be certain circumstances present in order to found a real doubt regarding the relationship.

Precautions:

(a) "*Remoto scandalo*:" Even though all other conditions be verified in a particular case the Ordinary, before applying the dispensation, must see to the removal of scandal if there be such. This condition refers to all scandal, whether already given in the past, or which may be given by the celebration of marriage itself. Past scandal must be repaired and future scandal obviated. This precept of law must receive special attention when there is question of convalidating a marriage that has been previously civilly contracted, or of uniting, in lawful wedlock, people who

[83] C. 1076, par. 3: "Nunquam matrimonium permittatur, si quod subsit dubium num partes sint consanguineae in aliquo gradu lineae rectae aut in primo gradu lineae collateralis."

[84] 2–3 June 1918, *A. A. S.*, X, 346.

have lived in concubinage. The natural law itself demands that every reasonable attempt be made to repair the past and to obviate future scandal. Prudence and experience will suggest the means by which this end can be best obtained. The manner of repairing the scandal given by one in major Orders or one solemnly professed, through a life of concubinage, was suggested by the Leonine Decree, and, though it cannot now be said to be obligatory, it might well be taken by Ordinaries as a *norma directiva* in the repairing of this and other kinds of scandal.[85] The decree laid down that if it were ever necessary to dispense one in major Orders or a religious solemnly professed, every possible means should be utilized to remove the scandal, either by inducing the parties to betake themselves to some place where their ecclesiastic or religious state is unknown, or, if this be not possible, by imposing salutary penances and a mode of life calculated to repair past excesses.[86] The obviating of scandal will demand that a dispensation from a public impediment be given publicly in foro externo, and the reasons for the same to be made known in some way.[87] The scandal of public concubinage is best removed by marriage which should be made known, in the best way possible, to those who have been scandalized.[88] On the other hand, to obviate scandal, it will at times be necessary that the dispensation and the celebration of marriage be kept secret and be inscribed, not in the public marriage register, but in the secret book in the Curial archives, as, for instance, if the two parties concerned were commonly reputed as husband and wife and really were living in con-

---

[85] Blat, *Commentarium Textus Codicis Juris Canonici*, Lib. III—P. 1—De Rebus, n. 435; De Smet, *o. c.*, II, n. 762, e; Wernz-Vidal, *Jus Canonicum*, V, n. 413.

[86] *Coll. de Prop. Fide*, 1685.

[87] Wernz-Vidal, *o. c.*, V, n. 413; Chelodi, *o. c.*, n. 41.

[88] Augustine, *A Commentary on the New Code of Canon Law*, V, (ed. III), p. 101.

cubinage. In case of occult impediments one must proceed very secretly.[89]

The complying with this precept, *"remoto scandalo,"* is necessary for the lawful use of the faculty of dispensing, but it is not required for validity. The terminological setting of the decree, 20 February, 1888, does not permit the condition of removing scandal to be considered as a requisite for the validity of the dispensation.[90] If the Ordinary, therefore, should find the total removal of scandal a practical impossibility, its partial removal, joined with the parties' promise, or, at least, willingness, to do more, will give him enough ground to grant the dispensation. Nay, more, he may proceed even if the scandal is irreparable; but if the parties out of mere obstinacy refuse to remove it, when the difficulties to be confronted are inconsiderable, a dispensation *should* not be given, because the least the Church exacts under such circumstances is compunction of heart for the wrong done and scandal created, which compunction is not to be conceived unless accompanied with readiness to embrace a little humiliation or inconvenience connected with the repairing of the scandal given.[91] However, in this whole question of the repairing and obviating of scandal, the Ordinary should lean towards leniency rather than severity. While striving to do well he should not overdo the good, for the Church frowns on anything which leads to abuse rather than eradication of abuse.

(b) *Cautiones:*

Should the case require a dispensation from the impediment of disparity of cult or of mixed religion, the customary cautiones should be subscribed to before the Ordinary proceeds any further. As to the nature and extent

---

[89] Chelodi, *Jus Matrimoniale,* n. 41; Wernz-Vidal, *o. c.,* V, n. 413; C. 1047.

[90] Motry, *Diocesan Faculties According to the Code of Canon Law,* p. 133; Petrovits, *o. c.,* n. 159; Cerato, *Matrimonium,* n. 35.

[91] Petrovits, *The New Church Law on Matrimony* (ed. II), n. 159.

of this very practical and serious condition there is much controversy, especially in very recent times. It will not, therefore, be amiss to preface the discussion with a few words on the precise nature and force of the cautiones.

Summarizing the evils which are associated with mixed marriages, Leo XIII wrote: "When minds do not agree as to the observances of religion, it is scarcely possible to hope for agreement in other things. Other reasons also proving that persons should turn with dread from such marriages are chiefly these: that they give occasion to forbidden association and communion in religious matters; endanger the faith of the Catholic partner; are a hindrance to the proper education of the children; and often lead to a mixing up of truth and falsehood, and to the belief that all religions are equally good."[92] These evils are manifestly so great that the divine law itself forbids such marriages. Until the prohibition of the divine law ceases, such marriages cannot be lawfully contracted, and it is obvious that the divine law permits of no dispensation by ecclesiastical authority. By the removal of the dangers to the faith of the Catholic party and of the offspring, or, at least, by rendering them remote—for scarcely ever can they be completely removed—, the divine law ceases to urge. The conditions under which the prohibition of the divine law is withdrawn have been frequently set forth by the Holy See, as, for example, by an Instruction of the Holy Office which requires: "that all danger of perversion be removed from the Catholic party, that all the children of both sexes shall be brought up in the Catholic religion, and that the Catholic party undertake the obligation of procuring the conversion of the non-Catholic."[93] The Church cannot grant a dispensation for a mixed marriage until she is morally certain that this prohibition of the divine law has ceased in the particular

[92] Ep. Encycl. *Arcanum*, par. 26, *Fontes*, 580.
[93] 3 Jan. 1871, *Fontes*, n. 1013.

case. This moral certitude will not be had, *as a rule,* unless the non-Catholic party formally promises to give full liberty to the Catholic party in the exercise of his or her religion, and in the complete Catholic education of the entire offspring.[94] It is for this end that the Church requires that this twofold promise by the non-Catholic party, regarding the divine and natural law, must precede the dispensation, namely, in so far as it is necessary to beget moral certainty that the prohibition of the divine law has ceased.[95] This twofold promise is generally known as "cautiones" or "guarantees." The Church's general law, as enforced for centuries, is restated (with some small exceptions) in Canon 1061 (summarized for cases of *"difference of worship"* in Canon 1071). The Church does not dispense unless:

(1) There is a just and grave cause;

(2) There be a guarantee given by the non-Catholic party to remove danger of perversion from the Catholic partner; and by both parties, that all the children will be baptized and brought up in the Catholic faith only.

(3) There be moral certainty that these guarantees will be fulfilled. These cautiones are but the concrete means demanded by the Church to secure the fulfillment of the conditions of the divine law, and to prove, in the external form, that the prohibition of the divine law has ceased. These are not conceivably the only means of obtaining this end, for it is not repugnant that moral certitude, as to the cessation of this prohibition, can be had without this formal promise.[96] But they are the necessary means demanded by the Church, so much so, that even if, in a particular case, it is certain that the conditions of the divine law are not in jeopardy, the ecclesiastical law demanding the cautiones still binds.[97]

---

[94] Gasparri, *De Matrimonio* (ed. III), I, n. 497.
[95] Gasparri, *l. c.*
[96] Gasparri, *De Matrimonio* (ed. III), I, n. 496.
[97] Gasparri, *l. c.*

Reference to these elementary matters has been made only to emphasize the distinction, always to be kept in mind, between the *conditions* under which the divine law ceases, and the *cautiones* or *guarantees* which the ecclesiastical law requires for the fulfillment of these conditions. Throughout the present discussion the ecclesiastical aspect of the cautiones only will be considered, as in all cases under discussion it will be presupposed that the demands of the divine law are satisfied, that is, that the *conditions* are fulfilled.

If a dispensation is granted for a mixed marriage in danger of death, the cautiones are to be given (*"praestitis consuetis cautionibus"*). All will admit that, even in danger of death, these guarantees *per se* must be asked *and* received. The Holy Office has declared this expressly: *"Cautiones etiam in articulo mortis esse exigendas."*[98] But what, if the non-Catholic party refuses obstinately to subscribe to the cautiones? This practical difficulty has given rise to a discussion among Canonists as to whether the giving of the cautiones, in danger of death, is a necessary condition for the validity of the dispensation,[99] so that without them the dispensation cannot be given under any circumstances. A number of Canonists can be found defending both opinions. The view that they are absolutely necessary for validity is espoused by Woywod,[100] Augustine,[101] Prümmer,[102] De Smet,[103] Noldin,[104] Simon,[105] Chelodi and

[98] 18 March 1891, *Coll. de Prop. Fide,* 1750.

[99] Hence for the validity of the marriage, if the impediment is disparity of worship; for the validity of the dispensation, not of the marriage itself, if it is merely mixed religion.

[100] *A Practical Commentary on the Code of Canon Law,* n. 1011; also in *H. P. R.*, XXIII, p. 1059.

[101] *A Commentary on the New Code of Canon Law* (ed. III), V, p. 101, c.

[102] *Manuale Theologiae Moralis* (ed. III), III, n. 866; also in *H. P. R.*, XXVII, 2, p. 194 ff.

[103] *De Sponsalibus et Matrimonio* (ed. IV), II, p. 36, nota 1; p. 217, n. 508, nota 1; n. 591, nota 4.

[104] *De Sacramentis* (ed. XIV), III, n. 608.

[105] *Faculties of Pastors and Confessors for Absolution and Dispensation,* p. 86.

Wernz-Vidal at least partially.[106] These Canonists found their opinion *mainly* on the decisions of the Holy See. They appeal first to the decision of the Holy Office, 18 March, 1891, already quoted. They also invoke a decree of 21 June, 1912: "An in concedendis ab habente a Sancta Sede potestatem dispensationibus super impedimento disparitatis cultus praescriptae cautiones semper sunt exigendae." The answer given was: "Dispensationem super impedimento disparitatis cultus nunquam concedi, nisi expressis omnibus conditionibus seu cautionibus."[107] The second question answered by the same Congregation has more bearing on the point at issue: "Utrum dispensatio super impedimento disparitatis cultus, ab habente a Sancta Sede potestatem, non requisitis vel denegatis praescriptis cautionibus impertita, valida habenda sit an non?" The answer was given thus: "Dispensationem, prout exponitur, impertitam esse nullam."[108] From the absoluteness of these declarations these Canonists conclude that an Ordinary could never dispense, in favor of a well-disposed Catholic, if the non-Catholic party refuses to subscribe to the cautiones.

Many other Canonists, however, maintain, as a probable opinion, that in case the cautiones are refused by the non-Catholic, provided the Catholic party is favorably disposed, and the conditions of the divine law are fulfilled in the case, the Ordinary can validly dispense. This view is defended by Petrovits,[109] Farrugia,[110] Genicot-Salsmans,[111]

---

[106] Chelodi, *Jus Matrimoniale* (ed. III), n. 41; Wernz-Vidal, *Jus Canonicum,* V, n. 413, c. Both express their view thus: "his (cautionibus) non requisitis aut denegatis dispensatio non certo valida sit."

[107] *A. A. S.,* IV, p. 442.

[108] *A. A. S.,* IV, 443.

[109] *The New Church Law on Matrimony* (ed. II), n. 160; n. 192.

[110] *De Matrimonio et Causis Matrimonialibus* (ed. X), n. 83, d.

[111] *Institutiones Theologiae Moralis,* II (ed. X), n. 523.

Cerato,[112] Vermeersch,[113] Pighi,[114] Kubelbeck,[115] O'Neill,[116] Mahoney,[117] De Becker,[118] King,[119] and Cappello.[120] They point out that there is nothing in the canon to demand that the asking and obtaining of the cautiones are necessary for validity; that this inference is legitimate from the fact that, according to the New Legislation, a rescript is not invalidated, though its use may be illicit, unless preceded by the conditional conjunction, *"if," "unless," "except," "provided,"* or any other belonging to the same class.[121] They furthermore contend that the use of the ablative absolute ("praestitis consuetis cautionibus") does not necessarily involve a condition that is required for validity. This latter reason, however, does not appear conclusive. Prescinding from the grammatical aspect of the question, it will suffice to quote the potent words of the prince of Canonists, Benedict XIV. Treating of rescripts he wrote: *"Certissimum est inter jurisperitos quod vera conditio ex ablativo absoluto consequitur: qua de re praetermitti nullo modo potest, licet gravissima incommoda jam exposita interponantur."*[122] The same Canonists also point out that the words of the Holy Office, *"cautiones in periculo mortis esse*

---

[112] *Matrimonium* (ed. III), n. 35.

[113] *Theologia Moralis,* III (ed. 1923), n. 758.

[114] *De Sacramento Matrimonii* (ed. II), n. 90, 6 a, who, with Cerato, maintains that in danger of death the cautiones are necessary "simpliciter" for liceity.

[115] *The Sacred Penitentiaria and its Relations to Faculties of Ordinaries and Priests,* p. 63, who writes: "if the Ordinary for no reason dispenses, without exacting the conditions, the dispensation would be valid but illicit."

[116] *I. E. R.,* XXVIII, pp. 634, 635.

[117] *H. P. R.,* LXXII, p. 510.

[118] *De Sponsalibus et Matrimonio* (ed. II), p. 278, nota 1; p. 243.

[119] *The Administration of the Sacraments to Dying Non-Catholics,* pp. 123–131.

[120] *De Sacramentis,* III, n. 232, f: "Probabilius affirmandum, positis conditionibus jure divino requisitis, quia non videtur Ecclesia urgere sub poena nullitatis observantiam legis canonicae in periculo mortis, ob damna gravissima quae secus forte obvenirent fidelibus. Quod si desit omnino tempus praestandi ejusmodi cautiones, pro certo tenemus legem ecclesiasticam tunc cessare, et matrimonium esse procul dubio validum."

[121] Canon 39: Cf. Petrovits, *l. c.*

[122] *Institutiones Ecclesiasticae,* II, Inst. 87, n. 68.

exigendas," should be interpreted as imposing an obligation to obtain the cautiones *"in quantum fieri potest,"* and to demand absolutely at least those which are prescribed by the divine law.[123] Lastly, they argue that the decree of the Holy Office, 21 June, 1912, quoted by their opponents, refers to ordinary cases, and not to those in which there is danger of death; that it speaks of the exercise of special faculties from the Holy See, and not of those conferred by common law; that the words *"prout exponitur"* actually imply that, in different circumstances, a different reply might be given, and that if there is another case ("prout exponitur") in which such a dispensation might be valid, surely that case is the danger of death.[124]

Perhaps there is no canonical question under dispute for which it is so difficult to obtain any tangible evidence as the one at present under discussion. The old law gives very little information to help clear the cloud of controversy. Such a dearth of evidence among the pre-Code authors is intelligible when one bears in mind that the faculties of 20 February 1888 *expressly* excluded mixed religion from the power they conferred. Truly indeed they did not put disparity of cult outside the pale of the dispensatory power of Ordinaries in danger of death, but unfortunately the commentators on that decree give nothing which has a practical bearing on the precise point at issue. Wernz[125] dismisses the question with the remark that the cautiones are to be demanded in danger of death, *especially* if it is the Catholic party who is in such danger. Gasparri[126] insists on the necessity of obtaining moral certainty as to the cessation of the prohibition of the divine law, but remarks that the cautiones, though the *necessary* means, are not the *only means* of acquiring this certitude. The only author who discussed the question "ex professo" decided in favor of the

[123] De Becker, *l. c.*
[124] Cerato, *l. c.*
[125] *Jus Decretalium,* IV (1904), p. 837, nota 33.
[126] *De Matrimonio* (ed. III), I, n. 497.

more benign interpretation: "*Nihilominus in gravissimo mortis periculo, si pars acatholica cautiones de prole catholice educanda recuset, sed tamen removeatur pro parte catholica periculum proximum perversionis et simul haec pars consuetas praestet cautiones, credimus ea sufficere ut dispensatio legitime concedatur. Neque, extra praedictum periculum, desunt casus in quibus Sedes Apostolica, ob graves rationes similiter dispensaverit, imo et sanationem in radice concesserit.*"[127] Previous to 1888 little evidence can likewise be obtained, which can also be explained by the fact that in the faculties attributed to Bishops at that time, on the plea of custom and presumed consent of the Supreme Pontiff, mixed religion and disparity of cult were *probably* excluded.[128] Hence the solution of the present discussion depends *practically* on the interpretation given by modern authors.

Theoretically it is not easy to come to a certain conclusion on this very difficult question. It is hard to give one unified answer which would cover all cases. It seems the far better opinion that when it is the catholic party who is in danger of death, the actual *acquisition* of the cautiones is necessary for the validity of the dispensation. A decision of the Holy Office, 6 July 1898, seems to favor this conclusion. Having been asked as to how a priest should act when called to attend a dying Catholic who is already civilly married to an infidel, and there are baptized children whom the civil law regards as legitimate, the Holy Office gave answer: "Episcopus vel parochus in casu uti poterit facultate Ordinariis concessa sub die 20 Febr. 1888, renovato consensu et *datis* cautionibus."[129]

But what if it is the non-catholic party who is at death's

---

[127] De Becker, *De Sponsalibus et Matrimonio* (ed. II), p. 278, nota 1; Cf. p. 243.

[128] See Part I, cap. III of this work: Cf. Benedict XIV, *De Synodo Dioecesana,* Lib. IX, cap. III, n. 2; Giovine, *De Dispensationibus Matrimonialibus* (1885), I, cons. CLXXI, n. 5; Feije, *De Impedimentis et Dispensationibus Matrimonialibus,* n. 613.

[129] *Coll. de Prop. Fide,* 2007, ad. 2.

threshold and he obstinately refuses to give the cautiones? No doubt the Church is unwilling that a direct dispensation, without the cautiones, should be given in such circumstances. The Church has undoubtedly expressed such unwillingness when the most she has consented to give in such circumstances (and that only to avoid a greater evil), is the power to grant a sanatio in radice without the cautiones.[130] However this decision is not so absolute as to prove with certainty that a direct dispensation without the cautiones would be invalid in such a case. She is clearly unwilling that such should be the general mode of action in such circumstances, but from the very fact that she did not forbid marriage absolutely, but permitted the giving of a sanatio in radice without the guarantees, seems to show that in extreme necessity, in a particular case, a direct dispensation, without the cautiones, would not be absolutely invalid. As has already been said, the cautiones are but the external means used by the Church to guarantee and safeguard the fulfillment of the requirements of the divine law. They are indeed the means, and the *necessary* means, demanded by the Church, but it must be admitted that, in the concrete, there *can* be moral certainty as to the cessation of the prohibition of the divine law, in a particular case, without the formal cautiones.[131a] Hence if, in a particular case, the non-catholic party is in extreme danger of death, and the celebration of marriage is necessary for the legitimation of children already conceived or born, and if the Ordinary is prudently satisfied that, notwithstanding the obstinate refusal of the non-catholic to give the cautiones, the requirements of the divine law are not in jeopardy, it seems quite reasonable to presume that the Church would not urge, in such circumstances, a law that is merely ecclesiastical, and that a dispensation in the case would be valid.

There can be no doubt that this opinion has received

[130] Holy Office, 12 April 1899, *Coll. de Prop. Fide,* 2042.
[131a] Gasparri, *o. c.,* I, n. 497.

the approbation of a sufficient number of canonists and theologians to render it probable. The division among authors on the point effects that the Church's law calling for the cautiones, in such straitened circumstances, under pain of invalidity, is a *lex dubia,* and lex dubia (dubio juris) non obligat.[131b]

In modern times the opinion which would not condemn, under pain of invalidity, a dispensation given in such extreme necessity, is gaining ground gradually, as far as external authority is concerned. Vermeersch, one of the outstanding canonists of to-day, has severed his allegiance from the stricter view and embraced the milder opinion. In 1922[132] he upheld the invalidity of such a dispensation, but in 1923[133] he accepted the opposite opinion as *probabilior:* "Si (cautiones) plene obtineri vel prudenter peti posse non videntur, Ordinarius *probabilius* valide agit qui, in his rebus extremis, conditionibus jure divino requisitis, contentus sit. Id tamen minus ex praesenti facultate, quam ex c. 81, colligitur quo, ubi in mora est periculum gravis damni, Ordinarius ad mentem S. Sedis dispensare permittitur." A similar change in view has been made by some canonists, and in face of this it is hard to see the justification for the article which came from the pen of Prümmer, a few months ago, on this very point at issue. He states, without substantiating his statement, that it was the common opinion before the Code that a dispensation, without the cautiones, in danger of death, is invalid. He moreover claims that of recent Theologians and Canonists, Cappello is almost the only one who teaches the contrary.[134] The number of Canonists quoted above as *actually* teaching the contrary is a sufficient refutation of this claim.

In practice, then, the only case that can be *considered* is

[131b] Canon 15.

[132] *Epitome Juris Canonici* (ed. 1922), 11, n. 348, d.

[133] *Theologia Moralis,* III, n. 758. Cf. *Epit. Juris Canonici* (ed. II), II, n. 306.

[134] *H. P. R.,* XXVIII, 2, pp. 194, 195.

one in which the non-Catholic is the party in danger of death. In all other cases the view that the cautiones must be asked and *received,* under pain of invalidity, seems to be beyond dispute. When the non-Catholic is at death's portals, and refuses obstinately to make the customary formal promises, at least orally, then the Ordinary and priest must rely on their own judgment having invoked the aid of the Holy Spirit. But, above all, they must remember that in no case can they dispense until they are morally certain that the prohibition of the divine law has ceased in the case. Regarding this latter point it may be well to bear in mind that the refusal of a non-Catholic to subscribe to the guarantees demanded by the Chruch does not *always* connote that the requirements of the divine law are in danger, even in so far as they depend on him; such a refusal is, at times, but the manifestation of unwillingness to submit to terms which are considered irksome.

If the cautiones are given by both parties, it is scarcely necessary to add that, if time does not permit otherwise, it is sufficient if they are given orally.

Given all these conditions the Ordinary can dispense both *in ordine ad matrimonium contrahendum* and *in ordine ad matrimonium convalidandum.* The general tenor of the canon justifies this conclusion.[135] The dispensation can be granted both for the internal and the external forums. If the impediment is public, to obviate scandal, the dispensation is to be given publicly and before witnesses (unless he dispenses from the form also). If the impediment is occult the dispensation must be given in the internal forum, whether sacramental or non-sacramental.[136]

The faculty of dispensing in danger of death, however, does not enable its recipient to grant a *sanatio in radice.* This was the accepted teaching before the Code,[137] and is

---

[135] De Smet, *De Sponsalibus et Matrimonio,* II, n. 761.

[136] Cappello, *o. c.,* III, n. 232, e; Noldin, *o. c.,* III, n. 608, h; Blat, *o. c.,* n. 435.

[137] Wernz, *Jus Decretalium,* IV (1904), p. 887, nota 67.

also taught by all commentators since the Code.[138] This faculty is not granted not only because the granting of a sanatio in radice is reserved to the Holy See,[139] but also because canon 1043 does not include a dispensation from the law "de renovando consensu." Hence when revalidating a marriage the Ordinary must see to the renewal of consent according to the requirements of canons 1133–1137. The renewal of consent must be a new act of the will ratifying a marriage which is known to have been null from the beginning,[140] and this renewal is required by ecclesiastical law for the validity of the revalidation,[141] even if both parties gave their consent in the beginning and never withdrew it. As to the form of this renewal, if the impediment is *public,* the consent must be renewed by both parties in the form prescribed by law (unless he dispenses too from the form of marriage when a public renewal is not required, but there must be a private renewal).[142] If the impediment is occult and known to both parties, a secret and private renewal by both parties will suffice.[143] If it is occult and unknown to one party, a private renewal by the party cognizant of the impediment is sufficient, provided, of course, the consent of the other perseveres.[144]

Subjects of the Dispensing Power:—On whose behalf the dispensation may be granted is determined by the words, *subjects,* and *actual residence.* The Ordinary may exercise this faculty on behalf of his subjects wherever they are. His subjects are those who have a domicile or quasi-domicile (diocesan or parochial) in his diocese.[145] Monthly sojourn ("menstrua commoratio") in his diocese does not

---

[138] Cf. Cappello, *o. c.*, III, n. 232, J; De Smet, *o. c.*, II, n. 761; Ayrinhac, *Marriage Legislation in the New Code of Canon Law*, p. 323.

[139] Canon 1141; Cf. Holy Office, 6 July 1898, ad. 3, *Coll. de Prop. Fide,* 2007.

[140] Canon 1134.

[141] Canon 1133, par. 2.

[142] Canon 1135, par. 1.

[143] Canon 1135, par. 2.

[144] Canon 1135, par. 3.

[145] Canon 94, par. 1.

make one his subject. He may also exercise the faculty in favor of all persons who are hic et nunc tarrying within the limits of his diocese, even though not possessing a domicile or quasi-domicile, or even "menstrua commoratio," there. There is this difference, however, between these two classes of persons. For his subjects his jurisdiction is *personal,* while for all others it is *territorial.* Hence he may exercise his power of dispensing on behalf of his subjects even when they are outside the limits of his diocese, while all others fall within his jurisdiction only when they are *hic et nunc* actually within the confines of his diocese. Of course at times he may have power over non-subjects when outside his diocese, namely, when the requirements of c. 1098 are fulfilled.

It may happen, at times, that there is not time to make the ordinary investigations which should precede marriage because of the proximity of death. In such circumstances, when no other proof can be secured, and signs do not point to the contrary, the sworn statement of the parties that they are baptized and labor under no impediment will suffice to admit them to the celebration of marriage.[146a] One should proceed prudently in these circumstances. If the parties have been living in concubinage, or in civil marriage, it will be wise to endeavour to find out why they did not marry "coram Ecclesia," and in this way one may discover the existence of an impediment. Special attention is to be given to the impediments of *crimen* and *ligamen.*

In dispensing in danger of death the "stylus Curiae" need not be observed,[146b] especially in cases of great urgency. Some form of dispensing like the following may be used: "By the authority granted to me by the Holy Church, I dispense you from this impediment and unite you in the holy bond of matrimony." Of course, should time permit, it would be well not to be satisfied with granting the dispen-

---

[146a] Canon 1019, par. 2.
[146b] Cf. Gasparri, *o. c.,* I, n. 445; *Contra,* Vlaming, *o. c.,* II, n. 416.

sation orally, but should give it in writing, drawing up an instrument in which would be enunciated all those things required by the "stylus Curiae," namely, (a) mention of the faculty whereby the dispensation is granted; (b) the verification of the causes required by law; (c) the act of dispensing.[146c]

Nature of power: It is practically the unanimous teaching of Canonists to-day that the power of dispensing conferred by canon 1043 is *"potestas ordinaria-vicaria,"* and, therefore, one which can be delegated.[147] Ojetti,[148] however, has defended, in a somewhat long treatise, the view that the powers of canons 1043–1045 are not ordinary but *delegatae a jure,* and that they cannot be sub-delegated. A full understanding of his opinion would not be possible without some consideration of the principal arguments he has put forth to maintain the doctrine he has propounded.

He starts out his discussion with the bold assertion that all other authors do not understand the sense of canon 197 rightly. This canon lays down that any power which is annexed to an office by law is ordinary. But this principle, he claims, can be understood in a twofold sense; namely, that whatever power is said in the Code to be conceded to Ordinaries thereby becomes ordinary; or that only that power is ordinary which the Code asserts, either *formaliter* or *equivalenter,* pertains to the office of Ordinaries. Authors generally interpret the principle in the first sense, but wrongly so. Accepting the second interpretation the power of canon 1043 cannot be said to be *ordinary.*

[146c] Cf. Vlaming, *l. c.*

[147] Augustine, *A Commentary on the New Code of Canon Law* (ed. III), V, p. 98; Cappello, *De Sacramentis,* III, n. 232, I; Vermeersch-Creusen, *Epitome Juris Canonici,* II, n. 307; Farrugia, *De Matrimonio et Causis Matrimonialibus,* n. 83; Blat, *Commentarium Textus Codicis Juris Canonici* (1924), Lib. III—P. 1—De Rebus, n. 435; Maroto, *Institutiones Juris Canonici,* I, n. 699, 7, a; Vlaming, *Praelectiones Juris Matrimonii* (ed. III), II, n. 400, n. 415; Wernz-Vidal, *Jus Canonicum,* V, n. 413; Hilling, *A. K. K.,* CIV., pp. 181–189; Haring, *L. Q. S.,* LXXIX, pp. 594, 595; Woywod, *A Practical Commentary on the Code of Canon Law,* n. 1012.

[148] *Gregorianum,* VI, pp. 436–441.

His second argument is a philosophical one and, it must be confessed, one that is not very tangible. Those faculties, he seems to infer, which the present law annexes to those offices which it has received from a superior law, and according to the preconceived idea of that law, constitute ordinary power; but those annexed to those offices constituted by itself, and according to its own preformed idea, are not ordinary but delegated. Hence, he concludes, the power of a Bishop to rule his diocese (the Bishopric is an office received from a superior law, and the Code annexed that power to it as essentially belonging to it) is ordinary; whereas the faculty of a Bishop to dispense in danger of death (an office constituted by the present law itself) is not ordinary.

His third argument is more to the point. Canon 81, he says, lays down the general principle that no Ordinary, inferior to the Pope, can dispense from the general laws of the Church, because the relaxation of a law in a particular case can be effected only by the legislator himself, his superior, successor, or delegates. When Ordinaries then are enabled to dispense, as they are by canon 1043, they dispense, not as legislator, his superior, or his successor, but as his delegates, and the power they exercise is only delegated.

Next he claims that his contention is not opposed to the nature of delegated power. Delegated power is not that which is committed to a physical person, but that committed to a person *simpliciter*. A person is either physical or moral, the latter being collegiate or non-collegiate. Hence jurisdiction which is given to a non-collegiate moral person, as is an *office,* is not ordinary but delegated.

He concludes by claiming that his view follows directly from the very concept of commission; for power which is committed, say to an Ordinary, is not proper to his office, but is superadded to it, so that he could never exercise that power were it not committed to him. When he does exercise it, he does not do so *"vi officii,"* but *"vi commissionis."*

"Quapropter ut aliqua potestas jurisdictionis dicatur ordinaria, non sufficit ut concedatur officio, sed insuper requiritur ut sit propria officii, id est, ut *per se* (et non solum per commissionem) pertineat ad officium secundum ideam praeformatam in jure constitutionale."[149]

A general comment on these arguments can be summed up in the remark that they admirably prove one thing, and only one thing, namely, that the powers conferred by canons 1043–1045 are not *"potestas ordinaria propria,"* which all must admit. They by no means militate against the claim that the power is *"ordinaria-vicaria."*

Ordinary jurisdiction may be propria or vicaria. Propria is that which belongs to an office of its very nature, so much so that without it the office, as such, cannot be conceived. Hence the power of a Bishop to rule his diocese is *ordinaria-propria;* it pertains to the very essence of the Bishopric. *Ordinaria-vicaria* is that which indeed belongs to the office as annexed to it by common law, but which does not essentially pertain to that office, so that without it the office, as such, could still exist. The holder of that office would not possess this power had it not been annexed, superadded as it were, to his office by the law itself.

Delegated jurisdiction is that which one possesses not by virtue of his office, but by special commission; and it is *delegata a jure* when the source of that commission is the common law itself. Hence the solution of the question, as to whether the power of canon 1043 is *"ordinaria-vicaria,"* or *"delegata-a-jure,"* depends on one point, namely, whether it is to be regarded as annexed to the office, in question, by the common law, or as a *personal* commission made by law.

It is not possible to conceive the power conferred by this canon as a personal commission made by law. The whole philosophy and background of the canon goes to show that the power it bestows is to be regarded as a power annexed to an office. When the Archbishop of Baltimore dispenses

[149] *L. c.*, p. 439.

in danger of death, by virtue of canon 1043, he dispenses, not as Archbishop Curley, but as Ordinary of Baltimore. It is immaterial who holds that office, but he who does hold it eo ipso possesses this power.

Moreover, the power in question possesses all the elements necessary for *"potestas ordinaria-vicaria."* This is essentially comprised of two elements, (a) it is annexed to an office, and (b) this annexation is made by law (canon 197). If either of these elements were wanting, the power is not ordinary but delegated. The primary element which determines the nature of ordinary power is the *officium;* it is the essential factor by which ordinary is distinguished from delegated jurisdiction. Authors teach generally that the officium must be one in the strict sense,[150a] but that an *"officium commissum"* is a sufficient title to vicarious power. No one will deny that the Ordinary of canon 1043 has an officium sufficient to meet the requirements of the law in this respect.

If the power is only delegated it must be the defect of the second element (annexation, by law, of the power to the office) which makes it so. Is the power to dispense, in danger of death, annexed by law to the office of Ordinaries? If so it is ordinary-vicarious power; if not it is only delegated. All that is necessary for vicarious power is that it be annexed by law to the office in such a way that the persons holding that office receive the power *mediante officio,* without any other act of concession, distinct from that by which the superior confers the office, being required.[150b] It must be annexed *permanently,* and *antecedently* to the persons on whom the office is bestowed; it must be so annexed as to be regarded as cohering with the office in a permanent way, and independently of the persons who obtain that

---

[150a] Maroto, *Institutiones Juris Canonici,* I, p. 674, nota I; Wernz-Vidal, *o. c.,* II, n. 366.

[150b] Wernz-Vidal, *Jus Canonicum,* II, n. 366.

office.[151] It is clear that the power of canon 1043 meets with these requirements.

Other arguments can also be given to show that the power of canon 1043 is ordinary. (a) *Historical Proof:* while it is true that many Canonists regarded the faculties of 20 February 1888 as delegated jurisdiction,[152] many others regarded them as ordinary.[153] But the powers attributed to Bishops for urgent cases previous to 1888, on the strength of custom and the common teaching of Theologians, were regarded by some as ordinary,[154] by others as quasi-ordinary,[155] but by none as *delegated.* Canon 1043 is to be interpreted not merely in the light of the Decree of 20 February 1888, but also, and especially, with an eye to the common and certain teaching of Theologians and Canonists previous to that year, which was the source of the powers exercised by Bishops in urgent cases, through many centuries, and which is the *ultimate* and fundamental foundation of canon 1043.

(b) *From the Code itself:* From canon 1043 to canon 1050 inclusive, the Code deals with three distinct species of dispensatory power, namely, (a) the power to dispense mentioned in canons 1043 to 1045 inclusive; (b) power granted by rescript, as referred to in canon 1047; and (c) that given by general indult, as dealt with in canon 1049. Then canon 1051 is inserted to declare the effect, regarding the legitimation of offspring, resulting from dispensations granted by each of these powers, and enumerates the same three species of powers, thus maintaining the same division established in the preceding canons. If the relation between

---

151 Maroto, *Institutiones Juris Canonici,* I, n. 699, 8, a; Wernz-Vidal, *l. c.*

152 Cf. Wernz, *Jus Decretalium,* n. 617, nota 63.

153 Cf. Gasparri, *De Matrimonio* (ed. 1904), n. 435; De Becker, *De Sponsalibus et Matrimonio* (ed. II), p. 316.

154 Sanchez, *De Sancto Matrimonii Sacramento,* lib. II, dis. XL, n. 14; D'Annibale, *Summa Theologiae Moralis,* I (ed. III), n. 231; Wernz, *o. c.,* IV, n. 618, nota 74; Gasparri, *o. c.,* n. 435.

155 Cf. Feije, *De Impedimentis et Dispensationibus Matrimonialibus* (ed. III), n. 633; Heiss, *De Matrimonio,* pp. 196, 197.

canon 1051 and its predecessors is to be maintained, it follows that the power bestowed by canons 1043 to 1045 is ordinary, as the latter two species of power mentioned in canon 1051 certainly answer two species of the power described in the preceding canons.

(c) All admit that the faculty given by canon 1043 includes the power to legitimate spurious offspring, excepting adulterous and sacrilegious. Canon 1051 does not mention *potestas delegata a jure,* and, hence, if the faculty of canon 1043 is not ordinary power, it would not be justifiable to attribute to it the above-mentioned effect.

The arguments given by Ojetti by no means weaken the accepted teaching of practically all other writers, namely, that the power, though vicarious, is ordinary. His interpretation of canon 197 seems too restrictive. The argument he deduces from canon 81 clearly contains a *petitio principii,* as he takes for granted that explicit or implicit concession made by law to Ordinaries, inferior to the Roman Pontiff, is delegation; which point is the very kernel of the dispute. His interpretation of "officium" as a "non-collegiate moral person," and its application to canon 197, par. 1, is somewhat far-fetched; nay, it would destroy the whole sense of that canon. "Potestas jurisdictionis ordinaria ea est quae ipso jure adnexa est officio; delegata, quae commissa est personae."[156] It is clear from these words that the radical element of the distinction between the two species of power is *officium,* in contradistinction to *persona.* If officium can be regarded as coming under the genus of *persona,* in this context, the fundamental factor of differentiation between ordinary and delegated power would indeed be rendered vague.

Blat, while admitting that the power of canon 1043 is ordinary, denies, however, that it can be delegated.[157] His argument is that the power to dispense from general laws,

---

[156] C. 197, par. 1.

[157] *Commentarium Textus Codicis Juris Canonici* (ed. II), Lib. II—De Personis, n. 148; Lib. III—P. 1, De Rebus (ed. 11), n. 435.

as conferred by canon 1043 and other canons throughout the Code, does not come under the principle enunciated in canon 199, par. 1, but under the exception made therein (*"nisi aliud expresse jure caveatur"*). His interpretation of that canon would be that ordinary power cannot be delegated except in cases where the power to delegate it is expressly mentioned. This interpretation is however opposed to the clear meaning of the words of the canon and to the teaching of practically all Canonists.[158] Moreover many of the older writers stated expressly that this power could be delegated.[159]

Hence the power conferred by canon 1043 is ordinary, and can be delegated "vel ex toto vel ex parte."[160]

---

[158] Cf. Hilling, *A. K. K.*, CIV, p. 193; Vermeersch-Creusen, *Epitome Juris Canonici*, II, n. 307; Haring, *L. Q. S.*, LXXIX, pp. 594, 595; Chelodi, *Jus de Personis*, n. 127; Maroto, *Institutiones Juris Canonici*, I, n. 699.

[159] Sanchez, *De Sancto Matrimonii Sacramento*, lib. II, dis. XL, n. 14: "dicendum est posse delegare quia jurisdictio . . . competens, non *personae*, sed perptuo dignitati, vel officio; non est delegata sed ordinaria et potestatis ordinariae jura habet." Cf. St. Alphonsus, *Theologia Moralis*, lib. VI, n. 1125.

[160] C. 199, par. 1.

CHAPTER VI

Danger of Death

Powers of Parish Priests, Priests, and Confessors

In eisdem rerum adjunctis de quibus in can. 1043 et solum pro casibus in quibus ne loci quidem Ordinarius adiri possit, eadem dispensandi facultate pollet tum parochus, tum sacerdos qui matrimonio, ad normam can. 1098, n. 2, assistit, tum confessarius, sed hic pro foro interno in actu sacramentalis confessionis tantum. (*Canon 1044.*)

Under the same circumstances described in the previous chapter, but *exclusively* in cases where no recourse can be had to the Ordinary of the place, the same extensive faculty to dispense is enjoyed by the Parish Priest, and by any priest who assists at marriage according to the norm of canon 1098, par. 2, and even by the confessor, the power of the latter being restricted to the internal forum and in the act of sacramental confession only.

This canon confirms and extends certain faculties which were conferred previous to the Code. By Article VII of the "Ne Temere" decree, when danger of death arose, and when the local Ordinary, or Parish Priest, or priest delegated by either to assist at marriages, could only be approached with grave inconvenience, and when, moreover, the marriage was advisable either for the purpose of soothing the conscience of the parties concerned, or of legitimating the children born or conceived, any priest might validly assist at the ceremony. In these circumstances, according to the decree of the Sacred Congregation of the Sacraments,[1] the priest assisting, whoever he might be, and, a fortiori, the parish priest, if he were present,[2] could dispense from all *diriment*

[1] *A. A. S.*, I, 468, 469.
[2] *S. Congr. Sacrs.*, 29 July 1910, *A. A. S.*, II, 650.

impediments of the ecclesiastical law, with the two exceptions of the priesthood and affinity, as in the Leonine Decree of 1888.

These decrees marked a considerable advance from previous legislation. Any priest might exercise the faculty. It made no difference whether the danger arose from disease, or any other cause. There was, however, still no provision made for impedient impediments, and both Bishops and Priests had to be content with whatever extension of faculties the principles of epikeia might suggest. But this is no longer, for the impedient impediments now fall into line.

Before the three classes of persons enumerated in Canon 1044 can validly use the faculty of dispensing, it will be necessary that all the conditions and circumstances of c. 1043, and as explained in the preceding chapter, be verified, and, moreover, that approach to the Ordinary for the dispensation be either physically or morally impossible.

ARTICLE I

The Parish Priest

Besides the conditions of urgent danger of death, the necessity of adjusting matters of conscience, or of legitimating offspring, a third very essential condition must necessarily be present before the parish priest can dispense. The phrase "Ordinarius adiri non possit" must be verified in every particular case. The only difference between the powers of the Ordinary, described in the preceding chapter, and those of the parish priest consists in this that the powers of the latter cannot be exercised unless it is impossible to approach the Ordinary. If this impossibility does not exist the parish priest is powerless, and must recur to the Ordinary for the dispensation.

What Ordinary is contemplated by the law? Petrovits[3]

[3] *The New Church Law on Matrimony* (ed. 11), n. 161.

interprets the canon as including both the proper Ordinary of either party in question (that is, the Ordinary by virtue of domicile or quasi-domicile), and the Ordinary of the place in which the parties tarry *hic et nunc.* If either can be approached in time, therefore, the parish priest could not dispense. This is quite reasonable, since both of these Ordinaries are competent to dispense by virtue of canon 1043.

"Adiri non possit." The impossibility of approaching the Ordinary does not mean absolute physical impossibility. It refers rather to the delay which such a course would inevitably necessitate. The impossibility is to be understood of moral impossibility, which is present whenever one of the parties is in danger of death and it is prudently feared that death or, at least, unconsciousness may supervene before recourse to the Ordinary can be made, and the dispensation obtained.[4]

The possibility of recurring to the local Ordinary must be understood of ordinary means. If the parish priest can come in contact with the Ordinary in person or by letter, even by "special delivery" letter, if necessary, in sufficient time to receive a dispensation, he is clearly bound to do so. If, however, the use of even these means would cause grave incommodum to the parties, arising especially out of the danger of violating a secret, then the condition "adiri non possit" is verified, and the parish priest can dispense.[5]

There is no obligation whatever to resort to the use of the telegraph or telephone. They are to be regarded as *extraordinary* means. "Censendum esse Ordinarium adiri non posse, si nonnisi per telegraphum vel telephonum ad eum recurri possit."[6] Not only is it not obligatory to use these extraordinary means of communication, but it is not advisable. In fact it is forbidden "ex regula ordinaria" to

---

[4] De Smet, *De Sponsalibus et Matrimonio,* II, n. 792; Wernz-Vidal, *Jus Canonicum,* V, n. 425.

[5] Vermeersch, *Theologia Moralis,* III, n. 758; Wernz-Vidal, *o. c.,* n. 425, 2.

[6] *Pont. Comm. pro Interp. Codicis,* 12 November 1922, *A. A. S.,* XIV, 662, 663.

use these methods for any dispensation. The letter of the *Cardinal Secretary of State* to the Bishops of Italy, 10 December 1891, declared that all applications for favors to the Roman Curia, made by telegraph, shall be ignored, and desired that all Bishops would introduce a similar practice in their diocesan Curia.[7] Even the validity of a dispensation may be endangered by the methods under consideration, especially in those cases in which many things are to be expressed *"de validitate,"* as may happen when Bishops dispense *"vi indultorum."*[8] As to the use of the telephone, its validity depends upon prompt, reliable, and secret service. The ordinary party line is no trustworthy and confidential means of communication. It is not only unsafe, but liable to abuse on account of the publicity involved. But in no case is the use of the telephone mandatory.

As to the use of the automobile, whether it is to be numbered among the ordinary or extraordinary means, may still be regarded as an open question. Much depends on the individual case. It is generally admitted to-day that *for many* the automobile is no longer to be regarded as an extraordinary means, and should be utilized, if time and convenience permit, to obtain the dispensation from the competent authority.[9]

One must, however, always bear in mind that only moral impossibility of reaching the Ordinary is required. One must not be overscrupulous in estimating the degree of urgency. The salvation and welfare of souls is far more important that quibbling over the words of a law. One must be careful not to give blind assent to the remarks of some nurses and doctors when interrogated on the state of a patient, for they often misunderstand the motives of the interrogations and over-exaggerate the chances of recovery. It is only when one is morally certain that there is time to obtain a dispensation from the Ordinary before the patient

[7] *N. R. T.*, XXIV, pp. 32, 33.

[8] Vlaming, *Praelectiones Juris Matrimonii,* II, n. 449.

[9] Cf. Wernz-Vidal, *Jus Canonicum,* V, n. 544.

becomes unconscious, or otherwise incapable of seeing to the affairs of conscience, that the pastor is bound to have recourse to him. In all other cases he can safely act on canon 1044, for, in doubt, he should always favor the party in danger.

If there is not enough time to have recourse to the Ordinary, would there be an obligation to apply to an ecclesiastic delegated by the Ordinary to dispense? Would the possibility of having recourse to such a one deprive the parish priest of power to dispense? Vermeersch[10] and Motry[11] deny that any such obligation can be urged for the validity of the dispensation, as there is nothing in the law to justify such a severe interpretation, and, moreover, that it is beyond the jurisdiction of the Ordinary to make recourse for the faculty of canon 1043 obligatory, because the power granted in canon 1044 is given by the highest lawgiver, whose authority overrules that of inferiors. Vlaming[12] and Owens,[13] however, without putting forth any argument in support of their view, would urge the obligation of recourse, in the case, under pain of invalidity to the dispensation. Theoretically there is no justification in the law itself for the imposition of such an obligation. The canon speaks of the impossibility of approaching the Ordinary, and it would be an unwarranted straining of the meaning of the words to include an Ordinary's delegate under the term *"Ordinarius."* Canon 198 enumerates all who come under the name of *"Ordinarius,"* and does not mention one who may be delegated. However, in practice, seeing that there is so little external authority in support of either view, it would be safer to approach one who has been delegated, when recourse to him is possible, to provide for the certain validity of the dispensation: "Attamen si saltem adiri possit cui Ordinarius hanc canonis 1043 facultatem delegaverit,

[10] *Theologia Moralis* (1923), III, n. 758.

[11] *Diocesan Faculties According to the Code of Canon Law,* p. 136.

[12] *Praelectiones Juris Matrimonii* (ed. III), n. 412.

[13] De Smet-Owens, *Betrothment and Marriage* (1925), p. 219, nota 1.

parochus, ne per seipsum invalide dispenset, ad illud tenebitur."[14]

When the conditions of urgent danger of death, the necessity of settling matters of conscience, or of legitimating offspring (all of which are to be understood here in the sense in which they have been explained in the preceding chapter), are present, and when, moreover, the competent authority to dispense cannot be reached in time, the parish priest enjoys the same power as the Ordinary. He can, therefore, dispense from the form to be observed in marriage and from all impediments of ecclesiastical origin, with the two exceptions mentioned in canon 1043, namely, priesthood and affinity in the direct line arising from a consummated marriage. Regarding the impedient impediments arising from the five simple vows it will be noted that he can dispense from the impediments only, and not from the vows themselves, which will still continue to bind outside of the lawful use of the actual marriage contracted by virtue of the dispensation. The parish priest is likewise bound by the obligations of removing scandal and of obtaining the cautiones, as explained in the preceding chapter.

His power to dispense extends to both forums. The choice of forum will depend on the nature of the impediment. If it is public, he will grant the dispensation in the external forum. If it is occult, he will dispense in the internal extra-sacramental forum.

The faculty is valid for the validation of marriages as well as for those to be contracted,[15] but the parish priest will take care to obtain the renewal of consent when there is question of convalidation.

The canon makes no restrictions, and, therefore, it is lawful to conclude that the power of the Parish Priest extendes to his parishioners, wherever they may be, and to all *hic et nunc* actually within the limits of his parish.

---

[14] Vlaming, *o. c.*, II, n. 412.

[15] Wernz-Vidal, *Jus Canonicum,* V, n. 425.

All who come under the name of "Parochus," in law, enjoy the faculty bestowed by canon 1044. Hence the following can dispense by virtue of this canon:

(1) All *parish priests* in the strict sense, that is, all those to whom a parish is given *"in titulum"* with the care of souls, to be exercised under the authority of the Ordinary of the place;[16]

(2) *Quasi Parochi,* that is, all those who rule a quasi-parish (the equivalent of a parish in missionary countries) in a Vicariate or Prefecture Apostolic;[17]

(3) *Vicarii paroeciales,* that is, all those who are endowed with full parochial power. Under this heading are to be enumerated, (a) *Vicarii actuales,* or all those who have the care of souls *exclusively* in a parish that is *pleno jure* united to, or incorporated with, any moral person to whom the parish is given "in titulum";[18] (b) *Vicarii oeconomi,* that is, all those who rule a parish, as administrators, during its vacancy,[19] (c) *Vicarii cooperatores,* that is, whoever, when a parish becomes vacant, assumes the rule of the parish until such time as the administrator ("oeconomus") is appointed. If there are several assistant priests in the parish, the first in rank, or, if all are equal in rank, the senior assistant, is to assume the office of pastor "ad interim"; if there are no assistant priests, the nearest parish priest is to assume the same office; in parishes which are entrusted to religious, the superior of the house is to act in the same capacity. Whoever assumes the "ad interim" administration of a parish, is equiparated to "parochus" in law, and enjoys the faculties of canon 1043;[20] (d) *Vicarius adjutor,* or one who is given by the Ordinary to a parish priest who, by reason of age, mental debility, blind-

---

[16] Canon 451, par. 1.

[17] Canons 451, par. 2, n. 1; 216, par. 3.

[18] Canon 471, pars. 1, 4; Cf. Vlaming, *o. c.,* II, n. 563; Ferreres, *Compendium Theologiae Moralis* (ed. 3), n. 1073.

[19] Canons 471, par. 1; 473. Cf. Vlaming, *l. c.;* Fanfani, *De Jure Parochorum,* n. 308.

[20] Canon 472, par. 2.

ness, or any other permanent cause, becomes incapable of discharging his duty properly;[21] and lastly, (e) *Vicarius substitutus;* or one who, with the approbation of the Ordinary, and only *after* his approbation, supplies the place of a parish priest "*in omnibus*" who, with the written permission of the Ordinary, is absent from the parish beyond a week;[22] also one who takes the place of the parish priest who, because of a sudden and serious cause, is compelled to leave the parish for an absence beyond a week. But this latter has not power until the Ordinary has been notified as to his identity, and, having been notified, has not determined otherwise. He need not however await the Ordinary's approbation.[23] The assistant who supplies the place of the parish priest whose absence does not extend beyond a week, does not enjoy, *qua parochus,* the faculty of canon 1043.[24]

Nature of the Power:

Many authors maintain that the power of the parish priest to dispense by virtue of canon 1044 is "ordinary-vicarious" power.[25]

The reason these authors imply is that the parish priest has an "officium," and to it is attached, by law, the *facultas*

---

[21] Canon 475; Cf. Vlaming *l. c.*

[22] Canons 474; 465, par. 4; *Pont. Com. pro Interp. Codicis,* 14 July 1922, *A. A. S.*, XIV, 527, 528.

[23] Canons 474, 465, par. 5; *Pont. Com. pro. Interp. Codicis,* July 14, 1922, *A. A. S.*, XIV, 527, 528.

[24] Cappello, *o. c.*, III, n. 236.

[25] De Smet, *De Sponsalibus et Matrimonio,* II, nn. 791, 799; Chelodi, *Jus Matrimoniale* (ed. III), n. 44; Petrovits, *The New Church Law on Matrimony* (ed. II), n. 162; Haring, *L. Q. S.*, LXXIX, pp. 594, 595; Augustine, *A Commentary on the New Code of Canon Law* (ed. III), V, pp. 102, 103; Cappello, *De Sacramentis,* III, n. 236, 2, f; Farrugia, *De Matrimonio et Causis Matrimonialibus,* n. 86; Vermeersch, *Theologia Moralis,* III, n. 758; Blat, *Commentarium Textus Codicis Juris Canonici,* Lib. III, P. I, De Rebus, n. 436; Hilling, *A. K. K.*, CIV, n. 193; Kubelbeck, *The Sacred Penitentiaria and Its Relations to Faculties of Ordinaries and Priests,* p. 70; King, *The Administration of the Sacraments to Dying Non-Catholics,* p. 118: "his power is certainly ordinary for the internal forum, and *probably* for the external forum"; Motry, *Diocesan Faculties According to the Code of Canon Law,* pp. 134, 135.

dispensandi. Other Canonists deny that this power is ordinary, because the office of the parish priest is one to which no jurisdiction in the external forum can be attached.[26]

It seems that the power in question is ordinary because it is annexed by law to an office. Even though "officium" in canon 197, par. 1, is to be taken in the strict sense, this contention would hold, for it cannot be denied that a parish priest holds an office in this strict sense, and the "potestas dispensandi" is annexed to it by law. The great difficulty against this opinion is that parish priests have no jurisdiction in the external forum, and that the granting of a dispensation in foro externo necessitates the exercise of such power. It is indeed true that a parish priest has no *"jurisdictio ordinaria propria"* in the external forum, but it is not repugnant to this fact that, through the concession of law, he be at times enabled to exercise *ordinary vicarious* power in that forum.

ARTICLE II

Priests

Besides the parish priest, this faculty to dispense is enjoyed by any priest who assists at marriage according to the norm of canon 1098, par. 2. This canon legislates that in case of danger of death, when the Ordinary, parish priest, or a priest who has been delegated by either to assist at marriages, cannot be reached, or be present, without grave inconvenience, marriage may be contracted validly and lawfully before witnesses alone. If, however, it is possible for a simple priest to be present he should assist also, but the marriage would, at any rate, be valid before the witnesses alone. If such a priest were present and does assist, canon

[26] Vlaming, *o. c.*, II, n. 415; Woywod, *A Practical Commentary on the Code of Canon Law*, n. 1012; Ojetti, *Gregorianum*, VI, p. 443.

1044 empowers him to dispense in the circumstances, and under the conditions, enumerated in canons 1043 and 1044.

The first essential requisite before a simple priest enjoys power to dispense is that there be danger of death, and that it be not possible, morally speaking, for the Ordinary, parish priest, or a delegate of either, to be present personally, or to be approached for the necessary faculties. In comparing canons 1044 and 1098, regarding the first condition, a slight difference is noticeable; the former canon speaks of *"urgente mortis periculo,"* the latter of, simply, *"periculum mortis."* Both expressions, however, in the present question are to receive the same interpretation. This is true even though the two *may* not agree objectively regarding the degree of danger (which is not likely), for *"urgens mortis periculum"* is the condition required in the whole context. The impossibility of reaching the competent authority *"sine grave incommodo"* is also to receive a similar interpretation to the phrase *"adiri non possit."* If it is prudently feared that death or unconsciousness may intervene before the necessary recourse is made, the priest can quite safely proceed to dispense. The doctrine set forth in the preceding article regarding the use of the telephone, telegraph, and automobile is to be applied here also.

One must be careful to discriminate rightly between the conditions necessary for the valid and lawful use of the extraordinary form of marriage, according to canon 1098, and those required for the valid and licit use of the power of dispensing, according to canon 1044 collated with canon 1098, par. 2. Two people may validly contract marriage before two witnesses alone if there is danger of death *plus* the impossibility of fetching, or going to, the Ordinary, parish priest, or a priest delegated by either to assist at marriages. If there is any other priest at hand, his presence would be required only for liceity. Now if the parties are bound by a diriment impediment and there is a simple priest at hand, then his presence too would be required for the validity of the marriage because of the presence of the impediment.[1] The impediment, and not the presence of such a priest, would, in this case, oppose the use of the extraordinary form. If there is an impediment to the marriage and a simple priest is, by chance, present, he is empowered to dispense from all the impediments mentioned in canon 1043, with the two exceptions so often referred to. But the danger of death, and the impossibility of getting to the competent authority, are not sufficient of themselves to justify the use of the faculty to *dispense.* The marriage must moreover be necessary *"ad consulendum conscientiae et, si casus ferat, legitimationi prolis."*[2] Otherwise the dispensation would be invalid. Hence all that has been said in Chapter V on the interpretation of this condition is to be applied here also.

The qualifying adjective *"alius"* seems to permit any priest to resort to this faculty even though he may be excommunicated, or suspended, or deprived of all jurisdiction. This conclusion seems to hold even in the case of a priest who is an *excommunicatus vitandus,* and in the case of one who is excommunicated, interdicted, or suspended, *per sententiam declaratoriam vel condemnatoriam,* as the canon draws no distinction. Precinding from the question as to the obligation and advisability of calling on such a priest to assist when his assistance would be required only for liceity (when there would be no diriment impediment), it seems that, in spite of canons 2264, 2275, and 2279, such a priest is endowed with the faculty of dispensing in danger of death, provided all the other conditions are present. Before the New Code, when the word *"quilibet"* was used

[1] It is not within the scope of this work to discuss the much mooted question as to whether the impediment would cease in such circumstances if there was no priest available. The only point discussed here is the power of a simple priest to dispense if he is de facto present, and the case needs a dispensation.

[2] This condition would not be necessary for the valid use of the privilege of contracting the marriage before witnesses alone, if there were no diriment impediment. Cf. Ferreres, *Theologia Moralis* (ed. XIII), nn. 1079, 1081.

instead of the present term "*alius*," this opinion seems to have been held by Wouters: "ne is quidem excluditur qui nominatim excommunicatus, vel ab officio suspensus est."[3] Since the promulgation of the New Code the opinion is expressly espoused by Petrovits,[4] and, at least implicitly, by Vlaming[5a] and De Smet.[5b] Their opinion seems quite reasonable in view of canon 2261, par. 3, for although this canon does not directly cover the case under discussion, it seems that, if it is interpreted in the light of canon 20, it gives sufficient foundation for the opinion that in danger of death any priest, no matter under what penalty he may labor, is endowed with the power of dispensing, provided, of course, the other conditions, referred to above, are present. Moreover, the general trend of the Church's legislation regarding cases of danger of death seems to show that she regards such priests as in good standing when, in such extremities, their presence is necessary for the spiritual welfare of her children.

Given all the conditions above mentioned, any priest can dispense from all the impediments mentioned in Canon 1043 with the two usual exceptions. Can he also dispense from the form? Yes, for although the presence of two witnesses would be required by canon 1098, when a priest is present he can dispense from their presence by virtue of canon 1044.

As to the nature of the dispensatory power of such a priest the greater number of canonists maintain that his power is "delegated by law," since he has not an "officium" capable of receiving ordinary jurisdiction.[6] There are some,

---

[3] *O. c.*, p. 54.

[4] *O. c.*, n. 162.

[5a] *O. c.*, II, n. 586.

[5b] *O. c.*, II, n. 133, who states that no special quality is called for in a priest in such circumstances.

[6] Vermeersch-Creusen, *Epitome Juris Canonici*, II, n. 311, 2; Vlaming, *Praelectiones Juris Matrimonii* (ed. III), II, n. 415; Blat, *Commentarium Textus Codicis Juris Canonici*, Lib. III, P. 1—De Rebus, n. 436; King, *The Administration of the Sacraments to Dying Non-Catholics*, p. 119.

however, who hold that his power is ordinary, and can, therefore, be delegated, on the ground that the context justifies the interpretation of officium, here, in the wide sense.[7] The question is more speculative than practical, since all priests in those circumstances are empowered to dispense, and there is no need of, or room for, delegation.

It has already been said that before a simple priest is empowered to dispense it is necessary that the Ordinary, parish priest, or a priest delegated by either to assist at marriages, cannot be present or approached except with grave incommodum. If a priest delegated to assist at marriages is present, or can be easily procured, a simple priest could not dispense. The question then occurs, could this delegated priest dispense in case the Ordinary or parish priest cannot themselves be conveniently approached? The question, at first sight, seems irrelevant, and even ridiculous, for surely he can dispense if a *simple* priest could dispense in his absence. But a serious doubt arises, as to his capacity of dispensing, from a consideration of canons 1044 and 1098. In canon 1044 the legislator enumerates *taxative* those on whom he confers the power, namely, the parish priest, the priest of canon 1098, par. 2, and the confessor. But the latter canon *per se* covers only the case of the non-delegated simple priest, and there seems nothing in the law on which to found the claim of a priest, who has been already delegated to assist at marriages, to dispense in danger of death. Owing to the apparent defect of evidence in the law some authors conclude that a "*sacerdos delegatus ad assistendum tantum*" does not possess, by common law, the power to dispense in danger of death.[8] Of course they admit if he becomes a confessor in the case he can dispense

[7] Cappello, *De Sacramentis,* III, n. 236, 2, f; De Smet, *De Sponsalibus et Matrimonio,* II, n. 791; Motry, *Diocesan Faculties According to the Code of Canon Law,* p. 135; Kubelbeck, *The Sacred Penitentiaria and its Relations to Faculties of Ordinaries and Priests,* p. 75.

[8] Wernz-Vidal, *Jus Canonicum,* V, p. 514, nota 90; Ayrinhac, *Marriage Legislation in the New Code of Canon Law,* p. 89; Vermeersch-Creusen, *o. c.,* II (ed. II), n. 311.

qua confessor. Many others, however, hold the opposite view.[9] They point out that it would be abnormal and ridiculous to ascribe the faculty to any other priest and deny it to the regularly appointed priest in this case; that it would be illogical to maintain that, because of his delegation, he should lose the faculty which he would have were he not delegated to assist. Considering these points they conclude that it is incredible that the lawmaker, who wished to provide for all cases of necessity, would make such an unintelligible restriction. Chelodi and Cappello[10] add that if he does not possess this power by virtue of canons 1044 and 1098, par. 2, he certainly acquires it by virtue of the general canon 200, which states that if delegated power (here to assist at marriage) is given to a person, the delegation is considered to include all other powers without which the delegated one itself cannot be exercised. This, however, is not a logical deduction, because the delegation of power guarantees the acquisition only of those powers of the same species which are necessary for the exercise of the delegated power; it does not eo ipso include other powers which do not pertain to the same species of power. Power to assist at marriage and power to dispense from matrimonial dispensations are a completely distinct species of power, since the latter entails the exercise of jurisdiction, while the former does not.

The conclusion, however, that a delegated priest is enabled by common law to dispense in danger of death is quite reasonable, but to be juridical, it must have some foundation in the law itself. Leitner[11] attempts to establish this by maintaining that a priest who is delegated to assist

---

[9] Cappello, *De Sacramentis*, III, n. 200, e; Chelodi, *Jus Matrimoniale* (ed. III), n. 44; Cerato, *Matrimonium*, n. 36; Fanfani, *De Jure Parochorum*, n. 306, c; Genicot-Salsmans, *Institutiones Theologiae Moralis* (ed. X), II, n. 523; Haring, *L. Q. S.*, LXXIX, pp. 505, 590; Arregui, *Summarium Theologiae Moralis* (ed. VII), n. 735; Leitner, *Lehrbuch des katholischen Eherects* (ed. III), p. 332.

[10] *L. c.*

[11] *Lehrbuch des katholischen Eherects* (ed. III), p. 332.

at marriages can assist at such, in danger of death, not only by virtue of canon 1095, par. 2, but also on the ground of canon 1098, par. 2, and, thereby, is enabled by canon 1044 to dispense in these circumstances. This reasoning, however, does not seem to meet the difficulty, for canon 1098, par. 2, covers only the case of the non-delegated priest regarding assistance.

However it must be affirmed that a priest who has been delegated, by virtue of canons 1095, par. 2, and 1096, to assist at all marriages within the parish, has power to dispense in danger of death when time does not permit recourse to the Ordinary or parish priest. The external authority in support of this doctrine is sufficient to justify its application in practice. Moreover it is undoubtedly the evident purpose of the law to cover all cases in such urgent necessity, but it would fail in its purpose if such a priest could not dispense in the circumstances described. It would, moreover, be unreasonable to assert that the lawgiver punishes, as it were, the delegating of one to assist by depriving him of the power to dispense. Would it not appear irrational that the legislator would intend that such a priest should possess less faculties than a simple priest, even than an excommunicated or suspended priest. It is inconceivable that the law should contain such an incongruity, and after all, in the interpretation of law one must look not merely to the words of the law itself, but also to the mind of the legislator.

Against this external reasoning, so to speak, it can still be urged that such an extension of power cannot be justified, as a principle, unless there is some foundation and justification for it in the law itself. It seems that the law itself does sufficiently justify the opinion in question. A close consideration of canon 1044 in conjunction with canon 1098 establishes this. Canon 1098, pars. 1, 2, legislates that even in case the Ordinary or parish priest cannot be present or approached without grave incommodum, a simple priest does not yet obtain the faculty to assist. It is still necessary that a priest delegated by either to assist cannot be approached, except with the same inconvenience. If such a delegated priest is present, a simple priest is powerless either to assist or dispense. Canon 1098 deals only with *assistance* at marriage. Canon 1044 treats of the power of dispensing. By referring to the former, the latter takes over its prescriptions regarding *assistance* and applies them to the power of dispensation. But canon 1098 presupposes that in case a priest delegated to assist is present he can assist (which is evident), and therefore canon 1044, by referring to it, lays down, at least implicitly, that such a priest can likewise dispense.

At least it must be admitted that this opinion is *probable,* and, therefore, by invoking canons 15 and 209, is safe in practice. To make assurance doubly sure, and to remove *every* doubt, it would be well if the parish priest, or, at least, the Ordinary, would delegate also the faculty of canon 1043 together with the general faculty of assisting at marriages.

ARTICLE III

The Confessor

In the same circumstances, and under the same conditions, the confessor is invested with the same power as the Ordinary, but he may exercise it only for the internal forum and in the tribunal of penance. Any priest may be the confessor of any person in the danger of death.[1]

In the case of the confessor it suffices that the Ordinary cannot be approached. The Code does not expressly condition the existence of his power on the impossibility of approaching the parish priest or a delegated priest if there be such. It would seem that if it were possible to recur to the parish priest or a priest delegated to dispense, without

[1] Canon 882.

danger to the sacramental seal or grave incommodum to the parties, the confessor would be bound to do so, but the canon mentions only the Ordinary, and since no author adds any further obligation, the only condition necessary is that the Ordinary cannot be approached. In practice, moreover, it will scarcely ever be possible to have recourse to the parish-priest or his delegate because of danger to the sacramental sigillum. Blat maintains that if there is question of a public impediment the confessor will be bound to recur to the parish priest (where such recourse is both physically and morally possible), at least for liceity, because of the words *"remoto scandalo."*[2]

The condition, *quando Ordinarius adiri non possit,* will be more easily verified in the case of the confessor than of other priests, because of the danger to the sacramental seal involved in the recourse. He is not bound to make use of the telephone or telegraph, and, as a rule, should not utilize these means, in order to safeguard the sacredness and secrecy of confession. Even though time does permit recourse to the Ordinary, but there is a prudent fear that such a course of action would endanger the sigillum, or the good name of the parties, he should proceed to dispense. The only occasion in which he is bound to recur is when he is morally certain that this action will not be prejudicial to the sacramental seal or the good of the parties. When the parties are bound by an *occult* impediment recourse will be, as a rule, impossible.

The confessor, however, can dispense only for the internal forum and in the act of sacramental confession only, so that neither the dispensation nor the subsequent marriage is valid in the external forum.[3] Hence his power is not as extensive as that of priests who are *not* confessors since he cannot dispense in the internal extra-sacramental

[2] *Commentarium Textus Codicis Juris Canonici,* Lib. III—P. I, De Rebus, n. 436; Cf. Woywod, *A Practical Commentary on the New Code of Canon Law,* n. 1012; Mahoney, *E. R.*, LXXII, p. 511.

[3] Canon 202.

forum, but is limited, as a *conditio sine qua non,* to the internal sacramental forum. He can, however, dispense even though the confession is null and void, provided there was sacramental confession, and even though he does not give absolution.[4] Seeing that the dispensation must be given in the act of sacramental confession, it is necessary that it be applied either during the confession strictly speaking, that is, before the prayers joined by the Church to the form of absolution (Passio Domini, etc.), or immediately after these prayers.[5]

Since the confessor can dispense only for the internal sacramental forum, the question at once arises as to the extension of his powers regarding impediments. Canon 1044 grants him the same power (*"eadem dispensandi facultate pollet"*) as conferred by canon 1043. On the other hand he is restricted "pro foro interno." These considerations have caused a division among canonists as to the confessor's powers over public impediments. A mere outline of the various views and arguments is all that will be given here, as a fuller discussion of them is reserved for a subsequent chapter on the *"casus perplexus,"* where its discussion will have more import.[6] Harping on the word *"eadem,"* Vermeersch,[7] Oesterele,[8] Chelodi,[9] and Augustine[10] maintain that the confessor can dispense from all impediments mentioned in canon 1043, whether public or occult, even from those which are public in nature and in fact. This contention is expressly denied by Hilling,[11] as an untenable opinion, on the ground that canon 1044 does not extend the old faculties in general, but only for the internal forum,

---

[4] Chelodi, *Jus Matrimoniale* (ed. III), n. 44; De Smet, *De Sponsalibus et Matrimonio,* II, n. 238.

[5] Blat, *o. c.*, n. 436, c.

[6] See Chapter IX of this work.

[7] *Epitome Juris Canonici,* II, n. 312.

[8] *Munsterisches Pastoralblatt,* LVII, p. 131.

[9] *Jus Matrimoniale,* n. 44.

[10] *A Commentary on the New Code of Canon Law* (ed. III), pp. 103, 104.

[11] *A. K. K.*, CII, p. 12, nota 2.

and that this extension holds only regarding the number of persons enabled to dispense, and not regarding the powers of dispensing themselves.

Others are less generous in their interpretation, and restrict the power of the confessor to impediments which are occult in fact, whether they are occult or public in nature. They would attribute to the confessor the faculty of dispensing from impediments which are public in nature provided they are occult in fact, that is, not known to more than seven or eight persons in a city, or five or six in a town.[12] This opinion is espoused by Genicot,[13] Arendt,[14] O'Donnell,[15] and the *IL Monitore,*[16] on the ground that the internal sacramental forum is capable of receiving a dispensation from *any* impediment that is occult in fact. If there is danger of divulgation and, consequently, of conflict between the external and internal forums, the confessor can *demand* from the penitent promises which would remove that danger, namely, to seek, afterwards, a dispensation for the external forum, or to permit the inscription of the marriage in the marriage register kept in the secret archives of the diocesan Curia, or to make recourse to the Sacred Penitentiary with a view to obtaining the inscription of the marriage in its own secret archives.[17]

Other canonists restrict the power of the confessor still more. They attribute to him power only over impediments which are occult in nature and in fact. They reject the other two opinions as untenable. This opinion is embraced by De Smet,[18] Cappello,[19] Wernz-Vidal,[20] Farrugia,[21]

---

[12] Cf. Benedict XIV, *Institutiones Ecclesiasticae,* II, Inst. Eccl. LXXXVII, n. 45.

[13] *Institutiones Theologiae Moralis* (ed. X), II, n. 523.

[14] *N. R. T.*, XLVII, pp. 261–274.

[15] *I. E. R.*, XVI, p. 408.

[16] *M. E.*, XXXII, p. 58 ff.

[17] Cf. Vermeersch, *Theologia Moralis,* III, n. 758, d.

[18] *De Sponsalibus et Matrimonio,* II (ed. IV), n. 794.

[19] *De Sacramentis,* III, n. 238.

[20] *Jus Canonicum,* V, n. 428.

[21] *De Matrimonio et Causis Matrimonialibus* (ed. X), n. 89.

Ojetti,[22] Vlaming,[23] and the editor of the *IL Monitore.*[24] They oppose the extension of the confessor's power to impediments natura sua public, because these must be removed not only for the internal, but also for the external, forum over which the confessor has no power. They deny that the words *"eadem dispensandi facultate pollet"* give any foundation for such an extension, because canon 1044 itself assigns the greatest difference between the faculty of the parish priest and the confessor, in so far as it enables the latter to dispense only for the internal sacramental forum. They urge that the other two opinions are untenable because of the many and great incommoda which would result from them when put into practice. Marriages would be valid in the internal forum and invalid in the external, so that if the parties wished to attack their marriage in the external forum there would be no means of upholding its validity, since no proofs can be brought forth to prove that a dispensation from the impediment was given, while the impediment itself can easily be proven. The confessor cannot furnish the necessary proof on behalf of the dispensation, for the evidence of a confessor, *as such* (even though he has received the penitent's permission to reveal his knowledge for this purpose), avails nothing in the *external forum.*[25] They also reject the suggestions put forth by those of the opposing opinion as to the means of overcoming the practical difficulties which may arise from the milder view. The confessor, they say, can, indeed, oblige the penitent to manifest to him *qua sacerdos canonis 1098, par. 2,* a public impediment, outside the tribunal of penance, but he cannot lawfully *demand* of the penitent permission to speak outside confession of those things heard in confession.

The theoretical aspect of this question will receive a fuller treatment in a subsequent chapter when dealing with

---

[22] *Jus Pontificium,* annus VI—Fascic. 1-11, pp. 56-61.

[23] *Praelectiones Juris Matrimonii* (ed. III), II, n. 414.

[24] *M. E.,* XXXII, p. 62 ff.

[25] Canon 1757, par. 3, n. 2.

the casus perplexus. Suffice it here to give a few suggestions as to how the confessor is to act in practice and, incidentally, a few remarks on the various opinions. The kernel of the dispute centers around the nature of the internal sacramental forum. If this forum is capable of receiving a dispensation from an impediment which is public in nature and in fact, or from one public in nature only, but not in fact, all *must* admit, whatever about the incommoda which may arise in practice, that the confessor can dispense from them, since canon 1044 endows him with the same power as that given to Ordinaries by canon 1043. Almost all admit that when the impediment is occult, at least *in nature,* given the other conditions, the confessor can proceed at once to dispense. Owing to the division among canonists, if the confessor detects in confession an impediment which is public in nature, but occult in fact, he should urge the penitent either to recur to the parish priest or any other competent authority, or, at least, to manifest the impediment to him, qua sacerdos, outside of the tribunal of penance, so that he may dispense, if all other conditions are present, for the internal non-sacramental forum, *and register* the marriage in the secret register.[26] If the impediment is public, not only in nature but also in fact, the necessity of obviating scandal will furthermore intervene as a more urgent reason for demanding a similar action, in order to enable him or the parish priest to dispense in the external forum, and duly register the marriage.[27] If this alternative is not operative in a particular case, either because of the extreme urgency of the case, or any other grave incommodum to any party concerned, the confessor can dispense in the internal sacramental forum. The objection that this forum is juridically incapable of receiving such a dispensation does not discredit this mode of procedure. That this forum does labor under such incapacity is not a juridically

---

[26] By virtue of canon 1098, par. 2; Cf. Cappello, *l. c.;* Wernz-Vidal, *l. c.*

[27] Cf. Arregui, *Summarium Theologiae Moralis* (ed. VII), n. 735, IV; *N. R. T.*, XLVII, p. 268 ff.

established fact. Proof of this will be given in a future discussion. Suffice it to point out here one analogical proof. All will admit that the confessor can dispense from the form of marriage in the danger of death. Nay, in practice, he will very often be well-nigh compelled to exercise his faculty in this respect. The form is not an impediment, but it is a *public* formality prescribed by the Church. If the confessor cannot dispense from public impediments, in the internal sacramental forum, the restriction of his power arises not *ratione impedimenti qua talis,* for all the impediments of canon 1043 fall under his power, but *ratione impedimenti qua publici.* The public nature of the form does not restrict his power, neither can the public nature of the impediment effect such a restriction. Regarding the incommoda, a treatment of them is likewise reserved for a future discussion. (See Chapter IX.) Suffice it to say here that the same objection can be urged against the restrictive opinion. An impediment which is occult in nature, but which is known only to two or three prudent persons so that there is no danger, except a remote one at most, of its being divulged, is still occult in fact, and therefore falls under the confessor's powers. Still the existence of the impediment *can* be proven in the external forum, but the dispensation from it cannot.

Vlaming restricts the confessor's powers to impediments which are occult "simpliciter," and therefore to those which *cannot* be proven in the external forum.[28] This would obviate the above incommoda completely, but would reduce the confessor's power to a minimum, seeing that, besides the impediments of crime and illegitimate consanguinity, very few, if any, impediments would be occult in this strict canonical sense.

This treatment is merely incidental. The reader is referred to the treatment of this question under canon 1045 (see Chapter IX), where the various opinions will be more

[28] *Praelectiones Juris Matrimonii,* II, n. 414; Canon 1037.

fully outlined and discussed. The confessor possesses in danger of death at least as much power as he has in urgent cases. The one point referred to here which will receive no reference in the subsequent discussion is that of public impediments, that is, those public in nature *and* in fact. Strictly speaking, and theoretically, the confessor has the power to dispense from them *validly* in danger of death. Perhaps with Blat,[29] it should be held that he is bound to recur to the Ordinary, or at least the parish priest, for liceity. In practice he need not, and should not, dispense from them *qua confessor*. He should urge, or even *command*, the penitent to manifest the public impediment to him qua sacerdos outside the tribunal of penance, and then dispense by virtue of canon 1098, par. 2, and register the marriage in the manner outlined in the following chapter.

[29] *Commentarium Textus Codicis Juris Canonici,* Lib. III—P. 1—De Rebus, n. 436.

CHAPTER VII

The Obligation of Reporting and Recording Dispensations Granted in Danger of Death

Parochus aut sacerdos de quo in can. 1044, de concessa dispensatione pro foro externo Ordinarium loci statim certiorem faciat; eaque adnotetur in libro matrimoniorum. (*Canon 1046.*)

Should the parish priest, delegated priest, or simple priest mentioned in the preceding chapter (not however the confessor), grant a dispensation in the external forum, he is immediately to notify the Ordinary of the place, and record the dispensation in the matrimonial register.

By the Ordinary of the place is understood the Ordinary of the diocese within whose territory the dispensation is given.[1] Dispensations granted in the external forum are public acts and, as such, should be recorded in the public register.[2] The Sacred Congregation of the Propaganda, 25 June, 1791, advised the priests of Ireland, not only to keep copies of dispensations which they granted, but also to record the same in the marriage register.[3] The validity of the dispensation does not, of course, depend on the fact of its being reported or recorded.[4]

A dispensation given by the confessor for the internal sacramental forum must not be reported to the Ordinary of the place, nor is it to be recorded, for it is a secret act needing no recording, and, moreover, it cannot be recorded, ex-

[1] Canon 198, pars. 1, 2.
[2] Petrovits, *The New Church Law on Matrimony*, n. 163.
[3] *Coll. de Prop. Fide*, 605
[4] Augustine, *A Commentary on the New Code of Canon Law*, V (ed. III), p. 110.

cept with permission of the penitent, without breaking the sacramental seal. Even with the penitent's permission he should not record the dispensation, whenever he dispenses *qua confessarius*. If he dispenses as the priest of canon 1098, par. 2, the case would be otherwise.

If the parish priest, delegated priest, or simple priest dispense only for the internal non-sacramental forum, he is not bound to report to the Ordinary his action of dispensing, but he is bound to record the fact in the special book kept for those purposes in the secret archives of the diocese.[5] The reason why there is no obligation to notify the Ordinary, or to record the matter in the *public* marriage register, in this instance, arises from the nature of the case. A dispensation will be given in the internal non-sacramental forum when the impediment is occult, and its divulgation would cause incommodum. To save the parties from disgrace, and to obviate scandal, the Church takes all these precautions. It, however, insists on the matter being recorded in the secret book in the archives in order to furnish means of proving the removal of the impediment in the external forum, should such a need arise.[6]

The obligation of notifying the Ordinary is grave *ex genere suo*. The Ordinary has the right and duty to see that no abuses should creep in, in this matter of dispensations, and also to see, in a manner dictated by prudence, that the various conditions and clausulae, required by law, are fulfilled in particular cases, especially the clause regarding the removal of scandal.[7] Hence the Church imposes the obligation of notifying him of each dispensation granted in the external forum.

This obligation urges *statim* after he has applied the dispensation. Hence a priest is bound to notify the local Ordinary within two or three days after he has dispensed unless a grave cause justifies a postponement for an extra

[5] Canon 1047, collated with canon 1046.

[6] Cf. Cappello, *De Sacramentis*, III, n. 242, 3.

[7] Cappello, *o. c.*, n. 241.

period.[8] The same word *statim* was used in the "Ne Temere" decree, Article IX, regarding the registration of marriages contracted in cases of urgency, and some commentators of the decree contended that the spirit of the law required that the record should be made within two or three days after the marriage had been contracted.[9] Others maintained that the obligation urged *immediately* after the marriage, but that a delay of two or three days would not involve a grave sin.[10] The same teaching may be applied to the matter of dispensations. The obligation is grave, it binds at once, but a delay of two or three days would not constitute a mortal sin unless it involved a *real* danger of omitting the notification completely. A just and reasonable cause would, moreover, excuse from mortal sin if the fulfillment of the obligation was protracted even beyond the specified time.

Not only must the matter be reported to the Ordinary, but the fact of dispensation must also be noted in the marriage register. This obligation is also a grave one, and one must be careful to do his duty in this respect as soon as possible. Unwarranted delay may easily cause the omission of this registration, and one cannot, with a safe conscience, postpone the recording of the dispensation beyond two or three days without exposing himself to the grave danger of completely omitting it and, therefore, of sinning gravely.

Canon 1046 speaks only of the recording of the *dispensation* in the marriage register, but if the marriage itself was actually contracted or revalidated, and in the external forum, this fact must also be noted in the same register.[11] The priest responsible for the registration must enter the marriage according to the manner prescribed by the Church.

---

[8] Cappello, *o. c.*, III, n. 241.

[9] Vermeersch, *De Forma Sponsalium ac Matrimonii post Decretum "Ne Temere,"* n. 79, 2.

[10] Wouters, *Commentarius in Decretum "Ne Temere,"* p. 64.

[11] Canon 1103, par. 1.

His registration must contain the names of the contracting parties, the place and date of marriage, the dispensation from the impediment, the validation of marriage, if it took place in the external forum, and the name of the witnesses who assisted, unless he had dispensed from the form, which fact too must be noted.

This obligation binds *quamprimum*.[12] While this word does not imply the same necessity of speedy compliance with the law as the term *statim* implies, nevertheless it would seem that a delay of four or five days should not be exceeded. There is no doubt that this obligation rests on the parish priest in the instances in which he assists. In the cases, however, in which the priest assists according to canon 1098, par. 2, it is difficult to say on whom precisely the obligation rests primarily. If canon 1103, pars. 1, 3, be taken as a norm the obligation would rest primarily on the priest.

The marriage must also be recorded in the baptismal register if one or both parties were baptized in the parish where the marriage was celebrated. In case one or both were baptized elsewhere, the parish priest of the place where they were baptized must be notified. The notification must be sent by the parish priest of the place where the marriage is celebrated, either personally, or through the diocesan Curia.[13]

In case either the parish priest or any other priest, who is not a confessor, dispenses in the internal extra-sacramental forum, the dispensation and marriage should be noted in the special book preserved in the diocesan archives, but not, however, in the baptismal register.

---

[12] Canon 1103, par. 1.

[13] Canons 1103, par 2; 470.

CHAPTER VIII

URGENT CASES

THE POWER OF ORDINARIES OF PLACES

Possunt Ordinarii locorum, sub clausulis in fine can. 1043 statutis, dispensationem concedere super omnibus impedimentis de quibus in cit. can. 1043, quoties impedimentum detegatur, cum jam omnia sunt parata ad nuptias, nec matrimonium, sine probabili gravis mali periculo, differri possit usque dum a Sancta Sede dispensatio obtineatur.

Haec facultas valeat quoque pro convalidatione matrimonii jam contracti, si idem periculum sit in mora nec tempus suppetat recurrendi ad Sanctam Sedem. (*Canon 1045*, pargs. 1, 2.)

Under the conditions laid down in the end of canon 1043, if an impediment is discovered when everything is ready for the marriage, and the ceremony cannot be delayed without the probable danger of grave evil until a dispensation is obtained from the Holy See, the Ordinaries of places can dispense from all the impediments mentioned in the same canon.

If a marriage has been invalidly contracted, the same faculties to dispense are granted if delay of the convalidation of the marriage is equally dangerous, and there is not sufficient time to have recourse to the Holy See.

A historical survey of the development of the powers conferred by this canon has already been given, and the reader is referred to Part 1, Chapter III, arts. I, II, as a knowledge of the old law will contribute much to a better understanding of the present legislation.

The New Code not only confirms the doctrine of the older canonists, by express approbation of it, but greatly extends the powers it attributed to Bishops. The many and great controversies which shrouded the whole question of urgency in the past now look small in the light of canon 1045. The new faculty is much more generous and extensive than the old. It is shared, not only by Bishops, but by all local Ordinaries. The clause restricting the faculty to impediments from which the Pope was accustomed to dispense gives little trouble now, since the power extends to all ecclesiastical impediments, with the two exceptions specified in canon 1043. There is no provision, in the case of revalidation, that the marriage should have been contracted in good faith, and be consummated. Above and beyond all the condition that the impediment must be occult has disappeared, so far as local Ordinaries are concerned, and carried many a controversy with it. Lastly, the power is no longer restricted to the internal forum.

The unexpected discovery of an impediment at the last moment when everything was ready for the marriage, and there was no time to have recourse to the competent authority for the necessary dispensation, was properly called the *casus perplexus* by canonists and moralists who wrote before the Code.[1] The New Legislation has sounded the death knell of the *casus perplexus, and interred* it with due pomp and funeral honors.[2]

The circumstances in which the dispensation may be granted are, I, if all preparations are made for the marriage, and II, if the ceremony cannot be postponed, without probable danger of serious evil, until a dispensation is obtained from the Holy See.

The special concession of canon 1045 is a particular application of the general provision of canon 81. The

---

[1] See Feije, *De Impedimentis et Dispensationibus Matrimonialibus* (ed. III), nn. 640–649.

[2] Chelodi, *Jus Matrimoniale* (ed. III), n. 41.

latter canon recognizes the power of the Ordinary to dispense when recourse to the Holy See is difficult, and, at the same time, there is danger of serious harm in delay, provided the dispensation in question is one which the Holy See usually grants. The particular application of this general concession with regard to matrimonial dispensations is limiting of its nature (*taxative*), so that the power to dispense in urgent cases cannot be extended beyond the limits of canon 1045. Nay, the particular goes further than the general concession, since the latter is confined to dispensations which are *usually* given by the Holy See, and therefore do not extend to all the impediments of canon 1043.[3] Vermeersch,[4] Chelodi,[5] and Cappello[6] maintain that canon 1045 does not exhaust the concession of canon 81 with regard to marriage dispensations, since the restrictions laid down in the former canon retract the powers of local Ordinaries in some cases of urgency contemplated in the latter. It is difficult, however, to conceive a case in which canon 81 would avail where canon 1045 would fail.

It is not required for the legitimate use of the powers granted in canon 1045 that the impediment be altogether unknown up to the time of the marriage, but it suffices that it has not come to the knowledge of the Ordinary until such time as it is impossible to obtain a dispensation from the competent authority.[7]

The question is raised by commentators whether the Ordinary can dispense in favor of a person who *mala fide*

---

[3] De Smet, *De Sponsalibus et Matrimonio* (ed. IV), II, n. 763; Blat, *Commentarium Textus Codicis Juris Canonici*, Lib. III, P. 1, De Rebus, n. 437; Farrugia, *De Matrimonio et Causis Matrimonialibus* (ed. X), n. 84.

[4] *Epitome Juris Canonici* (ed. 1922), II, n. 350.

[5] *Jus de Personis*, n. 87; *Jus Matrimoniale* (ed. III), n. 41, 3.

[6] *De Sacramentis*, III, n. 234, 2.

[7] *Pont. Com. pro Interp. Codicis*, 1 March 1921, *A. A. S.*, XIII, 178: "Clausula 'quoties impedimentum detegatur cum jam omnia sunt parata ad nuptias' intelligi debeat . . . quod impedimentum, quamvis antea cognitum, tunc solum tamen ad notitiam parochi aut Ordinarii sit delatum."

reserved the revelation of the impediment until such time as a state of urgency existed. Vidal[8] would not recognize the power of a Bishop to dispense in such a case, because the legislator, he maintains, in granting these very extensive faculties, embracing impediments from which the Holy See does not dispense, except in very exceptional cases and for a very grave cause, wished to provide for contingent necessity, and not to put a premium on fraud: "fraus sua nemini patrocinari debet."

The Ordinary can, however, dispense in these circumstances. The law does not call for good faith on the part of the parties concerned, and it is beyond the ken of the commentator to insert such a condition. The end of the law is not merely to provide for the good of the contracting parties, but also to obviate scandal, or any other grave evil. This reason may well be present even in cases where the contracting parties have been in bad faith all through.[9] An argument may also be adduced from analogy with canon 1098. This canon enables persons to contract marriage validly before two witnesses, without the assistance of a priest, when the Ordinary, parish priest, or a priest delegated by either to assist at marriages, cannot be procured, and this state of affairs is foreseen, with moral certainty, to last for a month. The Sacred Congregation of the Sacraments, 13 March, 1910, decided that this extraordinary form can be used by parties who, *in fraudem legis,* betake themselves to a place where this condition would be fulfilled.[10] The same holds true, *mutatis mutandis,* in the question at issue. *Fraus legis* is not to be punished by a denial of the dispensation. "Abuse or frivolous extension of the power need not be feared, for the publica-

---

[8] Wernz-Vidal, *Jus Canonicum,* V, n. 413, nota 59.

[9] Gasparri, *De Matrimonio* (ed. III), I, n. 249; Cappello, *o. c.,* III, n. 233, 5, g; Petrovits, *The New Church Law on Matrimony* (ed. II), n. 165; Pighi, *De Sacramento Matrimonii* (ed. II), n. 92, 3; Augustine, *A Commentary on the New Code of Canon Law,* V, p. 107.

[10] *A. A. S.,* II, 195.

tion of banns and the careful investigation and examination imposed on the pastor will naturally reduce such cases to a minimum. Besides, if the Ordinary is afraid of abuses creeping in, he may, and should at times, refuse to grant a dispensation, in order to procure the necessary respect for ecclesiastical laws."[11]

Some restrict the phrase "*cum jam omnia sunt parata ad nuptias*" to the canonical preparations, that is, to the publication of the banns, the examination of the parties, and all else required by law (canons 1020-1033).[12] But it is sufficiently probable that, even though these canonical preparations have not been made or completed, if the invitations for the wedding have been sent out, the day set for the wedding, and all other civil arrangements have been made, that the phrase "*cum jam omnia sunt parata ad nuptias*" is sufficiently verified in practice.[13] One should not be scrupulous in the interpretation of this and the other conditions of this canon, but should interpret it, "*moraliter, scrupulis abdicatis.*"[14]

Not only must the preparations be made for the marriage, but it is also required that the ceremony cannot be postponed, without probable danger of grave evil, until such time as the requisite dispensation is obtained from the Holy See. The impossibility of delaying the marriage celebration, until the dispensation can be procured, *must* arise, not from an arbitrary source, but from a real probable danger of grave evil. It need not indeed be morally certain that some grave evil will result from the postponement, but a prudent well-founded fear that such an inconvenience will arise is necessary. If the parties could, if they so wished, prevent the impending evil, without

[11] Augustine, o. c., V, p. 107.

[12] Cappello, o. c., III, n. 233, c; Augustine, *A Commentary on the New Code of Canon Law* (ed. III), V, p. 107.

[13] Reiffenstuel, *Jus Canonicum Universum* (ed. 1735), IV, Appendix, *De Dispensatione super Impedimentis Matrimonii*, n. 63; Petrovits, *The New Church Law on Matrimony* (ed. II), n. 164.

[14] Chelodi, *Jus Matrimoniale* (ed. III), n. 41, 3.

grave inconvenience, the Ordinary is destitute of power to dispense.[15]

The nature of the impending evil is not defined by the Code. Hence, no matter what kind of harm will result from the postponement of the ceremony, be it spiritual or corporal harm, provided it is *grave,* the Ordinary can proceed to dispense.[16] Thus, with regard to the impending celebration of marriage, a case may be considered urgent if the danger of grave inconvenience arises from the fact that an impediment, public in nature, is discovered immediately before the celebration of marriage, and the parties are soon to travel, or refuse delay, and are bent on a merely civil service. If the impediment is occult, urgency will, as a rule, be present, as injury to the reputation of the parties, or scandal to the people, may easily result from the postponement of the ceremony. Likewise, with regard to a revalidation, urgency would be present, not only when there existed ignorance of the invalidity of the marriage, and the impossibility of maintaining brother and sister relationship for several days, and perhaps weeks, and the separation of the supposed married couple could not be effected without danger of scandal or loss of reputation, but also it might arise in case of invalidity publicly known; for it might easily happen that the parties, on the one hand, might refuse to separate for the time necessary for appeal to Rome, or indeed could not do so without grave inconvenience, and, on the other hand, that they could not continue to live as married people without offense to the community.[17] The mere fact that recourse to the competent authority is *physically* possible does not, of it-

---

[15] Feije, *De Impedimentis et Dispensationibus Matrimonialibus* (ed. III), n. 635; Wernz, *Jus Decretalium* (ed. 1904), IV, p. 894, nota 88: "At prava voluntas *utriusque* partis certe non sufficit, quae, si velit, incommodum tollere possit."

[16] Blat, *Commentarium Textus Codicis Juris Canonici,* Lib. III—P. 1, De Rebus (ed. II), n. 437; Farrugia, *De Matrimonio et Causis Matrimonialibus* (ed. X), n. 84; Feije, *o. c.*, n. 642.

[17] De Smet, *De Sponsalibus et Matrimonio* (ed. IV), n. 764.

self, remove the danger of evil, but it suffices if the recourse is *valde difficilis,* as can happen in time of war or schism, and the celebration of the marriage will not brook delay.[18]

The Code speaks only of recourse to the Holy See and, hence, some conclude that if the time allotted is not sufficient to permit recourse to the Holy See itself, but certainly suffices for recourse to one possessing delegated power, as, for instance, the Apostolic Delegate, the Ordinary would not be bound, under pain of invalidity, to recur to one so delegated, but could dispense on the strength of urgency.[19] Under the old law, from which the present legislation is taken substantially, it was the far better and more common opinion that, in such a case, one with delegated powers should be approached, for, otherwise, a state of urgency would not be present.[20] Others, however, spoke only of approaching the Holy See or the Pope,[21] and Henriquez [22] denied expressly the obligation of having recourse to a delegate. Feije, however, while adhering to the first opinion, admitted the opinion of Henriquez as tenable.[23]

Hence since this canon must apparently be interpreted in the light of the old law [24] it would seem the better opinion, even today, that a delegate of the Holy See should be approached for the requisite dispensation. However,

---

[18] Reiffenstuel *o. c.*, n. 53; Cappello, *o. c.*, III, n. 233, 5.

[19] Blat, *Commentarium Textus Codicis Juris Canonici,* Lib. III—P. 1, De Rebus, n. 437; Motry, *Diocesan Faculties According to the Code of Canon Law,* p. 138.

[20] Reiffenstuel, *Jus Canonicum Universum,* IV, Appendix, *De Dispensatione super Impedimentis Matrimonii,* n. 49: "Nulla adest causa, vel necessitas, quod dispenset Episcopus, consequenter cessat ratio ob quam ei competit potestas." Sanchez, *De Sancto Matrimonii Sacramento* (ed. II), Lib. II, dis. XL, n. 8; Giovine, *De Dispensationibus Matrimonialibus,* I, consult. CCCXXV, n. 3; Gasparri, *De Matrimonio* (ed. III), I, n. 442; Wernz, *Jus Decretalium,* IV, n. 619; Feije, *De Impedimentis et Dispensationibus Matrimonialibus* (ed. III), n. 634, 4.

[21] Benedict XIV, *De Synodo Dioecesana,* lib IX, cap. II, n. 3; Bangen, *Instructio Practica de Sponsalibus et Matrimonio,* tit. II, p. 155.

[22] *De Matrimonio,* lib. XII, cap. XXIII, n. 1.

[23] *O. c.*, n. 534, 4: "contrarium tamen potest sustineri."

[24] Canon 6, n. 2.

seeing that the canon itself mentions only the Holy See, and, above all, since the legislator, knowing of the standing controversy, added no qualification in the canon, a strict obligation, at least under pain of invalidity, cannot be imposed. It would be well, nevertheless, to have recourse to the delegate, so that provision may be made for the *certain* validity of the dispensation. It may be well to add here that the time required for recourse from America to the Holy See would be from forty to fifty days.[25] The telephone or telegraph is not obligatory and, as a rule, should not be used.[26]

It is apparently stated in the canon, and commentators generally interpret it as such, that the two conditions, namely, that all things should have been prepared for the marriage, and the ceremony cannot be postponed without probable danger of grave evil, must be strictly present simultaneously before the Ordinary is endowed with power to dispense. De Smet [27] and Vermeersch [28] very strongly insist on this point and maintain that neither condition can be assimulated with the other; that the latter condition is distinct from the former, and is not to be considered equivalent to it; that if, on the one hand, all preparations have been made for the marriage, it does not follow that postponement is morally impossible, while, on the other hand, the mere fact that the marriage cannot be postponed is not sufficient ground of itself to justify the Ordinary to dispense. Now, it may easily happen in practice that, in a special case, the second condition is so fully verified that it involves more serious trouble than, in the normal run of things, would be involved in both together. For instance, illicit intercourse between two persons bound by an impediment has taken place with normal results. There

---

[25] Cappello, *o. c.*, III, n. 233, 5.

[26] *Pont. Com. pro Interp. Codicis*, 14 November, 1922, *A. A. S.*, XIV, 662.

[27] *De Sponsalibus et Matrimonio*, II, n. 764.

[28] *Epitome Juris Canonici*, II (ed. 1922), n. 350.

are no preparations made for the marriage, no date fixed, no expenses incurred, no friends invited. The man, home say on a holiday, is willing to contract marriage just now, but if the present opportunity is not availed of, he is more than likely to change his mind and marry some one else. Is it not true that, in such circumstances, the impending misfortune may be much greater than it would be in the case of two individuals, the preparations of whose marriage have already been fully made, and who are liable to some suspicion if the marriage is postponed, but who are determined, at all costs, to marry each other sometime. Ought not the one condition to be taken as equivalent to both?

In their treatment of such cases where the one condition, especially the second, is verified without the other, commentators have been brief and unsatisfactory. To meet practical difficulties which arise when both conditions are not present simultaneously, and yet the celebration of marriage is urgent, the authors have recourse to various means of escape. Cappello [29] considers a case in which preparations have not been made for the marriage which, however, cannot be postponed without danger of serious evil, and solves it by recourse to canon 81. But such a solution is not satisfactory, since the scope of canon 81, which certainly does not cover all the impediments of canon 1043, and consequently of canon 1045, is not as extensive as that of the power in question. Chelodi[30] and Vidal[31] consider the case when an impediment is discovered at a time when no preparations have been made for the marriage, and when there is sufficient time to have recourse to the Holy See. The petition for the dispensation is sent, the preparations are, in the meantime, made for the marriage, but the dispensation de facto has not arrived, for some reason or other, when the wedding day comes along.

---

[29] *De Sacramentis,* III, n. 233, 8.
[30] *Jus Matrimoniale,* n. 41, 3.
[31] *Jus Canonicum,* V, n. 413.

Such a case would not be covered by canon 1045, since no preparations were made when the impediment was brought to the notice of the Ordinary. These authors, however, acknowledge the power of the Ordinary to dispense, in the case, on the ground that the Church would be unwilling to urge her law in such a case. But this reason is truly a dubious one, notwithstanding the fact that Chelodi claims that he knows of a case in which the Holy See ratified a dispensation given in such circumstances.

The whole expression in canon 1045 par. 1 ("cum jam omnia sunt parata ad nuptias, nec matrimonium, sine probabili gravis mali periculo, differri possit . . .") indicating urgency, must be understood as referring to the time necessary for recourse to the right authority. There is, indeed, a condition expressed in the phrase *cum jam omnia sunt parata ad nuptias,* but, if the clause is interpreted widely, the condition will be fulfilled if from the moment the impediment is brought to the knowledge of the Ordinary to the time fixed for the marriage there is not sufficient time to have recourse to the competent authority. If this clause were interpreted strictly the consequence would be that the impediment would have to be discovered after the last preparations for the marriage had been made, so that if the parties make known the impediment at the very first day the Ordinary could not dispense, even though there would be no time to have recourse for the dispensation, and, at the same time, grave evil would be feared from a postponement of the marriage.[32]

A second consequence would be that all preparations for the marriage should have taken place, that is, a solemnity and publicity that would oppose its postponement. This would exclude from the benefit of the dispensation certain cases of urgency, for grave evil may often result

[32] Cf. Feije, *De Impedimentis et Dispensationibus Matrimonialibus* (ed. III), n. 640.

from the putting off of a marriage, even when the preparations have not been made.

The end of the law undoubtedly consists in furnishing the Ordinary with sufficient power to enable the faithful to contract marriage validly in all cases of urgency, that is, when there is no time to have recourse to the Holy See, or one of its delegates, for the dispensation, and there is danger of serious evil in postponing the marriage. This end would certainly not be obtained if the Ordinary could not dispense in all cases, but only in some, for, as the legislator has intended by canons 1043-1044 to provide for all cases in danger of death, so also has he evidently wished, by canon 1045, to provide for all cases of *real* urgency, outside the danger of death; otherwise the law would be incomplete, insufficient and contradictory.[33] Incomplete and insufficient, for there would be a class of marriages for which a dispensation would be really urgent, but for which there would be no provision; contradictory, because some cases would be urgent and not-urgent at the same time, since a dispensation could be, at the same time, necessary and impossible. It may at times be necessary for the Ordinary to give a dispensation, but he cannot give it because *"non omnia sunt parata ad nuptias."*

Hence the mind of the legislator is not at all doubtful. He has certainly intended to cover all cases in which it is no longer possible to recur to Rome, or, at least, one with delegated power. Among such cases he has taken, *as a type*, the famous *"casus perplexus,"* but he has not intended to exclude other cases of urgency, so much so that he has extended the faculty to all the impediments, even public, of the ecclesiastical law, with the two exceptions specified in canon 1043. He has, in no way, intended to make the power of the Ordinary depend on circumstances which respect the parish priest alone.[34] The legislator has

---

[33] *M. E.*, XXXVII, pp. 297–301.

[34] For the parish priest, the urgency was determined in the Old Law, but the faculty to dispense was not given him.

furnished the Ordinary with the power required for all cases of urgency, even for those extraneous to the *casus perplexus* in its proper sense, while the parish priets is endowed with power only for the *casus perplexus,* since its solution provides for all cases of urgency which may be encountered by him.

Granted that the legislator, by the clause *"cum jam omnia sunt parata ad nuptias,"* wished to enunciate a true and strict condition for the exercise of the power by the Ordinary, this condition could not be measured with the same rule as it would be in the case of the parish priest. For the latter two or three days, at the most, will suffice for recourse to the Ordinary, while the Ordinary will require a far longer time.

Hence not only does the phrase *"cum jam omnia sunt parata ad nuptias,"* of canon 1045, par. 1, permit of a wide interpretation, but it excludes the strict interpretation given it by authors a propos of the parish priest and the *"casus perplexus."*

This interpretation is by no means arbitrary. The conditions required by canon 1045, pars. 1, 2, are taken substantially, with, however, a few little minor modifications, from the pre-Code legislation, and, hence, are to be interpreted, substantially, according to the teaching of the approved authors of that period. *"Canones qui ex parte tantum cum veteri jure congruunt, qua congruunt, ex jure antiquo aestimandi sunt."*[35]

Under the old legislation the condition of urgency was stated in general terms, as, for instance, "quando urgentissima necessitas id postularet,"[36] or "requiritur ut absque scandali vel infamiae periculo matrimonium differi nequeat, donec . . . dispensatio obtineatur."[37]

[35] Canon 6, n. 3.

[36] Sanchez, *De Sancto Matrimonii Sacramento,* lib. II, dis. XL, n. 8; Reiffenstuel, *Jus Canonicum Universum,* IV, Appendix, *De Dispensatione super Impedimentis Matrimonii,* n. 62.

[37] Feije, *De Impedimentis et Dispensationibus Matrimonialibus* (ed. III), n. 635.

Having stated the condition thus, the authors added that the *principal* case of urgency occurred when all things were ready for the marriage, and the ceremony could not be postponed, without notable loss, until a dispensation was obtained. But they did not restrict cases of urgency to this particular case, but simply quoted it as the most cogent example. Sanchez, who was the first to propound the doctrine which is incorporated, with certain extensions, in canon 1045, pars. 1, 2, clearly brought out this distinction: "*Quando urgentissima necessitas id postularet. Exemplum fit, accedit mulier mane passura et reperitur habens impedimentum dirimens cujus detectio infamiam notabilem produceret et sunt jam omnia parata ad nuptias vespere celebrandas . . .*"[38] Reiffenstuel states the condition likewise and repeats, for consideration, the *case* given by Sanchez.[39]

From the constant consideration of the special case of urgency where all things were prepared for the marriage, the manner of stating urgency in general took on a stereotyped mode of expression in the form of "*cum jam omnia sunt parata ad nuptias,*" with the result that some authors simply stated urgency in this form.[40] Yet the idea that urgency embraced more that this typical case was emphasized, at least implicitly, down through the centuries, and even by the writers immediately preceding the codification of the law. De Becker stated the condition of urgency in quite general terms: "dummodo urgens adsit necessitas et differi non valeat matrimonii celebratio sine scandalo et famae periculo."[41] Feije likewise states the condition but adds: "*duo praecipue* casus indicari solent, casus moribundi . . . et casus quo omnia jam sint ad nuptias

---

[38] *De Sancto Matrimonii Sacramento,* lib. II, dis. XL, n. 8.

[39] *O. c.,* Appendix, n. 62.

[40] Cf. Benedict XIV, *De Synodo Dioecesana,* lib. IX, cap. II, n. 2; Giovine, *De Dispensationibus Matrimonialibus,* I, consul. CCCXXXV, nn. 2, 3.

[41] *De Sponsalibus et Matrimonio* (ed. II), p. 305.

parata,"[42] clearly repeating the idea given centuries before by Sanchez. Gasparri also makes a somewhat similar statement of the condition: "Ex una parte matrimonium protrahi nequit sine magno damno aut scandalo . . ., et ex alia dispensatio facile peti non potest," and then he adds: "*DD. rei explicandae gratia duo exempla afferunt*: si ageretur de matrimonio in periculo mortis . . .; item si parata essent omnia ad matrimonium ita ut absque scandalo et personarum infamia differi nequeat celebratio, et simile impedimentum deprehenderetur."[43]

From this it is clear that the biblical clause "*cum jam omnia sunt parata ad nuptias*" was chosen as a typical phrase for the expression of cases of urgency, but that authors by its use did not intend to exclude other cases of urgency from the benefit of the dispensation. There is no doubt that the same must be said of canon 1045, par. 1; the clause enunciates a real condition undoubtedly, but is to be interpreted as expressing a *type* of urgency, but one which is not exclusive of other cases of urgency.

A private decision, bearing directly on this point, was given by the Holy See to Cardinal Logue, Primate of All-Ireland. Although no apodictic argument can be deduced from it, since the decision has not been embodied in the "*Acta Apostolicae Sedis,*" there can be no doubt as to its authenticity, since the Cardinal personally gave permission for its publication, and it is here restated for what it is worth. The Cardinal had dispensed in a case of urgency when the preparations had not been made for the marriage ceremony, and, with a view to procuring a satisfactory pronouncement, he informed the Sacred Congregation of the Sacraments of his action. The reply, dated 12 September, 1919, was as follows: "Super a se concessa dispensatione Ordinarius acquiescat, et deinceps quoties matrimonium nequeat differi absque gravis mali periculo Ordi-

---

[42] *O. c.*, n. 635.
[43] *De Matrimonio* (ed. III), I, n. 442.

narius dispensando utatur jure suo."[44] The first clause, "*Ordinarius acquiescat*," could be taken as involving nothing more than a grant of a "*sanatio in radice*," and, if so, would throw little light on the situation. Even the general commission to dispense might be taken by the hypercritical as a personal concession to his Eminence himself. But the two final words settle the question. When the Ordinary does dispense, he merely exercises "*his right*"—the right guaranteed him by law. Neither may it be objected that canon 81 may be regarded as the source of the power here guaranteed by the Congregation, for canon 1045, pars. 1, 2, is the application of canon 81 to the matter of matrimonial dispensations. The practical conclusion is that when the second condition is *certainly* fulfilled, the first ("cum jam omnia sunt parata ad nuptias") need give little trouble, provided there is real urgency in the case.

It may be well to add here that the condition of adjusting matters of conscience, or of legitimating offspring, are not required in C. 1045. Also that the power to dispense is no longer restricted to Bishops, but is extended to *all* Ordinaries of places.

The faculty of dispensing extends to all impediments of ecclesiastical law with the exception of priesthood and affinity in the direct line, when the marriage occasioning the affinity has been consummated. The legislator requires that all scandal must be removed, and that the usual cautiones are to be obtained in case a dispensation should be given from an impediment of mixed religion or disparity of cult. The removal of scandal is not required as a condition for validity, but the Ordinary is to see that all past scandal is repaired, and scandal likely to result from the marriage itself be obviated, before he dispenses. He will follow, in this matter, the rules already laid down in the previous chapters concerning dispensations in the danger of death.

The question as to whether the requirement of the cau-

[44] *I. E. R.*, XVI, 2, p. 409

tiones is for the validity of the dispensation takes on a different aspect in this canon, because the cases there mentioned are by no means as urgent as the case of the danger of death. Nearly all authors maintain that the usual guarantees must be asked and *received* from both parties even for the validity of the dispensation. All those authors who favor the view that in danger of death the actual giving of the cautiones is necessary before the Ordinary can validly dispense, are, of course, to be quoted here as favoring the view that this condition is also necessary for validity in other cases of urgency. Most of those who have been quoted as favoring the milder view regarding the danger of death, here admit that the validity of the dispensation in all cases of urgency outside the danger of death depends on the *asking and receiving* of the guarantees.[45]

Cerato[46] and Pighi[47] are of opinion that even in these cases of urgency the obtaining of the cautiones is required only for the *liceity* of the dispensation. Their opinion, however, can scarcely be sustained, and scarcely enjoys either internal or external probability. Their main argument is that even though the cautiones are not given, the cause required by law (canon 84, n. 1) for the validity of a dispensation already exists, namely, the danger of grave evil if the marriage is not celebrated, as scandal or grave damnum, or the danger of a merely civil marriage.

Against this it can be urged that canon 1061 clearly distinguishes between the just cause necessary for the validity of the dispensation, and the obtaining of the cautiones. Granted that the urgency of the case and the danger of the evils which may follow do constitute the just cause, the requirement of the cautiones still continues to bind. Hence, in ordinary cases which are not urgent, even

---

[45] Cf. Cappello, *o. c.*, III, n. 233, 5, 2; Vermeersch, *Theologia Moralis*, III, n. 755, c; n. 758, a.

[46] *Matrimonium* (ed. III), n. 37.

[47] *De Sacramento Matrimonii* (ed. II), n. 88, 6, a.

though the just cause is present, the validity of the dispensation, and hence of the marriage, if the impediment is disparity of cult, still depends on the giving of the cautiones. The only question which remains, then, is whether the Church persists in urging this obligation, in urgent cases, under pain of the dispensation's invalidity. There is nothing to point to a relaxation of the Church's strictness in this context; nay, everything points to the contrary,[48] and hence the asking and actual reception of the customary guarantees from both the Catholic and non-Catholic is necessary for the validity of the dispensation.

Canon 1045 does not authorize a dispensation from the form of marriage. Consistently with his classification of the form of marriage among the diriment impediments De Smet maintains that the faculty includes also power to dispense from the form.[49] He is joined by Vermeersch in his contention.[50] A few authors do not expressly exclude the form from the Ordinary's power, and, therefore, may possibly be quoted as also espousing this view, at least indirectly.[51] Durieux[52] and Oesterle-Brenninkmeyer[53] are also quoted by De Smet[54] as favoring his opinion.

It must, however, be held that the form of marriage does not fall within the ambit of the power conferred by canon 1045. Canon 1043 draws a clear distinction between the impediments and the form. In canon 1045 the legis-

---

[48] Cf. Decrees of the Holy Office, 16 April 1890, and 21 June 1912, *A. A. S.*, IV, pp. 442, 443.

[49] *De Sponsalibus et Matrimonio,* II, p. 218, nota 2.

[50] *Theologia Moralis,* III, nn. 755, d, 758, c. It has been brought to the notice of the writer that he (Vermeersch) has changed his opinion (*Epitome Juris Canonici* (ed. II), II, n. 300).

[51] Genicot-Salsmans, *Institutiones Theologiae Moralis* (ed. X), II, n. 523,, who, however, undoubtedly excludes it in his *Casus Conscientiae* (ed. IV), casus 1070; Vlaming, *Praelectiones Juris Matrimonii* (ed. III), n. 401, 3; Boudinhon, *Revue du Clérge Français,* XCII, p. 107.

[52] *Le Mariage,* n. 167.

[53] *Dispensatiebevergdheden van huwelyks-beletselen in dringende gevallen,* p. 36 ff.

[54] *O. c., Supplementum* (1923), ad n. 764.

lator mentions only the impediments of canon 1043, and thereby *implicitly* excludes the form.

External authority is, moreover, strongly on the side of the stricter interpretation, as the view is espoused by Cappello,[55] Petrovits,[56] Blat,[57] Farrugia,[58] Ferreres,[59] Chelodi,[60] Cerato,[61] Prümmer,[62] Vidal,[63] Woywod,[64] Creusen,[65] Pighi,[66] and Simon.[67]

De Smet [68] maintains that although canon 1045 does not mention clandestinity expressly, as does canon 1043, from that it does not follow that the form of marriage is excluded from the faculty. The first argument he brings in support of this contention is that clandestinity is not excluded from the list of marriage impediments in the Code, even though it does not find a place in chapter IV, which deals with the diriment impediments. In reply to this it could be said, with equal weight, that the form is not *included* by the Code among the diriment impediments, and, undoubtedly with more weight, that the form is treated separately, and expressly distinguished, in many parts of the Code.[69] In dealing with the convalidation of marriage the legislator draws a consistent and sharp distinction between impediments and form.[70] Moreover, all

---

[55] *O. c.*, III, n. 233, c.

[56] *The New Church Law on Matrimony* (ed. II), n. 164.

[57] *Commentarium Textus Codicis Juris Canonici,* Lib. III, P. I. De Rebus (ed. II), n. 437.

[58] *De Matrimonio et Causis Matrimonialibus* (ed. X), n. 85.

[59] *Compendium Theologiae Moralis,* II (ed. XIII), n. 952, V.

[60] *Jus Matrimoniale* (ed. III), n. 41, 3.

[61] *Matrimonium* (ed. III), n. 37.

[62] *Manuale Theologiae Moralis* (ed. III), III, n. 867; *Manuale Juris Canonici* (ed. III), n. 332, 4.

[63] *Jus Canonicum,* V, n. 413.

[64] *A Practical Commentary on the Code of Canon Law,* n. 1014.

[65] *Epitome Juris Canonici,* II, n. 309. Cf. II (ed. 1922), n. 350.

[66] *De Sacramento Matrimonii* (ed. II), n. 88.

[67] *Faculties of Pastors and Confessors for Absolution and Dispensation,* n. 88.

[68] *L. c.*

[69] Canons 1043, 1137, 1139.

[70] Canons 1133–1137.

other authors maintain that the form does not constitute an impediment, in the strict canonical sense, in the present terminology of the Code.[71]

The second argument of De Smet is that the Index attached to the Code includes canon 1094, on form, in its enumeration of the diriment impediments. In reply to this it is hardly necessary to state that the Index, while of high authority, is a private compilation, and cannot be considered as an authentic interpretation of the Code. It is but a practical means of finding out, with facility, the canons which treat of a particular subject, but, beyond this, no juridical value can be attributed to it.[72]

Notwithstanding the weight of authority arrayed against him, De Smet insists, in 1923, on the probability of his opinion,[73a] which claim, however, can scarcely be sustained.

The power of the Ordinary extends to both forums, and is no longer restricted to the internal forum. The choice of the forum will depend on the nature of the impediment. If the impediment is public, he will grant the dispensation in the external forum, and inscribe the marriage in the public marriage and baptismal registers. If the impediment is *occult,* he will dispense in the internal non-sacramental forum, and will register the marriage in the secret book kept in the diocesan archives.[73b]

He can dispense in favor of his subjects wherever they are, and his faculty is operative also in favor of *all* who *hic et nunc* tarry within the limits of his diocese.

---

[71] Vermeersch, *Theologia Moralis,* III, n. 750: "defectus formae non est impedimentum. Et sic in Codice intelligitur"; Vlaming, *Praelectiones Juris Matrimonii* (ed. III), I, n. 183, c: "quae vero ex parte consensus aut non observatae legitimae formae matrimonio valide ac licite ineundo obstare possunt, ea Codex canonibus suis de impedimentis non comprehendit, sed seorsum moderatur"; Farrugia, *o. c.,* n. 84; Cerato, *o. c.,* n. 37.

[72] Cf. Wernz-Vidal, *o. c.,* V, p. 499, nota 60; Motry, *Diocesan Faculties According to the Code of Canon Law,* p. 141, note 31.

[73a] *O. c., Supplementum,* ad n. 764.

[73b] Canon 1047.

Revalidation of Marriage

The faculty to dispense is also applicable for the convalidation of marriages invalidly contracted. There is question here only of simple revalidation, since convalidation by means of a *"sanatio in radice"* is not included in the faculty.[74]

It is not, however, required, under the new legislation, that the marriage, although null, should have been attempted in good faith, nor that it should have been consummated, nor that the impediment must be occult.

Before the faculty becomes operative in the case of revalidation, the same condition of necessity must be present; only here the necessity arises in a different manner, and may result from different causes. Even though it be held that the condition that *"all things should be ready for the marriage"* must, in all its strictness, be considered as an absolutely distinct condition for the validity of a dispensation *"ad contrahendum,"* it is certainly not required when the case is one of revalidation. The canon requires only that the same danger of grave evil be present, that is, that the revalidation of the invalid union cannot be postponed, until such time as the necessary dispensation is obtained from the competent authority, without probable danger of grave evil. But the case must be urgent. Urgency in the case requires that recourse to the Holy See, or, at least, to one having delegated faculties, is either physically or morally impossible, or, where such impossibility is not present, that the revalidation cannot be postponed, without probable danger of grave evil, until the dispensation should arrive. The nature of the evil is not defined and, therefore, the word *"malum"* here is to receive a wide interpretation. A case, then, is to be considered urgent when the parties cannot be separated without danger of

---

[74] De Smet, *De Sponsalibus et Matrimonio,* II, n. 764; Ferreres, *Compendium Theologiae Moralis* (ed. XIII), II, n. 952, V.

grave scandal, or of serious injury to their reputation, or of some other grave evil, during the time required to obtain a dispensation, and, at the same time, cannot cohabit, as brother and sister, without danger of incontinency.[75] There is special danger of scandal or infamia resulting from separation when the invalidity of the marriage is not publicly known; and the difficulty of fraternal cohabitation is greatly increased if one of the parties is unaware, and unable to be informed, of the invalidity of the marriage.[76] If, however, in a particular case, separation without scandal, or cohabitation without danger of incontinency, is possible, there is no urgency, and the Ordinary cannot dispense; but, in practice, either alternative will, as a rule, be impossible.[77] If both parties are in good faith they are to be left so until the necessary dispensation is obtained.[78]

By *marriage contracted* is meant here one which has the appearance of a marriage (*species matrimonii*).[79]

According to some,[80] the "species" or "figura matrimonii" consists in the expression of matrimonial consent, even though this does not produce a *vinculum matrimonii* because of the existence of a diriment impediment. In general it can be said that the "species or figura matrimonii" consists in the expression of consent *servata forma substantiali;* the form gives it the *figura matrimonii.* Hence, strictly speaking, only those marriages of the faithful have the *appearance of a marriage* which are contracted, even though not validly, in the form prescribed by the Church.[81a]

---

[75] Reiffenstuel, *Jus Canonicum Universum,* IV, Appendix, *De Dispensatione super Impedimentis Matrimonii,* n. 49; Sanchez, *De Sancto Matrimonii Sacramento,* lib. II, dis. XL, n. 3.

[76] Cf. De Smet, *o. c.,* II, p. 219, nota 1.

[77] Cf. Feije, *De Impediments et Dispensationibus Matrimonialibus* (ed. III), n. 634, 3.

[78] Gasparri, *De Matrimonio* (ed. III), I, n. 440; Feije, *o. c.,* n. 634, 1.

[79] Blat, *o. c.,* n. 437; Ayrinhac, *Marriage Legislation in the New Code of Canon Law,* p. 92.

[80] Cf. Gasparri, *De Matrimonio* (ed. III), I, n. 46; Feije, *De Impedimentis et Dispensationibus Matrimonialibus* (ed. III), nn. 406, 768; Wernz, *Jus Canonicum* (ed. 1904), IV, p. 28, nota 11.

[81a] Gasparri, *l. c.;* Wernz, *l. c.*

If the form has been observed, but is defective for some reason, as, for instance, because the incompetency of the assisting priest to assist, it seems that such a marriage would have the "appearance of a marriage."[81b] If two Catholics are married outside the Church it is hard to see how their union would have the "species matrimonii," seeing that such unions have been termed *"turpis atque exitialis concubinatus."*[82] Others, however, seem to hold that such a union would have the "species matrimonii": "ubicumque cap. Tametsi viget, tantum ille consensus matrimonialis fidelium *in rigore* habet speciem matrimonii, qui in forma Tridentina datus est . . . At *si sola natura rei spectetur* verus consensus matrimonialis (etsi inefficax) exprimi potest etiam aliis modis sine forma Tridentina in loco capiti *Tametsi* subjecto. Id, quod patet ex matrimonio civili ibidem *mala fide* et invalide a sponsis celebrato et nequaquam putativo, at postea nihilominus a R. Pontifice *in radice* sanato."[83]

As to the marriages of Catholics with Protestants or infidels outside the Church, it seems sufficiently probable that such can be regarded as having the "figura matrimonii" if marriage consent was really manifested by both parties (even though inefficaciously) and *"si juxta mores regionum* vel infidelium vel hereticorum *formam* matrimoniorum tenent et legitima reputantur."[84] If, however, such a marriage were contracted in a place (even though according to the customary form of that place) where clandestine marriages are held *notorie* as invalid it can scarcely be said to have the "species matrimonii."[85]

Perhaps all this is confirmed by a comparison of the

[81b] Gasparri, *l. c.*

[82] *Instr. S. Poent.*, ad 3, 15 January 1866. *Coll. de Prop. Fide,* 1280; Cf. Feije, *o. c.*, n. 634, 2; Gasparri, *o. c.*, n. 440.

[83] Wernz, *o. c.*, IV, p. 28, nota 11; Cf. Woywod, *A Practical Commentary on the Code of Canon Law,* n. 1015.

[84] Wernz, *l. c.;* Gasparri, *o. c.*, I, n. 46.

[85] Feije, *o. c.*, n. 768.

old and new legislation on the point in question. The old law required, as a necessary condition for the exercise of the faculty of convalidation, that the marriage, though invalid, should have been celebrated *"in facie ecclesiae,"* so that in the absence of the form, in *any* case, the Ordinary could not use his faculties.[86] The New Law, however, does not repeat this condition, but some, nevertheless, maintain that the faculty of canon 1045 par. 2, holds only for those marriages, contracted indeed in the prescribed form, but invalidly because of some dispensable impediment of the ecclesiastical law.[87] However, since the condition of the old law is not repeated, it seems that any invalid marriage which has the *"species matrimonii"* falls within the Ordinary's power. Where the "figura matrimonii" is absent he must have recourse to the faculty of c. 1045, par. 1.

Seeing that the faculty to revalidate marriages does not include the power to grant a *sanatio in radice,* the Ordinary must see to the renewal of consent.[88] Since he has not power to dispense from the *form* of marriage, the renewal of consent must be given publicly, in the prescribed form, by both parties, if the impediment is public. If it is occult, and known to both parties, the consent must likewise be renewed by both parties, but a private renewal suffices. Where the impediment is occult, and known only to one party, a private renewal by that one party suffices, provided it is certain that the consent of the other party perserveres.[89] If the defect of form has been the only cause of invalidity, the convalidation must take place in the form prescribed by the Church.[90]

---

[86] Feije, *o. c.*, n. 634, 2; Gasparri, *o. c.*, n. 440.

[87] Blat, *Commentarium Textus Codicis Juris Canonici,* Lib. III—P. 1, De Rebus, n. 437; Ayrinhac, *Marriage Legislation in the New Code of Canon Law,* p. 92; *M. E.*, XXXVII, pp. 310, 311.

[88] Cf. Holy Office, 6 July 1898, ad 3, *Coll. de Prop. Fide,* 2007.

[89] Canons 1133–1135.

[90] Canon 1137.

The power of dispensing is *ordinaria-vicaria* and, therefore, can be delegated. As to the views of others on this point the reader is referred to the discussion on the nature of the power conferred by canon 1043.[91]

---

[91] See Part II, Chapter V.

CHAPTER IX

Urgent Cases

Faculties of Priests and Confessors

In iisdem rerum adjunctis, eadem facultate gaudeant omnes de quibus in can. 1044, sed solum pro casibus occultis in quibus ne loci quidem Ordinarius adiri possit, vel nonnisi cum periculo violationis secreti. (*Canon 1045*, par. 3.)

This paragraph ushers in the solution of the *casus perplexus* as it was strictly and technically understood in the old law. The *perplex case* arose, (1) when all preparations had been made for the ceremony which could not be postponed until a dispensation could be got from the proper authority in an occult impediment now detected for the first time; (2) when, after marriage, one of the parties discovered such an impediment, and found it morally impossible to avoid living a married life during the period required to secure a dispensation in the ordinary way.[1]

Various methods for escaping the difficulty were suggested. It was a fairly common view that the impediment *probably* ceased in both cases, but that, for precaution's sake at least, a normal dispensation should be secured as soon as possible. It was noted by some that the most satisfactory course would be to have the Bishop delegate to his priests the power he enjoyed himself in the circumstances.[2]

---

[1] Cf. Gasparri, *De Matrimonio* (ed. III), n. 246 ff.

[2] Feije, *De Impedimentis et Dispensationibus Matrimonialibus* (ed. III), nn. 640–649; Marc, *Institutiones Morales Alphonsianae* (ed. 1885), II, n. 2048.

Now, under the new legislation, the conjectures of the past have given place to definite teaching. The priest is no longer merely able to *declare* that the impediment has ceased (even the most favorable view granted him only this much), for he is now officially commissioned to grant a dispensation.

In the same circumstances as specified in canon 1045, pars. 1, 2 (as explained in the preceding chapter), the same power of dispensing is enjoyed by all those mentioned in canon 1044, that is, the parish priest, the priest delegated to assist at marriages (in accordance with the interpretation of canon 1044 given in chap. VI, Art. II), the priest who assists at a marriage in virtue of canon 1098, par. 2, and the confessor, but only in occult cases in which even the local Ordinary cannot be approached at all, or only at the risk of violating a secret.

The activities of all four are, therefore, restricted to cases in which three conditions are fulfilled: (1) the case must be urgent; (2) the case must be occult; (3) a timely dispensation from the Ordinary, or, at least, from his delegate, if there be such, is either impossible, or possible only at the risk of violating a secret.[3]

First it is necessary that the case be urgent. The question of urgency, however, takes on a different aspect in the case of the parish priest or confessor than in the case of the Ordinary. The urgency is not to be measured by the same rule for each case, for the expressions "*nec tempus suppetat*" and "*cum jam omnia sunt parata ad nuptias*" do not mean the same for both. Recourse to the Ordinary by the parish priest or confessor is a question only of a few days at most, while recourse to the proper authority in the case of the Ordinary may require, at times, weeks and even months. It will be noted that the parish priest had need only of the solution of the technical "*casus perplexus*" to arm him against contingent necessities, so that for him

[3] De Smet, *De Sponsalibus et Matrimonio* (ed. IV), II, n. 793.

the phrase "cum jam omnia sunt parata ad nuptias" now, as in the old law,[4] is to receive a stricter interpretation. For the parish priest and the others, the "perplex case" has been codified without change.[5]

It is moreover necessary, before the parish priest or confessor can dispense, that the Ordinary, or his delegate, cannot be approached, either because recourse to him is physically impossible, or because the celebration or convalidation of the marriage cannot be postponed, without probable danger of grave evil, until the necessary dispensation is received from him, or because the case, being occult, cannot be stated to him without danger of violating the sigillum or revealing a secret.[6]

In estimating the possibility of recourse, outside the question of the danger to a secret, ordinary means only must be considered. As has been so often said the telephone or telegraph are extraordinary means, and, therefore, do not take from the urgency of the case; nay, as a rule, they should not be used, especially by the confessor.[7]

The opinion of Cappello[8] that the automobile, train-service, motor cycle and bicycle, are to be numbered among the extraordinary means, is really doubtful. The automobile may, indeed, in certain cases, be still considered an extraordinary means, but for a large number it must be regarded as ordinary, for today it is no longer regarded as a mere luxury, but is used ordinarily as a means of contracting the ordinary businesses of life. A train journey can scarcely be considered something extraordinary, unless the journey to be traveled is considerable and one which would entail large expenses. Likewise no one would seriously hold that the use of the motor cycle or bicycle is a use of extraordinary means, except in certain cases, where the

[4] Cf. St. Alphonsus, *Theologia Moralis*, lib. VI, n. 613; Feije, *o. c.*, n. 640.

[5] Cf. *M. E.*, XXXVII, pp. 297–301.

[6] Cf. De Smet, *o. c.*, II, n. 793.

[7] *Pont. Com. pro Interp. Codicis*, 12 Nov. 1922, *A. A. S.*, XIV, 662; Holy Office, 10 December 1891, *Coll. de Prop. Fide*, 1775.

[8] *De Sacramentis*, III, n. 236, 2, a.

extraordinary element would arise from some extrinsic reason, as, for instance, bad stormy weather, the necessity of a long journey over bad roads.

Perhaps the principal source from which the impossibility of approaching the competent authority will arise, in practice, will be the danger of violating a secret. The Code speaks simply of the danger to a secret. Since there are various kinds of secrets, natural, professional, and sacramental, it is not justifiable to restrict the secretum in this context to the sacramental sigillum.[9] When the Code wishes to impose such a restriction it does so expressly,[10] and it, moreover, recognizes the official secret of priests, officials, physicians, midwives, and others.[11]

As to the sacramental seal, there can be no doubt that its danger of violation excuses from having recourse for the necessary dispensation. This danger will be often present, since the confessor is not *bound* to ask the permission of the penitent to reveal what he has heard in the confession, and thus obviate any danger to the sigillum, and the penitent is not bound to grant it. If, however, recourse could be made without danger to the seal, by giving fictitious names, and supposing that the time permits the recourse, a dispensation must be sought from the competent authority.[12]

As to other secrets, natural and professional, there can be likewise no doubt that the danger of violating them excuses also from making recourse which would otherwise be necessary. The secret here intended is, of course, that which is concomitant with the occultness of the case.[13]

---

[9] Augustine (*A Commentary on the New Code of Canon Law* [ed. III], V, p. 108), so restricted it, but he seems to have withdrawn the restriction later (*Rights and Duties of Ordinaries*, p. 275).

[10] Cf. Canons 889, 2369.

[11] Canon 1755, par. 2, n. 1. Cf. Leitner, *Lehrbuch des katholischen Eherects* (ed. III), p. 335.

[12] Woywod, *A Practical Commentary on the Code of Canon Law*, n. 1016.

[13] Blat, *Commentarium Textus Codicis Juris Canonici* (ed. II), Lib. III —P. 1, De Rebus, n. 437.

On the condition that it is prudently feared that communication with the proper authority involves danger to the secret confided by the revelation of the case, the parish priest can proceed to dispense. The fact that the case is occult, and is likely to remain so, and that the parties so wish it for a *reasonable cause,* constitutes a sufficient ground for the use of this faculty.[14]

When the case is occult the parties are not bound to reveal it in the external forum in order to render recourse to the Ordinary possible, where such a revelation would cause serious harm. If, however, the parties themselves freely consent to such a revelation, the parish priest or priest would not be empowered to dispense.[15]

Some are of the opinion [16] that the law here does not include the Ordinary among the persons with whom the secret is to bc preserved, so that if application to him for the necessary dispensation does not endanger the secret regarding others (even though it involves a revelation of the secret to him), the parish priest and other priests are destitute of dispensatory power, and are bound to recur to the Ordinary for the faculty to dispense: *"Si non deesset tempus recurrendi ad Ordinarium, vel ad eum adeundum in casu non adesset periculum revelandi aliis secretum, casus referri Ordinario deberet."*[17]

The disciples of this opinion maintain that the expression: *"pro casibus occultis, in quibus ne loci quidem Ordinarius adiri possit,"* gives sufficient foundation for this interpretation. They imply that the impossibility of approaching the Ordinary is to be considered a distinct condition, to the extent that the keeping of the secret, con-

---

[14] Cf. Vermeersch-Creusen, *Epitome Juris Canonici,* II, n. 311; Vlaming, *Praelectiones Juris Matrimonii* (ed. III), II, n. 412; Fanfani, *De Jure Parochorum,* n. 306.

[15] Cappello, *De Sacramentis,* III, n. 236, 2.

[16] Cf. Farrugia, *De Matrimonio et Causis Matrimonialibus* (ed. X), n. 88; *M. E.,* XXXII, pp. 62–68.

[17] Farrugia, *l. c.*

nected with the occultness of the case, has no reference to him. But such an interpretation is obviously false, for the above phrase is immediately followed by the words "*vel nonnisi cum periculo violationis secreti,*" which go to show quite clearly that the law contemplates the danger to the secret, in the case of the Ordinary himself, as a source from which impossibility of recourse to the Ordinary may arise. There may, moreover, at times, be very grave reasons for keeping the secret from the Ordinary himself, which reasons will often be present when the persons, whom the occult case concerns, are related to him in consanguinity and affinity.[18] Practically all Commentators on this canon espouse the latter view.[19]

At times it may happen that, while recourse to the Ordinary or his delegate would endanger the secret, such a danger would not accompany recourse to the Holy See itself, or to the Apostolic delegate. In such a case would a parish priest, priest, or confessor, enjoy the faculty of dispensing, or would they be bound to have recourse to either of the latter two if time permitted? There can be little doubt that such a case could not be considered urgent, and that a normal dispensation will have to be procured. Paragraph three of canon 1045 speaks of cases "pro quibus ne loci *quidem* Ordinarius adiri posset . . .," implying that if the higher authority, mentioned in paragraph one, is approachable, recourse to him is obligatory. Moreover, the foundation of the power conferred by canon 1045 is the urgency of cases. Such urgency does not exist where the Holy See or its Delegate can be approached in time, and without danger to the secret, and where there is no urgency, there is no power to dispense: "quando nulla adest necessitas . . . consequenter cessat ratio, ob quam ei

[18] Cappello, *o. c.*, n. 236, 2, c.

[19] Cf. De Smet, *De Sponsalibus et Matrimonio* (ed. IV), n. 793; Cappello, *l. c.;* Blat, *o. c.*, n. 437; Vermeersch, *Theologia Moralis,* III, n. 758; Genicot-Salsmans, *Institutiones Theologiae Moralis* (ed. X), II, n. 523, Bis.

competit potestas dispensandi."[20] Moreover, many authors embrace this opinion expressly.[21a]

Regarding the danger to the secret, it is not necessary that there be either physical or moral certainty that recourse to the proper authority would entail such danger. The Code requires only *periculum violationis secreti,* and certitude is more than periculum. Hence it suffices that there be a prudent well-founded fear that the secret might be betrayed by such an action.

Neither is it necessary that there be danger of a *direct* violation of the secret. If only an indirect violation is feared, as may happen when the parties needing the dispensation belong to a small community or to some institute, the parish priest may proceed to dispense if the other conditions are present.

In conformity with the interpretation given to canon 1044 in chap. VI, Art. II, it is to be held here that a priest who is delegated by the parish priest or Ordinary to assist at marriages in the parish, but who has not been delegated by him to dispense, enjoys the faculty of canon 1045, par. 3, that is, he can dispense in urgent cases if the necessary conditions are present, principally, if the case is occult, and the Holy See or its Delegate, the Ordinary or his delegate, or the parish priest himself, cannot be approached without the inconveniences already so often referred to.[21b]

The priest referred to in canon 1098, par. 2, is also endowed with the faculty of dispensing in urgent cases. This canon legislates that when the Ordinary, parish priest, or priest delegated by either to assist at marriages, cannot

---

[20] Reiffenstuel, *Jus Canonicum Universum,* IV, Appendix, *De Dispensatione super Impedimentis Matrimonii,* n. 10.

[21a] Cerato, *Matrimonium* (ed. III), n. 38; Blat, *o. c.,* n. 137; Farrugia, *o. c.,* n. 87. De Smet, *o. c.,* n. 793, uses language which would seem to imply the other opinion, *"requiritur et sufficit . . . quod Ordinarius adiri non posset."*

[21b] Chelodi, *Jus Matrimoniale* (ed. III), n. 44, 2; Fanfani, *De Jure Parochorum,* n. 306; Leitner, *Lehrbuch des katholischen Eherects* (ed. III), p. 336; Cappello, *o. c.,* III, n. 236, 2, c.

be present or reached, without grave incommodum, and when, moreover, it is foreseen, with moral certitude ("ex notorio vel inquisitione"),[22a] that this state of affairs will last for a month, any priest may assist at the marriage. The assistance of this priest, however, is necessary only for liceity *ex capite formae,* but if a diriment impediment is present, his presence would be necessary for the validity of the marriage because of the necessity of removing the impediment. But in order that he be endowed with this power of *dispensing,* it is necessary that the conditions demanded by canon 1045 be also verified. These conditions are: that the impediment be detected when all things have been prepared for the marriage, and the ceremony cannot be postponed until such time as the power to dispense can be obtained from the competent authority, and provided, of course, that the case is occult.[22b]

A very clear and distinct difference is drawn by the legislator between the faculties enjoyed by the Ordinary in urgent cases, and those enjoyed by the parish priest, delegated priest, simple priest, and confessor, in similar circumstances. The former may dispense from all impediments of ecclesiastical origin, with, however, the two exceptions specified in canon 1043, regardless of the nature of the case, it being immaterial whether the case is public or occult. The latter class of persons, however, can dispense from the same impediments but only in occult cases. A further restriction must also be made in the case of the confessor, since his power is limited to the internal sacramental forum. Canon 1045, par. 3, does not explicitly lay down this latter restriction, with the result that some have concluded that the confessor can, like other priests, dispense also in the internal non-sacramental forum.[23] But

[22a] *Pont. Comm. pro Interpt. Codicis,* 10 November 1925, *A. A. S.,* XVII, 583.

[22b] Cf. Simon, *Faculties of Pastors and Confessors for Absolution and Dispensation,* p. 89; *I. E. R.,* XIII, p. 198.

[23] Leitner, *Lehrbuch des katholischen Eherects* (ed. III), p. 336.

this is not so. Canon 1044 expressly restricts the confessor's powers to the internal sacramental forum, and canon 1045, par. 3, in referring to this canon, thereby, at least implicitly, imposes the same restriction. Moreover, it is not likely that the legislator should intend that the confessor should possess more ample faculties in ordinary urgent cases than in the danger of death.[24]

The phrase "*pro casibus occultis*" has occasioned much controversy among the commentators on the Code. As this is the most practical of the conditions necessary for the validity of the dispensation, it is all important that every priest should have a clear and definite idea of the exact meaning of the clause, and as to how for it can, with safety, justify a priest to dispense. As special difficulties surround this condition in its application to the confessor, because of the peculiar nature of his power, an attempt will first be made to give the precise meaning of *occult cases* as such, and, then, the condition in its particular application to the confessor will receive some consideration.

In interpreting *occult cases* three opinions are, strictly speaking, put forward by commentators. Some opine that *occult cases* are the same as *occult impediments,* and that, therefore, neither the parish priest, priest, or confessor can dispense, in urgent cases, from impediments which can be proven in the external forum.[25] This view is embraced by Ojetti,[26] Vidal,[27] Augustine,[28] Simon,[29] and Pighi.[30] Others, however, go further and extend the faculty to all impediments of the internal forum. Hence, when there is question of contracting marriage, the parish priest, priest,

---

[24] Vermeersch-Creusen, *Epitome Juris Canonici,* II (ed. 1922), n. 353; Cappello, *o. c.,* III, n. 238; De Smet, *o. c.,* II, n. 794; Farrugia, *De Matrimonio et Causis Matrimonialibus* (ed. X), n. 89, b.

[25] Canon 1037.

[26] *Jus Pontificium,* annus VI—Fascic. 1–11, pp. 56, 61.

[27] *Jus Canonicum,* V, n. 428.

[28] *A Commentary on the New Code of Canon Law* (ed. III), V, p. 108.

[29] *Faculties of Pastors and Confessors for Absolution and Dispensation,* p. 88.

[30] *De Sacramento Matrimonii* (ed. II), n. 90, 3, a.

or confessor can dispense only from impediments which are occult in nature and in fact. Such impediments are not, strictly speaking, the same as occult impediments as understood in canon 1037. An impediment is to be considered *occult in fact* when it is not known to more than five or six discreet and prudent persons in a town, or to more than seven or eight in a city, so that there is no immediate danger of its becoming publicly known.[31] But an impediment known to so many may be capable of proof in the external forum, even though it is occult in nature, and, therefore, may be public in the terminology of the Code. When there is question of convalidating an invalid marriage, the faculty extends not only to impediments occult in nature and in fact, but also to *certain* impediments which are public by nature but actually secret, notably, spiritual relationship, and consanguinity or affinity in the third degree, and even in the second, if the impediment has remained secret for at least ten years and the parties had contracted marriage publicly, have lived together, and have been regarded as legitimate husband and wife.[32] This second view is espoused by De Smet,[33] Farrugia,[34] Hilling,[35] and Leitner.[36]

The third and most extensive interpretation comprehends under *occult cases* all impediments that are occult in fact. The faculty extends, therefore, also to impediments that are public by nature, provided they are occult in fact in the sense already explained. The greater number of commentators espouse this opinion, such as, Cappello,[37] Blat,[38]

---

[31] Benedict XIV, *Institutiones Ecclesiasticae,* II, Inst. Eccles. LXXXVII, n. 45.

[32] Benedict XIV, *o. c.,* Inst. Eccles. LXXXVII, nn. 7–11; *Pastor Bonus,* 13 April 1744, *Bullarium,* I, Const. XCV, n. 40.

[33] *De Sponsalibus et Matrimonio* (ed. IV), II, n. 466.

[34] *De Matrimonio et Causis Matrimonialibus* (ed. X), nn. 87, 89.

[35] *A. K. K.,* CII, pp. 1–13.

[36] *Lehrbuch des katholischen Eherects* (ed. III), pp. 334, 335.

[37] *De Sacramentis,* III, n. 236, d.

[38] *Commentarium Textus Codicis Juris Canonici* (ed. II), Lib. III—P. I, De Rebus, n. 437.

Oesterle,[39] Chelodi,[40] Fanfani,[41] Genicot,[42] Vermeersch,[43] Cerato,[44] Linneborn,[45] Petrovits,[46] the editor of the *Il Monitore Ecclesiastico,*[47] Woywod,[48] Arendt,[49] Koudelka,[50] Kubelbeck,[51] Motry,[52] and O'Donnell.[53]

For a better understanding of these three theories and of the arguments put forward by the disciples of each opinion, it may be of value to give a resumé of a little controversy that has been conducted in the European magazines on this precise point. It will serve to indicate the difficulties felt by experts on this matter, and will, at the same time, give the arguments on which one must rely in coming to a practical conclusion.

The controversy began by a contribution from the pen of a writer, who signed himself "Socius," to the *Il Monitore Ecclesiastico* in 1920. He cited a dozen or more of the commentators who had written on the subject up to his time and found them, on the whole, unsatisfactory. Some merely copied or translated the words of the canon. Some committed themselves so far as to underline the words *occult* or *occult cases.* Others were inclined to restrict the faculty to impediments naturally occult. A few supported this last view indirectly by drawing attention to the char-

---

[39] *Münsterisches Pastoralblatt,* LVII, p. 186 ff.

[40] *Jus Matrimoniale* (ed. III), nn. 40, 44, 2.

[41] *De Jure Parochorum,* n. 306, c.

[42] Genicot-Salsmans, *Institutiones Theologiae Moralis* (ed. X), II, p. 487, nota 2; *Casus Conscientiae* (ed. II), casus 1074, 1075, 1076.

[43] Vermeersch-Creusen, *Epitome Juris Canonici,* II, n. 311; Vermeersch, *Theologia Moralis,* III, n. 758, c.

[44] *Matrimonium* (ed. III), n. 38.

[45] *Grundriss des Eherects* (ed. II and III), p. 117.

[46] *The New Church Law on Matrimony* (ed. II), nn. 166, 167.

[47] *M. E.*, XXXII, pp. 62–68.

[48] *H. P. R.*, XXIII, p. 1061; Cf. *A Practical Commentary on the Code of Canon Law,* n. 1010.

[49] *N. R. T.*, XLVII, pp. 261–274.

[50] *H. P. R.*, XXIII, I, pp. 403–405.

[51] *The Sacred Penitentiaria and Its Relations to Faculties of Ordinaries and Priests,* pp. 72, 74.

[52] *Diocesan Faculties According to the Code of Canon Law,* p. 139.

[53] *I. E. R.*, XVI, pp. 404–408.

acteristics of an *occult impediment;* while others still, in more or less halting fashion, declared for an extension of the power to cases like those outlined by the correspondent. The canon has "interred the casus perplexus with all funeral honors," but, in view of the difference of opinion among experts, what is to be thought of the canon itself? Socius, with due deference to the writers who think otherwise, declared in favor of the view which extends the powers of the parish priest, priest, and confessor, in urgent cases, to impediments naturally (natura sua) public but actually (de facto) occult. He prefaces his arguments with the remark that one cannot speak with certainty today of the cessation or suspension of a diriment impediment, or of the use of epikeia, in a case of urgency. The reasons for his view, in so far as they can be epitomized, may be stated as follows.[54]

(1) The third paragraph of canon 1045 speaks of the same power as that mentioned in the first, and the first section, beyond all doubt, covers both public and occult impediments, as does canon 1043 to which it refers.

(2) The word *"cases"* is not synonymous with *"impediments,"* and, therefore, there is every reason for emphasizing the fact that the third section speaks, not of occult *impediments,* but of occult *cases.*

(3) The same third paragraph indicates, as one of the circumstances that lead to a grant of the faculty, the possible violation of a secret. The secret binds everybody, parish priest, priest, and confessor, in relation to *everyone,* the Ordinary not excluded. It is no longer necessary to advise the Ordinary if such an action would endanger the secret, and the obligation of observing the secret *may* urge even in the case of a naturally public impediment that remains actually occult. Therefore, even in this case, the Ordinary is not to be approached, and the parish priest, priest, and confessor are thrown on their own resources.

---

[54] *M. E.*, XXXII, pp. 59-62.

His theory, however, he admits, which seems to be the logical interpretation of the law, leads to very serious practical difficulties. Supposing the impediment becomes actually public after the *confessor* has dispensed, what is to be done? A dispensation given in the sacramental tribunal is of no avail in the external forum (can. 1047). What if one of the parties repudiates the marriage? The impediment can be proven, the dispensation cannot, and thus the way is open to grave abuse and gross injustice. One remedy is, of course, to induce the penitent to disclose the matter to the parish priest; he *can* give a dispensation and, at the same time, have it recorded in the secret book kept in the Curial Archives, which can be called upon if the need should arise. This will save the secret, and, at the same time, safeguard the dispensation in the external forum in all contingencies (canon 1047). He regards, however, as too rigid, the opinion of those who hold that the penitent must be obliged so to reveal an impediment of its nature public. What if the penitent cannot be induced to reveal the impediment to the parish priest? "Socius" finds himself driven, by a verbal interpretation of the canon, to hold that, even in that case, even when the parties are *mala fide,* the confessor is bound to give the dispensation; and he sees no way out of the *impasse* until the lines of escape are indicated by a special decree of the "Commission for the Authentic Interpretation of the Code."

In a long contribution immediately following that of "Socius," the editor of the *Il Monitore Ecclesiastico* accepts the view of the writer, in all its details, except as regard to the confessor. What "Socius" regards to be the principal, and even the only, element in the discussion, namely, the expression *"pro casibus occultis,"* is, instead, only secondary. He agrees fully with him in his view that "occult cases" embrace impediments which are naturally public. The word *casus* is not equivalent to *impedimentum,* and the basis of such equivalency, as given by those who maintain so, is fundamentally wrong. Moreover, he claims, canons 1044 and 1045 are based on the "*praesumptio juris et de jure*" that the Ordinary, if he could be approached, would dispense in the case. The material impossibility of reaching him, at least where it does not depend on the will of the parties, must not deprive them of the benefit which he would give. In other words, the parish priest, priest, and confessor are here to be considered as the extension, if the expression may be used, of the personality of the Ordinary, to dispense in so far as he can dispense.[55]

The editor, however, declares himself strongly on the opposite side to "Socius" regarding the Confessor. Transferring the discussion from the exact meaning of *occult cases* to a consideration of the nature of the power exercised by the confessor, he sees an open contradiction in a dispensation given in the internal sacramental forum from an impediment (natura sua publicum) which, of its very nature, pertains to the external forum, and which, in the hypothesis, continues to exist in that forum, even though, accidentally, it remains, so far, occult. The canon speaks of cases and not of impediments. True, but this matters little; the whole context suggests the limitation. In danger of death the parish priest has full power over all impediments, public as well as occult. Can he, therefore, select any forum he pleases? Certainly not, for if he grants in the internal sacramental forum a dispensation from a public impediment, his action would be invalid. "*Quidquid recipitur, ad modum recipientis recipitur:*" to dispense means to eliminate the impediment, and for this it is necessary that the impediment should no longer remain after the act of dispensing: the act must be equivalent, in everything, to the nature of the impediment. The same must be said of the confessor; the dispensation must correspond to the impediment, and a dispensation in the internal sacramental forum is absolutely useless—nay, in fact, a con-

[55] *M. E.*, XXXII, pp. 62–68.

tradiction in terms—unless it falls on impediments pertaining essentially to that forum, and which are, therefore, both naturally and actually occult.

The interpretation given by "Socius" would, moreover, leave a very wide opening for frauds of all kinds against the law. It would accentuate the undesirable discrepancy that sometimes arises between the divine and the ecclesiastical forum, and increase enormously the number of cases in which the Ordinary would have to condemn marriages valid in the sight of God (canon 1990). The remedies proposed to eliminate these very grave and enormous inconveniences would not only always remain insufficient, as "Socius" himself realizes, but would eventually destroy the very nature of the juridical institution which they purpose to help, by insisting, in the last analysis, on the insufficiency of the internal forum with the substitution of a dispensation in the internal non-sacramental forum. This cannot be the logical intention of the legislator who must have intended each forum to be sufficient in itself, and for its own functions, without the necessity of recurring from one to the other. The legislator does not deserve such a grave criticism in a matter so delicate and important.

If the faculty is restricted in the case of the confessor, the difficulties mentioned by "Socius" will disappear. There will be no room for fraud, for canons 1046 and 1047 guarantee the necessary proof in case of recalcitrance; the secret will be preserved in regard to everyone, except the Ordinary, and that suffices; the regulations made for each forum will be adequate and will need no supplementing; and if it be objected that this interpretation reduces the confessor's power almost to vanishing point, the answer is "yes," in so far as the diriment impediments are concerned, but the impedient impediments still leave a wide field open.

Such an interpretation is, without doubt, restrictive, but it is enough that it be logical, and consonant with the spirit of the law and the nature of things. What is the use in widening a faculty when such an extension ends in the destruction of the law, by making the existence or non-existence of a sacrament depend on the malice of men. The confessor's duty is plain. When an impediment naturally public (though actually occult) is revealed, he is to tell the penitent that he cannot give a dispensation unless the whole transaction is recorded in the secret archives of the diocesan Curia or of the Penitentiary. A hard law? Yes: *"dura lex sed lex;"* and there is no need to apply to the Commission.

The next to enter the arena of discussion is M. Arendt, Penitentiary theologian and consultor to the Holy Office. He discussed the whole matter at great length in *Nouvelle Revue Theologique.*[56] He quite agrees that there is no need to appeal to the Commission, his reason being that "Socius' " view is amply borne out by the words of the law, and that, if practical difficulties arise, their solution can be found in the generally accepted rules of Moral Theology. The supposed impossibility of giving in the internal forum a dispensation from an impediment naturally public is quite without foundation. A dispensation cannot be even conceived unless it renders the person dispensed juridically capable of performing those things which he could do were he never subject to the impediment. Regarding the *habilitas* of the person dispensed, no distinction can be admitted between one *habilis* naturally, or by common law, and one *habilis* as the result of a dispensation. The difference between a dispensation granted in the external forum and one given in the internal cannot be such as to deny to one dispensed in the latter forum the *formal* effect of a dispensation, which consists in the returning of the juridical capacity for the act. Whether the dispensation is given in the internal or external forum, the essential effect is the same—juridical capacity for marriage, and the only difference is that further steps are necessary to have this effect

[56] XLVII, pp. 261-274.

and its consequences *recognized* by the external society to which the penitent belongs. To assert that the second dispensation supplies an essential defect in the first is to be guilty of a "worse contradiction in terms" than "Socius" could ever possibly be accused of. This is confirmed by canon 1047, according to which a dispensation given in the internal non-sacramental forum, in order that it may be recognized as valid in the external, does not need renewal in that forum, but merely inscription in the secret book of the Curial Archives.

Canon 1044 certainly enables the confessor to give, in the internal forum, *all* the dispensations which the parish priest can grant in the external, for "when the law does not distinguish, neither should we." If further evidence be desired as to the *essential* equality between the two classes of dispensations, it will be found in the regulations governing a kindred matter—absolution granted in the internal forum from censures incurred in the external.[57]

Once that is granted, the only question that really arises is whether the conditions enumerated in the third paragraph of canon 1045 are fulfilled or not, that is, whether there is serious danger involved in delay, and whether the Ordinary can be conveniently approached. As for the dangers, the ordinary rules hold—the claims of charity and justice, the welfare of the parties themselves and of others, the needs of the church, and such like, are to be taken into account. And, on the second count, the necessity of taking steps to prevent a subsequent repudiation of the marriage must not be lost sight of. If the impediment, naturally public, is in no way defamatory, and there is no special reason for keeping it secret, the penitent must be told that he is *morally* obliged to make it a matter of the external forum, and have the dispensation registered. If it *is* defamatory, or there is special reason for secrecy, the con-

[57] Canon 2251.

fessor will arrange, with the penitent's consent, to inform the Penitentiary and follow its instructions.[58] If the penitent refuses to follow such a reasonable suggestion,—one that guarantees secrecy, and, at the same time, provides for the validity of the marriage in the external forum should the impediment ever become *actually* public—he must be informed that a dispensation will not be given; for, after all, the confessor, though empowered to act, is not *obliged* to use his faculties in favor of a man who violates obvious moral obligations, and is clearly indisposed for sacramental absolution. With these precautions the law will be saved from abuse, except such abuse as every human law entails.

The last contribution to the controversy has come from the pen of Ojetti.[59] He defends the opinion that "*occult cases*" are simply equivalent to "*occult impediments.*" He prefaces his arguments with the remark that none of the arguments of Arendt are conclusive; that nothing but the general axioms used by him have the species of conclusive argumentation. But general axioms help very little, for very rarely are they used legitimately and justifiably. The general axiom: "*Ubi lex voluit, dixit; ubi noluit, tacuit,*" if understood in a general sense, is false. It would exclude *all* restrictive interpretation which, on the admission of all, must, at times, be given. Nay, it would exclude the very end of *all* interpretation, which is to inquire into the mind of the legislator. So also the axiom: "*Ubi lex non distinguit, nec nos distinguere debemus,*" if understood in a general sense, would likewise exclude all restrictive interpretation. The use of such an axiom is legitimate only when there is no reasonable foundation in the law itself to justify a restrictive interpretation. But in the question at issue valid reasons for such a restriction are at hand.

The word "*cases*" is synonymous here with the word

---

[58] Canon 1047.

[59] *Jus Pontificium,* Annus VI—Fascic. 1-11, pp. 56-61.

"impediments." The grammatical construction of the canon proves this clearly. The term *cases* was used in order to observe congruity with the formation of the period; for the words *"in quibus nec loci quidem Ordinarius adiri posset"* were to follow immediately, and it would be more grammatical to speak of *"cases,"* in which the Ordinary could not be approached, than of *"impediments" in which* he could not be approached.

A comparison of paragraphs three and one also calls for this restrictive interpretation, for the first paragraph speaks only of *"impediments,"* so that the reference to it by paragraph three necessitates the acceptance of the term *"cases"* in the sense of *impediments.*

The extensive interpretation is altogether alien to the mind of the legislator who must be presumed to have wished to provide for the stability and indissolubility of the marriage state rather than permit frequent conflict between the ecclesiastical and divine forums, with such sinister consequences to souls and the marriage state.

Such are the many and various arguments put forth by the various disciples of the different opinions. Very little remains to be said, and it is perhaps difficult, in view of such difference of opinion and variety of evidence, to come to any certain conclusion. However, the opinion which would attribute not only to the parish priest and assistant priest, but also to the confessor, power over impediments naturally public and actually occult, in urgent cases, is, at least theoretically, the better, and perhaps the true, opinion. The principal reason for this conclusion is one taken from the history of the canon in its general relation to the present legislation. When one considers carefully the history of the powers conferred by canon 1045, and keeps it in mind in interpreting the present-day law, many of the difficulties created by authors will disappear, or, at least, will be greatly modified. For a fuller knowledge of the history the reader is referred to Part I, Chapter III, Articles I and II, as its repetition here will bring with it only what is barely necessary to establish the argument.

Under the old legislation, the common and certain teaching of theologians and canonists attributed to Bishops, in urgent cases, power to dispense, under certain well-defined conditions, from occult impediments, but limited the faculty to the internal forum. In cases in which the Bishop could not be approached in time, parish priests were advised to rely on the use of epikeia, and on the theory of the cessation of the impediment. The term *"occult impediments"* certainly excluded impediments that were public in nature and in fact, and certainly *included* those occult in nature and in fact. As to impediments which were public in nature but occult in fact, there was not agreement as to whether they fell within the ambit of the faculty. In the earlier days perhaps it was the more common opinion that these impediments should be excluded, on the ground that greater power should not be attributed to the Bishop than to the Major Penitentiarius.[60] Many authors, however, defended the extension of the Bishop's powers to these impediments; it was certainly a growing opinion, and was embraced by mostly all those authors who were the immediate predecessors of the Code and the eventful year of 1918.[61] To show how solidly probable was their doctrine, it will suffice to quote the words of Feije:[62] *"Non obstantibus gravibus hisce rationibus, non audemus pro praxi negare episcopi potestatem in impedimentis natura sua publicis, sed per accidens occultis."*

The use of epikeia, which the fairly common teaching

[60] Cf. Benedict XIV, *De Synodo Dioecesana,* lib. IX, chap. II, n. 1 ff; Feije, *De Impedimentis et Dispensationibus Matrimonialibus* (ed. III), n. 634.

[61] Cf. Pignatelli, *Consultationes Canonicae,* III, consul. XXXIII, n. 3 ff; Sanchez, *De Sancto Matrimonii Sacramento,* lib. II, dis. XL, n. II; Reiffenstuel, *o. c.,* IV, Appendix, nn. 44-46; Marc, *Institutiones Alphonsianae,* II, n. 2046; Gasparri, *De Matrimonio* (ed. III), nn. 440, 442, who, in this edition, changed his opinion in favor of the broader view; Wernz, *Jus Decretalium* (ed. 1904), p. 890, nota 79.

[62] *O. c.,* n. 634, 7.

of canonists vindicated for the parish priest, extended to the same impediments from which the Bishop could dispense.[63]

The two principal cases of urgency were given by these canonists as the danger of death and the urgency now considered in canon 1045.

Under the new legislation the conjectures of the past have given place to very definite teaching. As to the Bishop, he is empowered to dispense, in danger of death and other cases of urgency, not only from impediments by nature public, but from all impediments, even though public in fact, with the two exceptions made in canon 1043. The parish priest and assistant priest (whatever about the confessor) are endowed with the same power of *dispensing,* in danger of death, as the Bishop. But in other cases of urgency, outside the danger of death, his power is restricted to occult cases. What then is the natural and logical interpretation to be given to "occult cases"? If the general relation established between canons 1043–1045 and their counterparts in the old law is to be logically maintained, "occult cases" must be taken as including impediments that are naturally public, provided they are occult in fact. The mere probability of the doctrine which, in the old law, extended the power of Bishops to these impediments, has now given way to certitude. The use of epikeia, in the case of the parish priest, has been supplanted by the conferring of actual power of dispensing, and, taking these two points conjointly, it seems sufficiently clear that occult cases embrace also impediments naturally public and actually occult.

Ojetti's argument that the grammatical construction of canon 1045, par. 3, demands that cases be taken in the sense of impediments is somewhat far-fetched, and, far from proving his view, is, on the contrary, a very strong argument for the doctrine under defense. If the terms "*casus*" and "*impedimentum*" were synonymous, why

[63] Cf. Roncaglia, *De Matriionio,* q. V, c. 1.

should the legislator confuse the minds of his subjects by such a statement as *"pro casibus occultis"*; by the promiscuous use of *"case"* and *"impediment"* in the law which is supposed to be an exact and brief expression of the mind of the legislator. But, moreover, the terms are not synonymous; the word *"case"* neither etymologically or in common usage bears the sense of impediment; and that occult cases must be extended beyond occult impediments is clear from the very use of the word *"case,"* for if it were synonymous with "impediment" it would have been far simpler, and certainly far clearer, to have expressed the faculty in some such words as: "in such circumstances all those mentioned in canon 1044 have the same faculties as Ordinaries of places, but only when the impediments are occult."

Hence *"occult cases"* of canon 1045, par. 3, are to be taken as corresponding to the occult impediments of the *old law,* and, therefore, as including, at least with solid probability, impediments naturally public. The change introduced by the Code in the concept of public and occult impediments[64] necessitated the replacement of the word "impediments" by the term *"cases."* Today, the deciding element between a public and an occult impediment is no longer, as it was in the old law, the *knowledge* of, or danger of divulgation to, the impediment, but the *fact* as to whether it is capable of being proven in the external forum or not. If it can be proven in the external forum, by any juridical means, it is public; otherwise it is occult. In the old law an impediment was still considered occult if it were not known to more than five or six persons in a town or seven or eight in a city,[65] and there was no immediate danger of its becoming publicly known; but under the present discipline such an impediment would no longer be occult, but public, and, hence, some expression should be found to

---

[64] Canon 1037.

[65] Benedict XIV, *Institutiones Ecclesiasticae,* II, Inst. Eccles. LXXXVII, n. 46; Gasparri, *o. c.,* n. 260.

replace the use of the term "*occult impediments,*" unless the powers of canon 1045, par. 3, were to be more restricted than in the past, and the term "*occult cases*" was the one chosen, and which, perhaps, was the only one possible.

When then is a case to be regarded as occult? The Code nowhere defines an "occult case," and, therefore, in conformity with the interpretation given above, a case must be considered occult according to the rule given in the old law to determine the occultness or publicness of an impediment. Although absolute certainty was not arrived at regarding this point, the conclusion come to by Benedict XIV, the prince of all canonists, was, by far, the better, and perhaps, the generally accepted rule. Having weighed the opinions of those who were intimately connected with the Sacred Penitentiary (such as Prosper Fagnanus, Marcus Paulus Leo, P. Thesaurus, Tiburtius Navarrus, and Syrus of the Franciscan Order) and who, therefore, were in a position to know when the Sacred Penitentiary regarded an impediment as occult, Benedict XIV fostered the view: "*Res adhuc est occulta, si in oppido est nota quinque aut sex personis, in civitate vero septem, aut octo, adhuc occulta censeri debet, modo scilicet ab illis non fuerit divulgata.*"[66]

Three elements must be considered in determining the occultness or publicness of a case, (1) the number of persons to whom the impediment is actually known, (2) the quality of the persons to whom it is known, and (3), as a consequent to this second element, the degree of danger of divulgation present: If the persons who have already acquired knowledge of the fact are prudent, discreet, and trustworthy, and especially if they are relations of the parties concerned, proximate danger of divulgation is not, as a rule, to be feared. If, however, the persons are not endowed with such qualities, this danger is greatly to be feared, *and where there is proximate danger of divulgation* the case must be considered as already public. Perhaps at

---

[66] *Institutiones Ecclesiasticae,* II, Inst. Eccles. LXXXVII, nn. 44–46.

the present day one need not be mathematically held down to the number of persons laid down by Benedict XIV. The danger of a case becoming known within a short time is less likely today, and hence, perhaps, the maximum number of persons, to which the impediment should be known, may receive a little extension. St. Alphonsus professes to know of a case where the Sacred Penitentiary dispensed from a certain impediment of consanguinity that was known to ten persons,[67] and Gasparii claims that a similar dispensation was given by the Penitentiary from an impediment known to seven or eight persons in a city of nine thousand souls.[68] Hence the conclusion is that the rule handed down by Benedict XIV will always serve as a safe norm in practice.[69]

Some present-day authors[70] confuse the terms "*impedimentum natura sua publicum sed facto occultum*" and "*impedimentum natura sua et facto occultum,*" with the terms "*impedimentum materialiter publicum sed facto occultum*" and "*impedimentum formaliter et materialiter occultum*" respectively. This latter distinction had reference mainly to the impediment of crime. By a "*formally occult*" impediment was meant one in which the fact ("crime") from which the impediment arose was known, but it was not known, except to a few at most, that an impediment resulted from such a fact; or, as was generally said, that the fact "*ut criminosum*" was known, but the fact "*secundum rationem impedimenti*" was not known. An impediment was regarded as "*materially occult*" when the mere fact from which the impediment arose was known, but there

---

[67] *Theologia Moralis,* lib. VI, n. IIII.

[68] *De Matrimonio* (ed. III), I, n. 260.

[69] This is confirmed by a parallelism with canon 2197. The publicness and occultness of crimes is to be decided in somewhat the same manner as that which has been given for "cases."

[70] Cf. Cappello, *De Sacramentis,* III, n. 236, 2, d.

was general ignorance as to the imputability of the fact ("crime").[71]

No one denied that an impediment that was *"materialiter et formaliter occultum"* could be considered as an occult impediment, and, therefore, as falling within the ambit of the dispensatory power of the Bishop. But regarding one *"formaliter occultum et materialiter publicum"* it was vehemently disputed as to whether such an impediment fell under the Bishop's powers, and, consequently, as to whether it should be regarded as an "occult impediment" simply: "nos ipsi jurejurando affirmare possumus per tot annos, quibus Sacrae Poenitentiariae addicti fuimus, suffragiumque nostrum, cum res ejusmodi proponerentur . . . semper in more positum fuisse, ut impedimentum publicum *materialiter* spectaretur, et nunquam eo nos devenisse, ut examen fieret, an impedimentum *formaliter* occultum censendum esset."[72] Others, however, held that such an impediment could be regarded as occult, and, therefore, as coming under the power of the Bishop,[73] and their view seems to have been confirmed by a decision of the *Congregation of the Council,* 29 January 1881.[74]

Such an impediment, if it can be conceived as existing at the present day, would undoubtedly be regarded as public, since the elements constituting it are, ex hypothesi, known by a few, and, therefore, the existence of the impediment could be proven in the external forum.[75] It could however easily constitute an *"occult case,"* and where the fact that the criminal act constitutes an impediment is known only to a few, so that there is no proximate danger of its becoming public, there is, de facto, an occult case.

When occult cases are considered in reference to the

---

[71] Cf. Benedict XIV, *Institutiones Ecclesiasticae,* II, Inst. Eccl. LXXXVII, n. 48.

[72] Benedict XIV, *o. c.,* n. 48.

[73] Cf. Gasparri, *De Matrimonio* (ed. III), I, n. 442.

[74] *A. S. S.,* XIV, pp. 155–165.

[75] Cf. Cappello, *o. c.,* III, n. 200.

confessor further difficulties present themselves for discussion. The faculty of the confessor is restricted to the internal sacramental forum, and, because of this restriction, many have concluded that he can dispense only from occult impediments, even if the term "*occult cases*" were to receive the broader interpretation. This conclusion is accepted even by some of those who admit that "*occult cases*" comprehend impediments naturally public and actually occult.[76]

This restriction in the case of the confessor arises from the supposed impossibility of giving in the internal sacramental forum a dispensation from an impediment that is of its nature public. But this claim is without foundation. A dispensation given in the internal forum *per se* is not valid in the external.[77] This is true both of the internal non-sacramental forum and of the internal sacramental forum. Special exception is, however, made in favor of the former by canon 1047. This legislates that a dispensation granted in the internal non-sacramental forum is valid in the external if it be registered in the secret book of the Curial Archives. Previous to this registration the essential effect of the dispensation is produced, namely, the person dispensed is rendered juridically capable of contracting a valid marriage. But this juridical capacity is not yet recognized in the external forum of the Church until the fact of the dispensation is registered in the proper book. Hence the mere fact of registration does not change the nature of the power exercised in the internal non-sacramental forum; neither does it add to, or take from, the *essential* capacity of the forum itself. A dispensation given in the internal sacramental forum is indeed valid in that forum and before God, and, therefore, produces the same essential effect as one granted in the non-sacramental forum, namely, it gives

---

[76] Cappello, *o. c.*, III, n. 238; Vlaming, *Praelectiones Juris Matrimonii* (ed. III), II, n. 414; Editor of the *Il Monitore Ecclesiastico,* XXXII, pp. 62-68; Motry, *Diocesan Faculties according to the Code of Canon Law,* p. 135.

[77] Canon 202, par. 1.

juridically capacity for the contracting of marriage. But the dispensation can be registered in *no* book, no matter how secret, and, therefore, this capacity can never be recognized in the external forum. Hence it follows that there is no *essential* difference between these two fora: both possess the same *"potestas juridica recipiendi."* But no one will deny that a dispensation from an impediment *natura sua* public can be granted in the internal non-sacramental forum. Canons 1043 and 1044 certainly endow the parish priest with dispensatory power over public impediments in danger of death. But he is not free to choose arbitrarily whatever forum he should so desire. If infamia, scandal, or any other grave evil, would result from the revelation of an impediment that is naturally public but de facto occult, he must grant the dispensation from it in the internal non-sacramental forum. No one will deny him the right to do this; authors impose on him this obligation. Hence the internal non-sacramental forum is capable of receiving a dispensation from an impediment naturally public, and the same capacity must be attributed to the internal sacramental forum, if there is no essential difference between both fora.

Moreover, as has already been pointed out, Bishops, in the past, enjoyed power to dispense from occult impediments. It was sufficiently probable that this power extended to impediments of their nature public. But all insisted that this power was restricted to the internal forum, and if this were incapable of receiving such a dispensation, the teaching of the past would have contained two contradictory elements.

Again the Sacred Penitentiary has been in the past, as it is today,[78] the competent tribunal for the internal forum. It is from this tribunal that the confessor is to receive any extraordinary power which he may need. The power of the Penitentiary has, as a rule, always been restricted to

[78] Canon 258, par. 1.

occult impediments (at least to those occult in the pre-Code sense). But all power over impediments public by nature was not absolutely denied it. Regarding the revalidation of marriages, this Tribunal possessed power over certain impediments by nature public, notably consanguinity, affinity, and spiritual relationship: "In contractis vero matrimoniis, a dispensatione . . . in gradibus primo et secundo tantum, consanguinitatis, vel affinitatis ex copula licita, etiam in occultis, pariter abstineat; praeterquam si in secundo tantum gradu praedicto impedimentum saltem per decennium duraverit occultum, et oratores simul publice contraxerint, et convixerint, et uti conjuges legitimi reputati fuerint. In tertio autem et quarto gradibus occultis in contractis possit dispensare."[79] No matter how long the impediment may have remained occult, it is always public by nature, and, therefore, the internal forum, including the sacramental, is capable of receiving validly a dispensation from an impediment that is naturally public.

The second argument given by those who sponsor the view which restricts the confessor's power to occult impediments, is one taken from a consideration of the many inconveniences which would arise in practice from the broader interpretation. They claim that if the confessor were to possess power over impediments by nature public, frequent conflicts would arise between the internal and external forum, and, consequently, between the divine and ecclesiastical forum. Many marriages would be valid before God and in the internal forum, and yet invalid in the external forum of the Church, with the result that the parties would always be in a position to repudiate efficaciously in the external forum marriages valid before God. But the legislator cannot be accused of occasioning such frequent and serious conflict.

The possibility of such conflict, however, proves nothing.

---

[79] Benedict XIV, *Pastor Bonus,* n. 40, 13 April 1744, *Bullarium,* I, const. XCV; *Institutiones Ecclesiasticae,* II, Inst. Eccles. LXXXVII, n. 8.

Many laws have existed, and still exist to-day, where such conflict is possible, and even probable. Previous to 1907, in places not bound by the Tridentine form of marriage, clandestine marriages were valid; a valid marriage could be contracted *"extra faciem ecclesiae"* without the assistance of a priest. Sometimes indeed it was possible to prove such marriages in the external forum. If witnesses had been present, they could prove the fact of marriage against the denial of the parties who had contracted. At times the marriage could have been proven from civil documents. But what, if beside the assertion of the parties themselves, no other proof could be secured? Such was the case when marriages were celebrated altogether secretly without even the assistance of witnesses.[80] In such circumstances these marriages could be efficaciously assailed in the external forum. If, after such a marriage, a second had been contracted (and invalidly because of the impediment of *ligamen*) in the Tridentine form, an ecclesiastical judge should decide in favor of the validity of the second, against that of the first. Notwithstanding the danger of such conflict, this Church law on the form of marriage existed for centuries.

Even under the present legislation some of the Church's laws are not free from this bane of conflict. A person may be bound to observe a censure in the external forum and yet be absolutely free from it before God and in the internal forum. He may never have actually incurred the censure because of the absence of imputability in the committal of the crime, and yet be censured in the external forum,[81] or, having actually been under censure, he may be freed from it, in the internal forum, through absolution in that forum, and yet be bound by it in the external forum.[82]

It is also said, in accusation, that the extensive inter-

---

[80] Wernz, *Jus Decretalium,* IV (1904), nn. 187, 188.
[81] Canon 2218, par. 2.
[82] Canon 2251.

pretation of canon 1045, par. 3, in its relation to the confessor, would encourage fraud, would jeopardize the spiritual welfare of men, thus putting a premium on vice, and that no law should be so interpreted. No law, it must be admitted, can have the promotion of vice as its purpose, primary or subsidiary; but many laws, and good ones too, furnish occasion for fraudulent dealing, and do not remove the temporal advantagements that attach to their violation. The lawgiver tolerates evil results in consideration of advantages that could not otherwise be obtained. What of taxation laws, even the best and most equitable? Do they not mulct the honest man and let the dishonest go free? What of conscription laws, even the best? Do they not send the decent man to his death, and give freedom to the wretch who maims himself just beyond the standard? Laws of legal procedure, ecclesiastical or civil, will punish the truthful man, and let the perjurer go free. In all departments of business some advantage will be secured by fraud, at least if it be of the intelligent type. To give an instance closely related to the present case, the fraudulent man can obtain the privilege of the Church regarding the extraordinary form of marriage, when the straight-forward man would be placed beyond its reach.[83] The dishonest man cannot be excluded without involving the innocent man in disaster. If he is refused his premium greater evils will result to others and to the community at large. About which of the two should the law be more anxious?

Finally, if it is urged that this leaves the Church's law at the mercy of any one or two of the type described, who are perverse enough to conspire against it, it may be permitted to remark that there is hardly a law of the Church which may not be robbed of its good effects by the deliberate malice of the men and women it was intended to benefit. If the devil may quote Scripture, degenerates may sometimes utilize the Church's law to occasion the gratification

---

[83] C. 1098; *S. Cong. Sacrs.* ad 3, 13 March 1910; *A. A. S.*, II, 195.

of passion. This eventually will do them little good, and it will do the law little harm, for where there is even a fair degree of truth and honor, the probability of such a case arising is so slight that the law, as a whole, is unaffected.

Hence it remains that the parish priest, and even the confessor, can dispense, in urgent cases, from impediments that are by nature public, provided they are occult in fact. But from this it does not follow that eo ipso that such an impediment exists it falls within the ambit of their power. All the other conditions must be present; all things must be prepared for the marriage, and approach to the Ordinary must be either physically or morally impossible. It may be well to note that no secret may be involved in the application to the Ordinary for the dispensation from such an impediment, or that the manifestation of the impediment in the external forum necessarily causes grave evil. If so, recourse must be made to the Ordinary, and the others are destitute of power. The confessor, as a rule, will experience greater practical difficulties than the others. He must take steps to prevent a subsequent repudiation of the marriage. If the impediment (naturally public) is in no way defamatory, and there is no special reason for keeping it secret, the penitent must be told that he is obliged to make it a matter of the external forum, and either approach the parish priest, or Ordinary, for the dispensation, or, at least, have the dispensation registered. If it is defamatory or there *is* special reason for secrecy, the confessor will arrange (with the penitent's consent) either to register the marriage in the secret book of the Archives or, if this be not possible, to inform the Penitentiary and follow its instructions.[84] If the penitent refuses to follow such a reasonable suggestion—one that guarantees secrecy and, at the same time, provides for the validity of the marriage in the external forum, should the impediment ever become actually public—he

---

[84] Vermeersch, *Theologia Moralis*, III, n. 758, d; Pighi, *De Sacramento Matrimonii* (ed. II), n. 93; Cerato, *Matrimonium* (ed. III), n. 172.

must be informed that a dispensation will not be given; for, after all, the confessor, though empowered to act, is not obliged to use his faculties in favor of a man who violates obvious moral obligations, and is clearly indisposed for sacramental absolution. With these precautions the law will be saved from abuse, except such abuse as every human law entails.

When there is question of the revalidation of marriage, the parish priest and confessor must obtain the renewal of consent in the manner already laid down in Chapter VIII. A practical difficulty at once presents itself in the case of the confessor, a difficulty which, unfortunately, has received no attention from the authors. If the confessor dispenses from an impediment which is by nature public it would seem, from canon 1135, par. 1, that a private and secret renewal, even by both parties, does not suffice, but that the renewal must be made publicly by both parties in the form prescribed by the Church. Since he cannot dispense from the form, the renewal must be made in this public form. If he cannot obtain this, for any reason, his hands are tied, and nothing remains for him but to await a "*sanatio in radice*" from the competent authority, and, if the parties are bona fide, to leave them so.[85]

Authors generally impose the obligation on the parish priest and priest to notify the Ordinary whenever they dispense in urgent cases.[86] They found their contention on canon 1046. But such an obligation cannot be urged. Canon 1046 demands that the Ordinary be notified only when a dispensation has been granted in the external forum. The power conferred by canon 1045, par. 3, is, *ex natura rei*, restricted to the internal non-sacramental forum (except in the case of the confessor, when a further restriction is to be made), since the faculty is enjoyed only in occult

[85] See Genicot-Salsmans, *Casus Conscientiae* (ed. IV), casus 1076.

[86] Cf. Farrugia, *De Matrimonio et Causis Matrimonialibus* (ed. X), n. 88; Cerato, *Matrimonium* (ed. III), n. 38; Vermeersch-Creusen, *Epitome Juris Canonici*, II, n. 311.

cases.[87] Hence canon 1045, par. 3, does not fall under the prescriptions of canon 1046.

Moreover parish priests and priests enjoy the faculty of dispensing only when the Ordinary cannot be approached, or where recourse to him involves danger to a secret. This same secret may, and, as a rule, will, still continue to bind after the marriage has been contracted, and if danger to it excuses from the obligation of seeking a dispensation from the Ordinary, a fortiori does it release him from the obligation of notifying him of the dispensation granted.[88]

When the dispensation is granted in the internal non-sacramental forum, registration of it is to be made in the secret book kept for that purpose in the Curial Archives,[89] in order to provide for the validity of the marriage in the external forum.[90] Blat, however, denies that the registration obtains this effect when the impediment dispensed from is public by nature, since 1047 speaks only of occult impediments, and advises, as a canonical refuge, recourse to the Ordinary to obtain a ratification of the dispensation already granted.[91] Vermeersch, however, denies this assertion,[92] and Hilling maintains that the term *"occult impediments,"* in canon 1047, is to be understood according to the notion of *"occult impediment" in the old law.*[93]

There is nothing, however, to prevent the registration, in the secret book of the diocesan Archives, of a dispensation from an impediment that is naturally public. Canon 1047, it is true, speaks only of occult impediments, but this is intelligible when one remembers that the canon refers *mainly,* if not solely, to the Sacred Penitentiary, whose

[87] Blat, *Commentarium Textus Codicis Juris Canonici* (ed. II), Lib. III, P. I, De Rebus, n. 438.

[88] Farrugia, *o. c.,* p. 88, denies that the secret is to be kept from the Ordinary in either case.

[89] Canon 1047.

[90] Vermeersch-Creusen, *o. c.,* II, n. 311; Cerato, *o. c.,* n. 172; Genicot-Salsmans, *Institutiones Theologiae Moralis* (ed. X), II, 532, 5.

[91] *O. c.,* n. 441.

[92] *Epitome Juris Canonici,* II, n. 311.

[93] *A. K. K.,* CII, pp. 1-13.

powers are limited to occult impediments. The end of the registration is simply to supply a means of proving the marriage in the external forum, if the necessity of such a proof should ever arise. This end will be necessary in cases where the impediment is one public by nature, and there is no valid reason for holding that the registration, according to canon 1047, will not obtain its end in such cases.

Lastly, it may be well to point out that a dispensation granted by virtue of the faculties of canon 1045 brings with it *eo ipso* the legitimation of all offspring, either conceived or already born, with the exception of adulterous and sacrilegious.[94] No other act distinct from the act by which the dispensation is granted is necessary; the two effects, the removal of the impediment and the legitimatization of the offspring, are simultaneously produced by the one act of dispensing.[95]

---

[94] Canon 1051.

[95] Vermeersch, *Theologia Moralis,* III, n. 758, d; Chelodi, *Jus Matrimoniale* (ed. III), p. 43, nota 3.

CHAPTER X

Impedient Impediments

The present legislation enumerates but three impedient impediments, namely, the impediment of vow, legal relationship or adoption, and mixed religion.[1] The older canonists spoke of several impedient impediments, many of which have now been abrogated by the New Code, like the impediment of cathechism, public penance, that resulting from sponsalia, and various crimes.[2] Some authors to-day[3] include *unworthiness* resulting from apostacy, from affiliation with condemned societies,[4] and from censure and public sins,[5] among the impedient impediments. But these latter are not impediments in the strict canonical sense. Everything which opposes the licit celebration of marriage cannot be called a "canonical impediment." Since marriage is not only a contract, but also a sacrament,[6] and since one cannot exist without the other in the marriages of those baptized, anything which opposes their licit celebration in any way can indeed be called an impediment in the wide sense. Hence mortal sin is an impediment in this sense, since matrimony is one of the sacraments of the living. But the Church recognizes as real canonical impediments only those things which directly oppose marriage *ut contractus.*[7] Those things which oppose marriage directly *ut sacramentum* do not con-

---

[1] Canons 1058–1066.

[2] Ayrinhac, *Marriage Legislation in the New Code of Canon Law*, p. 111.

[3] Cf. Petrovits, *The New Church Law on Matrimony* (ed. 2), n. 199.

[4] Canon 1065.

[5] Canon 1066.

[6] Canon 1012, pargs. 1, 2.

[7] Cf. Wernz-Vidal, *Jus Canonicum*, V, n. 200; Noldin, *Summa Theologiae Moralis*, III, *De Sacramentis* (ed. XIV), n. 560.

stitute matrimonial impediments in the present terminology of canon law. Hence *unworthiness*, which is but a defect of a disposition required in the subject-minister, as in all other sacraments of the living, is not a canonical impediment.[8] Moreover, one cannot speak of removing *Unworthiness* by dispensation; this obstacle is removed by *absolution and* emendation of life; and the Church must, at times, permit marriage with those who are unworthy.[9]

Whoever is in the state of mortal sin is forbidden by the divine law from lawfully contracting marriage. If the sin is occult, it is remitted in the internal forum. If, however, it is public, account must be taken of it in the external forum, especially when spiritual danger to the other party and the offspring is to be feared. It is for this reason that canon law has given specific canons on public unworthiness.[10]

Of the three impedient impediments, only one class falls within the ambit of the dispensatory power granted by common law to those inferior to the Roman Pontiff. The Code nowhere concedes the power of dispensing from mixed religion and adoption (except in cases of urgency already considered, and in doubtful cases, as will be shown in the following chapter), and, hence, the only impediment that comes up here for consideration, in the matter of dispensation, is the impedient impediment resulting from vows.

"Matrimonium impedit votum simplex virginitatis, castitatis perfectae, non nubendi, suscipiendi ordines sacros, et amplectendi statum religiosum.

Nullum votum simplex irritat matrimonium, nisi irritatio speciali Sedis Apostolicae praescripto pro aliquibus statuta fuerit."[11]

---

[8] Blat, *Commentarium Textus Codicis Juris Canonici* (ed. II), Lib. III, P. I, De Rebus, n. 452; Cerato, *Matrimonium* (ed. III), n. 61.

[9] Chelodi, *Jus Matrimoniale* (ed. III), n. 65; Genicot-Salsmans, *Institutiones Theologiae Moralis* (ed. X), II, n. 65.

[10] Cf. Chelodi, *l. c.*

[11] Canon 1058, pargs. 1, 2.

Hence five vows render marriage illicit, but not invalid, namely, the simple vow of virginity, the simple vow of perfect chastity, the simple vow not to marry, or celibacy, the simple vow to receive sacred orders, and the simple vow to embrace the religious state.

The impediment resulting from the taking of any one of these five vows is only impedient, and, therefore, does not render marriage invalid, but only illicit. By special legislation, however, the simple vows taken, after the two years' novitiate, by the *scholastics* and *coadjutores temporales* of the *Society of Jesus,* are endowed with the force of nullifying marriage.[12]

There is question here only of *simple* vows, for solemn vows not only render marriages illicit, but also invalid.[13] Simple vows are those which are not solemn.[14] Solemn vows are those which are recognized by the Church *as such.*[15] Whatever be the real *foundation* for this distinction, only those vows are now, and have been for a long time, recognized as solemn which are taken in perpetual religious profession made in an order strictly so called.[16] Vows made in the world, those made in all modern religious congregations, in an Order strictly so called, but previous to the solemn profession, and those of some nuns who *de jure* should be solemnly professed, but who, de facto, because of peculiar circumstances, are only simply professed, are all simple vows.[17]

A simple vow can be either public or private; public, when it is accepted in the name of the Church by a legitimate superior; otherwise it is private.[18] Only those vows

---

[12] Gregory XIII, const., *Ascendente Domino,* nn. 20–23, 25 May 1584, *Fontes,* 153.

[13] Canon 1073.

[14] Canon 1308, par. 2.

[15] Canon 1308, par. 2.

[16] Canon 488, par. 2.

[17] Canons 488, n. 2; 488, n. 7; 574, par. 1; 1308.

[18] Canon 1308; *Pont. Com. pro Interpt. Codicis,* 1 March 1921, ad 3, *A. A. S.,* XIII, 178.

are public which are taken in a religious order or Congregation.

Vow of Virginity:

A vow of virginity is a deliberate promise made to God by virtue of which one imposes on oneself a voluntary obligation to preserve one's body intact from acts which violate its integrity, or which are instrumental to *primus opus carnale consummatum.*[19] This vow has for its direct object bodily integrity, and is, consequently, broken by a voluntarily gravely sinful act of sexual intercourse, or by pollution. In women the vow is broken by a gravely sinful act of unchastity by which virginal integrity is lost.[20] A vow of virginity, therefore, is not consistent with the consummated sexual act, and cannot be validly elicited by a person who has ever performed that act. If it has been validly elicited, it ceases immediately when such an act takes place. Hence this vow impedes the licit celebration of marriage both by divine and canonical law, and persons who, bound by such a vow, would contract marriage, without a dispensation, would marry indeed validly, but would commit a twofold sin; one against the divine law, by exposing himself or herself to the proximate danger of violating the vow, being bound to render the debitum conjugale to the other party lawfully demanding it, and also because such an action *per se* implies the intention of consummating the marriage, which is equivalent to a formal violation of the vow:[21] one against ecclesiastical law, by contracting while bound by an impedient impediment.

It may be well to note here regarding this vow (and also the other vows), that in so far as it opposes marriage from the divine law, the prohibition would not be *ex se* absolute, for supposing a grave cause and the absence of danger of

---

[19] Petrovits, *The New Church Law on Matrimony* (ed. II), n. 181; Farrugia, *De Matrimonio et Causis Matrimonialibus* (ed. X), n. 126.

[20] Woywod, *A Practical Commentary on the Code of Canon Law*, n. 1031.

[21] Cerato, *Matrimonium* (ed. III), n. 52; Petrovits, *o. c.*, n. 186; De Smet, *De Sponsalibus et Matrimonio* (ed. IV), II, n. 489.

violating the vow, it would be lawful, in so far as the divine law is concerned, to contract marriage, provided there was the agreement to exclude the use of marriage. But the canonical impediment would still remain, and as long as it stands marriage is not permitted by the Church.[22]

Once marriage is contracted, even though unlawfully, it is not lawful for the person bound by the vow to seek the conjugal debt, but he must render it.[23] But the vow is formally broken by the first act of consummation, by which integrity is lost, and once broken, it is lawful not only to *render*, but also to seek, the debitum conjugale. It is then no longer possible to fulfill the vow, and, therefore, every obligation arising from it ceases.[24]

Once the vow is formally broken it does not revive, so that if the first marriage is dissolved for any reason, as, for instance, by the death of the other party, the vow would not not oppose a second marriage.[25]

Vow of celibacy, or, not to marry:

By eliciting this vow one promises God simply not to embrace the marriage state. This vow has for its direct object abstention from the marriage contract. Hence it is diametrically opposed to the marriage state, and he who contracts, without a dispensation, sins directly against his vow, and also against ecclesiastical law. Once marriage *is* contracted, the vow no longer binds, because its fulfillment is rendered impossible, at least as long as the bond of this particular marriage lasts.[26] Having contracted marriage he can both seek and render the debt, without any further

---

[22] Wernz-Vidal, *Jus Canonicum*, V, n. 158.

[23] Gasparri, *De Matrimonio* (ed. III), I, n. 480; De Smet, *o. c.*, II, n. 489.

[24] Cerato, *l. c.;* Farrugia, *l. c.;* Cappello, *De Sacramentis*, III, n. 299.

[25] Chelodi, *Jus Matrimoniale* (ed. III), n. 54; Pighi, *De Sacramento Matrimonii* (ed. II), n. 32, 3a.

[26] Genicot-Salsmans, *Institutiones Theologiae Moralis* (ed. X), II, n. 511; Vermeersch-Creusen, *Epitome Juris Canonici*, II (1922), n. 303; Cerato, *o. c.*, n. 52.

requirement, because the vow has for its object *unicus actus ineundi matrimonium.*[27]

Some authors hold, *as probable,* that if the first marriage is dissolved, the vow does not revive, and that, therefore, there is no obstacle to the contracting of a second marriage.[28] However, the other opinion is far more common, and is, perhaps, the true doctrine, on the ground that once the marriage is dissolved the object of the vow again becomes possible, and, hence, the obligation arising from the vow again urges.[29] The practical solution of the question will depend on the intention of the person at the time the vow was elicited. If he intended to vow abstention from marriage absolutely and perpetually (which intention is to be presumed), during the first marriage the obligation of the vow was not extinguished, but merely suspended, so that when the bond of that marriage is dissolved, the vow again begins to bind, "nisi ob specialem intentionem voventis vel appositam limitationem temporis aliud sit statuendum."[30]

Vow of Perfect Chastity:

This vow implies abstinence from every carnal gratification whether external or internal. It extends to internal as well as external acts, but, *qua talis,* it does not oblige to embrace the religious state, because the obligation arising from a vow cannot be extended beyond the intention of him who made it. For one who lives outside of the marriage state, this vow excludes all carnal pleasure, and this is known as a vow of perfect chastity. If one vows abstention

---

[27] Feije, *De Impedimentis et Dispensationibus Matrimonialibus* (ed. II), n. 562; Sanchez, *De Sancto Matrimonii Sacramento,* lib. IX, dis. XXXIII, n. 22; Farrugia, *o. c.,* n. 126.

[28] Farrugia, *o. c.,* n. 127, 3; Prümmer, *Manuale Theologiae Moralis,* III (ed. II), n. 775.

[29] Giovine, *De Dispensationibus Matrimonialibus,* I, consult. CLI, n. 3: "mortuo autem altero conjuge, plena voti obligatio in suo robore exstat"; Feije, *o. c.,* n. 562; Gasparri, *o. c.,* I, n. 479; Cappello, *o. c.,* III, n. 301; Chelodi, *o. c.,* n. 54; Wernz-Vidal, *o. c.,* V, n. 160.

[30] Wernz, *Jus Decretalium,* IV (1904), p. 819, nota 15.

only from illicit carnal gratification, the vow is not one of perfect chastity.[31]

This vow differs from that of virginity in so far as it forbids, not only those external acts by which virginal integrity is lost, but also all internal acts against chastity.[32]

The vow of perfect chastity is per se immediately opposed to marriage, because it obliges to abstention from all delectatio venerea.[33] Therefore he who contracts without a dispensation from this vow sins gravely, not indeed because he thereby acts *directly* against his vow, but because he exposes himself to the proximate danger of not fulfilling his promise, nay, places himself in a position in which this is morally impossible, since he must *render* the marriage debt. If, moreover, the other party is ignorant of the existence of the vow, an injury is certainly done to him.[34] In a particular case, however, a sin may not be committed against the divine law, if both contracting parties mutually agree not to use their marriage rights, and there is no grave danger of incontinency. But the ecclesiastical prohibition still remains, so that a grave sin is *always* committed where one contracts without a dispensation from the impediment resulting from the vow.[35]

Even when marriage is contracted, the party under vow can never lawfully seek the marriage debt until a dispensation from the vow is received. But he must *render* it to the other party, since the conjugal obligations bind in justice, and prevail over the obligations arising from the vow.[36] If the first marriage is dissolved, and the vow has

---

[31] Cappello, *o. c.*, III, n. 300; De Smet, *o. c.*, II, n. 489.

[32] Cf. Augustine, *A Commentary on the New Code of Canon Law*, V, p. 136.

[33] Chelodi, *o. c.*, n. 54; Farrugia, *o. c.*, n. 126.

[34] Gasparri, *De Matrimonio*, I, n. 481; Wernz, *Jus Decretalium*, IV, n. 566; Genicot-Salsmans, *o. c.*, II, n. 510; Noldin, *Summaria Theologiae Moralis*, III (ed. XIV), n. 561.

[35] De Smet, *De Sponsalibus et Matrimonio*, II (ed. IV), n. 489; Cerato, *Matrimonium*, n. 52.

[36] Feije, *De Impedimentis et Dispensationibus Matrimonialibus* (ed. III), n. 559; Gasparri, *o. c.*, n. 481.

not been dispensed from, the contraction of a second marriage would be unlawful unless the vow had been made only temporarily, and the time had already elapsed.[37]

The three vows of virginity, celibacy, and chastity are often confounded by ordinary folk, and, hence, in practice, it will at times remain doubtful as to which of these vows precisely had been elicited. If one can discover the real *object* of the vow which had been made, then all doubt will be removed. To find out this it will be helpful to try to ascertain the *motive* which prompted the vow. If the vow was elicited for the purpose of escaping the burdens of married life, it may be presumed a vow of celibacy, unless there is certain evidence to the contrary. If the possession of the special heavenly reward promised virginity, or the desire to preserve oneself intact, inspired the vow, it may be concluded that virginity, in the strict sense, was promised to God. If the love of the virtue of purity is the motive of the vow, it may be considered a formal vow of chastity. This last case is the most frequent in practice.[38]

The Vow of Receiving Sacred Orders:

By the positive law of the Church this vow renders marriage illicit, because by marriage one would take upon oneself a state of life which, according to the same law, is incompatible with the state of higher orders, the first of which is that of subdeaconship.[39] This vow is, however, opposed to marriage only *mediate,* because of its incompatibility with that state.[40] He who contracts marriage notwithstanding the existence of this vow, contracts validly but commits a twofold sin, firstly, because he exposes himself *regulariter* to the proximate danger of rendering its

[37] Wernz, *Jus Decretalium,* IV, n. 566; Augustine, *o. c.,* V, p. 188.

[38] Gasparri, *o. c.,* I, n. 482; Vlaming, *Praelectiones Juris Matrimonii* (ed. III), I, n. 199; Genicot-Salsmans, *o. c.,* II, n. 510; Noldin, *o. c.,* III, n. 539.

[39] Canons 1058, par. 1; 987, n. 2.

[40] Chelodi, *o. c.,* n. 54; Farrugia, *o. c.,* p. 126.

fulfillment impossible, and, secondly, because he contracts without a dispensation from an impedient impediment.

Once marriage is contracted the party under vow does not sin by *seeking* or rendering the marriage debt. Some maintain that the consummation of the marriage would be unlawful in the case, but that, once consummated, the party is then altogether free in ordine ad debitum conjugale.[41] But this is not so, because the principal obligation of receiving orders having ceased, or at least, been suspended, the secondary and consequent obligation of observing chastity eo ipso ceases also. Chastity does not directly fall under the object of this vow.[42]

Others maintain that even when the marriage has been celebrated unlawfully, thc party bound by the vow is first bound to seek permission from the other party to receive Sacred Orders, notwithstanding the marriage bond; that the latter, however, is not bound to give this consent; and that it is only after this obligation has been fulfilled that the *vovens* (on the hypothesis that the consent of the other party has not been given) can lawfully ask and return the debitum conjugale.[43] Seeing, however, that those bound by the marriage bond are impeded from receiving orders,[44] and that such are not *bound* to seek a dispensation,[45] this opinion is scarcely sustainable.

Therefore once marriage is contracted the vow ceases, at least as far as that particular marriage is concerned. If the bond is dissolved, per se the vow revives, and the obligation of receiving sacred Orders again urges. In practice, however, this obligation can rarely be urged, for the obligation to support and educate the offspring of that marriage,

---

[41] Augustine, *o. c.*, V, p. 138.

[42] De Smet, *o. c.*, II, n. 232; Gasparri, *o. c.*, n. 483, Feije, *o. c.*, n. 501; Cappello, *o. c.*, III, n. 302; Genicot-Salsmans, *o. c.*, II, n. 510, who gives the doctrine as *probable*.

[43] Prümmer, *Manuale Theologiae Moralis* (ed. III), n. 776, d; Pighi, *De Sacramento Matrimonii* (ed. II), n. 33, 3a; Farrugia, *o. c.*, n. 127.

[44] Canon 987, n. 2.

[45] De Smet, *De Sponsalibus et Matrimonio*, I, n. 232.

if there has been such, or of fulfilling other obligations, which may have likewise arisen, will often free the vovens from any further obligation arising from the vow: "*votum saepe, ob mutata omnino adjuncta, non urgebit.*"[46] But the ecclesiastical impediment to marriage will remain all through until such time as a dispensation from it will be received.

Vow to Embrace the Religious State:

By a religious *state* must be understood every religious community with solemn or simple vows, perpetual or temporary; or, in other words, every religious organization whose members pronounce the three religious vows of chastity, poverty, and obedience, and lead a common life.[47] From a vow to embrace such a state, whether in an order or in a congregation, arises an impedient impediment to marriage, since it obliges to enter a state which is incompatible with married life. This vow opposes marriage only *mediate,* because of this incompatibility.[48]

Hence, if one should contract marriage while bound by this vow he would sin gravely against the divine law, because he exposes himself to the grave danger of rendering the fulfillment of the vow impossible. He also sins against the ecclesiastical law, by contracting with an impedient impediment.[49]

Once marriage is contracted, however, practically no further obligation remains, at least as long as the present matrimonial bond holds, and the party under vow can both seek and render the debitum conjugale, without need of any further dispensation.[50]

Some commentators hold that the obligation of the

---

[46] Vermeersch-Creusen, *Epitome Juris Canonici,* II, n. 327, 2; Cf. Wernz, *Jus Decretalium,* IV, n. 566; Cappello, *o. c.,* III, n. 302.

[47] Canon 487.

[48] Chelodi, *o. c.,* n. 54; Noldin, *o. c.,* III, n. 561.

[49] Feije, *o. c.,* n. 560; Genicot-Salsmans, *o. c.,* II, n. 510; Cappello, *o. c.,* III, n. 303.

[50] De Smet, *o. c.,* I, n. 232; Vlaming, *o. c.,* I, n. 200; Genicot-Salsmans, *o. c.,* II, n. 511.

vow continues to run until such time as the marriage is consummated, and that the vovens, if not dispensed, sins by the first act of consummation.[51] But this does not seem to be correct teaching under the present legislation. The sin is committed when the marriage has been actually contracted, and not by the act of consummation.[52] When the principal obligation of embracing the religious state ceases, the secondary obligation of preserving chastity likewise ceases.[53] The actual contraction of marriage renders the fulfillment of the vow practically impossible during the present marriage, for an existing bond of matrimony is an obstacle which renders admittance to the novitiate invalid,[54] and, consequently, to profession likewise,[55] and the vovens is not *bound* to seek a dispensation for the removal of this obstacle, even though the marriage is ratum tantum.[56] Augustine, Petrovits, and those who hold the opposite view, seem to confuse the old law with the new. Under the old legislation he who vowed to enter religion was permitted to refuse the marriage debt to the other party for the first two months after marriage had been contracted in order to provide time for sufficient deliberation.[57] Hence authors taught that the seeking or rendering of the debt during that period was unlawful, because the vow still continued to run, but after consummation once took place, both parties were free regarding the use of their marriage rights.[58] But this privilege no longer holds, as it is implicitly abrogated by canon 542, n. I,

---

[51] Augustine, *A Commentary on the New Code of Canon Law* (ed. III), V, p. 138; Petrovits, *The New Church Law on Matrimony* (ed. II), n. 183; Farrugia, *o. c.*, n. 127; Prümmer, *o. c.*, III, n. 776.

[52] Cappello, *De Sacramentis*, III, n. 909.

[53] De Smet, *De Sponsalibus et Matrimonio* (ed. IV), I, n. 232.

[54] Canon 542, n. 1.

[55] Canon 572, par. 1, n. 3.

[56] Genicot-Salsmans, *Institutiones Theologiae Moralis* (ed. X), II, 511.

[57] Reiffenstuel, *Jus Canonicum Universum*, IV, Appendix, *De Dispensatione super Impedimentis Matrimonii*, n. 560; Sanchez, *De Sancto Matrimonii Sacramento*, lib. IX, dis. XXXIII, n. 23.

[58] Cf. Gasparri, *o. c.*, I, 484; Feije, *o. c.*, n. 560. Wernz, *Jus Decretalium*, IV, n. 566, 3, seems to have held the opposite.

which constitutes the bond of an existing marriage an impediment to valid admission to the novitiate.[59] With this aspect of the law abrogated, the old teaching, it seems, must also lapse with it. Hence the debitum conjugale can be lawfully both asked and returned, even immediately after the marriage has been contracted.[60]

Chelodi[61] and Cerato[62] make a distinction and, while admitting that the first consummation of marriage is not sinful when the religious institute, which is the object of the vow, has only *simple* vows, deny liceity to this act when the religious state is one with solemn vows. They give no reason for this distinction, but, it seems, that the argument given by some under the old law can alone be the only justifying reason. Gasparri[63] and Marc[64] held the same doctrine on the ground that the vow to enter a religious institute with solemn vows was reserved to the Holy See, while a vow to embrace a religious state with simple vows was not. But these authors, in speaking of consummation, refer to consummation within the first two months after marriage had been contracted, during which time the vow continued to bind and, in case the vow referred to an institute with solemn vows, was reserved. But with the abolition of this two months' privilege, it seems that the other aspect of the old teaching does not hold.

If the first marriage is dissolved the vow revives, and per se the obligation to fulfill it urges once more, for the vow does not cease *absolutely* by the contraction of marriage, but is only suspended during the time of marriage.[65] However, in practice, this obligation will not as a rule urge,

---

[59] Cappello, *o. c.*, III, n. 299, 5, claims that the privilege of the old law is abrogated by canon 1111, while Vlaming, *o. c.*, n. 200, invokes canon 6, n. 4, which apparently is a misprint for canon 6, n. 6.

[60] Cf. Cappello, *l. c.;* Vlaming, *l. c.;* Farrugia, *o. c.*, n. 127.

[61] *Jus Matrimoniale* (ed. III), n. 54.

[62] *Matrimonium* (ed. III), n. 52.

[63] *De Matrimonio* (ed. III), I, n. 484.

[64] *Institutiones Morales Alphonsianae*, II, n. 1992, 3.

[65] Wernz, *o. c.*, IV, n. 566, 3; Feije, *o. c.*, n. 560; Genicot-Salsmans, *o. c.*, II, n. 511.

because of the change in circumstances, as, for instance, the necessity of supporting the children born of the first marriage, or unfitness for the religious life because of age, or any other cause, which will often render the fulfillment of the vow impossible. But it must be remembered that, since the vow still continues to bind, at least theoretically, the impedient impediment to future marriages remains until dispensed from.[66]

Power of Dispensing:

From what has been said it is clear that a dispensation is necessary before one who has elicited any one of the five vows may lawfully contract marriage. As long as the vow remains the impedient impediment remains, and thereby constitutes a second obstacle to licit celebration. If the vow ceases absolutely and completely, of course the impediment thereby also ceases, but where the vow is only *suspended,* the impediment still continues to bind.

Besides the Roman Pontiff, no one can dispense, even from impedient impediments, unless this power is conceded by the Holy See, either by common law, or by special indult.[67]

Only those powers conferred by common law will be considered here.

1. *Power of Dispensing from Private Simple Vows:*

"Vota non reservata possunt justa de causa dispensare, dummodo dispensatio ne laedat jus aliis quaesitum:

1. Loci Ordinarius quod attinet ad omnes suos subditos atque etiam peregrinos;

2. Superior religionis clericalis exemptae quod attinet ad personas quae can. 514, par. 1, enumerantur:" (canon 1313, nn. 1, 2).

---

[66] Cf. Vermeersch-Creusen, *Epitome Juris Canonici,* II, n. 327, 2.

[67] Canon 1040.

Hence those vows which the Holy See has not reserved to itself can be dispensed from by the local Ordinary, and the Superior of an exempt clerical religion. Of the private vows, two only are reserved.

"Vota privata Sedi Apostolicae reservata sunt tantummodo votum perfectae ac perpetuae castitatis et votum ingrediendi in religionem votorum sollemnium, quae emissa fuerint absolute et post completum decimum octavum aetatis annum."[68]

Of the private vows, therefore, the Holy See reserves only two, namely, the vow of perfect and perpetual chastity, and that of entering a religion with solemn vows, *provided,* in both cases, the vows were made absolutely, and after the eighteenth year of age had been completed. When these two vows are made under these conditions, no one, save the Holy See, can dispense from them *in ordinary cases* unless special power for this is received.

If, however, any of the above conditions is wanting in a particular case, the vow is no longer reserved, and, therefore, the local Ordinary and the Superior of an exempt clerical religion can dispense from the matrimonial impediments resulting from them without need of any further delegation.

Before the vow of chastity is reserved it must be, (a) a vow of *perfect* chastity (b) elicited *absolute,* and (c) after eighteen years of age had been completed. It must be perfect *ex parte materiae,* that is, abstinence from all venereal pleasure, whether by internal or external acts, must be *vowed in perpetuum.* If the object of the vow extends to external acts only, or if the obligation is assumed only for a time, the vow is not perfect, and therefore not reserved.[69] It must be perfect also *ex parte actus,* that is, the obligation must be assumed with perfect liberty, and under a

[68] Canon 1309.

[69] De Smet, *o. c.,* II, n. 767; Farrugia, *De Matrimonio et Causis Matrimonialibus* (ed. X), n. 83, b, nota 1; Genicot-Salsmans, *o. c.,* II, n. 329.

grave sanction. If any fear, even light, unjustly inflicted from outside, influenced the making of the vow, it is not a perfect vow; neither is it perfect when only a light obligation to fulfill it is imposed upon oneself.[70] Secondly, the vow must be taken *absolute,* that is, unconditionally. This element is present when the obligation imposed upon oneself has attached to it no condition as to time, circumstances, or to the matter itself. If any such condition is attached to the obligation, the vow is conditional, and, consequently, not reserved. A disjunctive vow is really conditional, and, therefore, cannot be considered as falling under the reservation.[71]

The question here arises as to whether a vow taken conditionally becomes reserved when the condition afterwards is fulfilled. The question, of course, presupposes that a real condition had been attached, which, however, is not the case when the word "si," by which the condition is placed, bears the sense of "*quando.*"[72] In the first place it is absolutely certain that the vow is not reserved as long as the condition remains unfulfilled. When it is fulfilled, it is at least solidly probable that even then the vow is not reserved.[73] The reason for this opinion is well put by Giovine: "Reservatio voti, utpote voventi onerosa, comprehendit tantum vota ex natura sua perfecta. Talia vero dici nequeunt vota conditionata, etiam post conditionis eventum, quandoquidem perfectio voti nedum metienda est ab effectu, idest ab obligatione ex eo consurgens, impleta conditione, sed et ab ejus radice, seu ab affectu, quo emissum

---

[70] Giovine, *De Dispensationibus Matrimonialibus,* I, consult. CLV, n. 6: "Hac in re uniformes sunt D. D., qui ea ratione ducuntur, quod reservatio ista, utpote odiosa, est restringenda"; Cf. De Smet, *o. c.,* II, n. 767; Farrugia, *o. c.,* n. 83, b; Sebastiani, *Summarium Theologiae Moralis* (ed. VI minor), n. 210; Cappello, *o. c.,* III, n. 305, 2.

[71] Sebastiani, *o. c.,* n. 210; Cappello, *o. c.,* III, n. 305, 2; Augustine, *o. c.,* V, p. 139.

[72] Giovine, *o. c.,* consult. CLVI, n. 4; Farrugia, *l. c.*

[73] De Smet, *o. c.,* II, p. 220, nota 2; Genicot-Salsmans, *o. c.,* II, n. 329, 4; Giovine, *o. c.,* consult. CLVI, n. 3: "Probabilius est, non esse reservatum. Ita sane docent gravissimae auctoritatis DD."

fuit. In sua radice autem vota conditionata imperfecta censentur etiam post conditionis eventum, quia affectus voventis in primitivo actu, quo votum emisit, divisus erat inter rem promissam, et objectum conditionis; et haec imperfectio non cessat post conditionis eventum; ac proinde videtur non esse reservata."[74] This reasoning is admirably in conformity with the wording of canon 1309 which clearly shows that the vow must be *absolute* actually at the time it is taken, "*quae emissa fuerint absolute.*" Hence, since it is solidly probable that such a vow is not reserved when the condition is fulfilled afterwards, it is *practically certain* that the local Ordinary can dispense, potestate ordinaria, from the impediment resulting from it.[75] It is scarcely necessary to add that, if the vow had been taken conditionally, but was *renewed* unconditionally after the condition had been fulfilled, the reservation is then present.

The third and very essential condition requires that the vow must have been elicited after the eighteenth year of age had been completed. The assuming of an obligation by means of a reserved vow is a serious matter requiring much discretion, and consequently, the Church establishes the age of eighteen as the minimum age for such an imposition.[76] Hence, if the vow is elicited before the age of eighteen has been completed it is not reserved, and does not become reserved after the completion of that age. If, however, it is *renewed* at that time it is accompanied with the reservation.[77]

The second private vow reserved by law is that of entering a religion with solemn vows, provided this too has been elicited *absolute,* and after the eighteenth year has been completed. The vow to embrace a religious state in which only simple vows are taken is not reserved. Solemn vows

---

[74] *O. c.,* consult. CLVI, n. 3; Cf. Genicot-Salsmans, *l. c.*

[75] Canons 15, 209.

[76] Cf. De Smet, *De Sponsalibus et Matrimonio* (ed. IV), II, p. 220, nota 2.

[77] Genicot-Salsmans, *o. c.,* I, n. 329.

are taken by men of all religious Orders, in the strict sense, in their perpetual religious profession.[78] The vows taken in the temporary profession which precedes the solemn profession in strict orders, and those taken by men in congregations, even in their final profession, are all simple vows.[79] Regarding the religious institutes of women, it is necessary also that solemn vows must be actually taken by their members, before the vow to enter them is reserved. In this country solemn vows are taken only by nuns of the five Visitation orders in Georgetown, Mobile, St. Louis, and Baltimore,[80] and by the Carmelite nuns in Philadelphia.[81]

The vow to enter a religious institute of women, the constitutions of which demand the taking of solemn vows and solemn religious professions, but whose members, by special prescript of the Holy See, *de facto* take only simple vows,[82] is not reserved.[83]

Having established the vows that are reserved, and shown the conditions under which they are reserved, we deduce, at once, that local Ordinaries, and the Superiors of exempt clerical religions, that is, the Superiors of exempt religions the most of whose members are priests,[84] can dispense, *potestate ordinaria,* from the impedient impediments resulting from the following private vows, namely, of celibacy; of virginity; of receiving major orders; of entering a religion with simple vows; of entering a religion whose members de facto take only simple vows, even though the constitutions call for solemn vows; of perfect chastity when taken conditionally; of perfect chastity when taken before the eighteenth year of age complete; of

---

[78] Canon 488, n. 2.

[79] Cf. Benedict XIV, ep. encycl., *Inter Praeteritos,* n. 41, 3 Dec. 1749. *Fontes* 404.

[80] *Litt. Sacrae Cong. Epp. et Reg.,* 30 September 1864, *Coll. de Prop. Fide,* 1263, *Fontes,* 1995.

[81] *Decretum,* n. 49877, *Sac. Cong. de Prop. Fide,* 10 June 1902.

[82] Canon 488, n. 7.

[83] Genicot-Salsmans, *Institutiones Theologiae Moralis,* II (ed. X), n. 85, 4, who quotes the *Sacred Penitentiary,* 23 Dec. 1835.

[84] Canon 488, n. 8.

chastity when taken temporarily; of entering a religion with solemn vows, when taken conditionally, or before the eighteenth year of age had been completed.

The exercise of this dispensatory power is, however, subject, under pain of invalidity, to two conditions, namely, there must be a just cause, and the strict right of a third party must not be violated.

There must be a just and proportionate cause, not only for the licit, but also for the valid, use of this faculty.[85] These causes can be reduced to four great classes:

(a) *Imperfectio actus;* as, for instance, if the vow was made before the age of puberty has been attained; if it had been made under fear, or in moments of great sorrow and despondency;

(b) *Infirmitas voventis;* as, for instance, if vehemence of passion, or frailty of the flesh, renders the fulfillment of the vow morally impossible;

(c) *Detrimentum voventis;* as, for instance, if the existence of the vow is the occasion of many scruples and anxieties to liberate himself from which the vovens has tried in vain;

(d) *Bonum commune;* as, for instance, if marriage would confer notably to the allaying of family discords; or if the good of religion would call for the conservation of a noble family.[86]

The second condition requires that the strict right of a third party be not violated by the relaxation of the vow. This condition also seems to be necessary for the validity of the *dispensation* (not however of the marriage), since it is introduced by the particle "*dummodo*":[87] "semper exceptis (iis) quae a tertio acceptata fuerint seu in quibus agatur de praejudicio tertii."[88]

---

[85] Canons 84, par. 1; 1313.

[86] Wernz, *Jus Decretalium,* IV, n. 570; Vlaming, *Praelectiones Juris Matrimonii,* I, n. 201.

[87] Canon 39.

[88] Benedict XIV, Litt. Encycl., *Benedictus Deus,* n. 4, 25 December 1750, *Fontes,* 409.

The violation of the right of a third party can happen in two ways; (a) if a public vow is taken in a religious institute *per modum contractus onerosi.* In such a case a dispensation from the vow, or the impediment, cannot be given without the consent of the superior;[89] (b) if a vow is made in favor of a person, physical or moral (as, for instance, a poor girl, or a pious and charitable institute), with the intention of obliging oneself *sub grave ex justitia,* and was accepted by that person, the vow cannot be dispensed from without the latter's consent; otherwise justice would be violated.[90] If, however, the vovens intended to oblige himself only in fidelity, or if the vow covered only light matter, there is no *jus strictum,* and the vow can be removed without his consent. Even if a grave obligation in justice was assumed, but the interested party did not accept the promise, the vow can likewise be removed without his consent.[91] The same teaching is to be applied, as, at least, probable, to a case in which a vow is made *principaliter* in God's honor, and only *secundario* in favor of a third person, for the latter party acquired his right dependently on the obligation contracted in the virtue of religion.[92]

Local Ordinaries are endowed with the power of dispensing, under the above conditions, in favor of their subjects, even though outside his diocese, and also in favor of all peregrini who are here and now actually within the diocesan limits. The Superior of an exempt clerical religion has the same power in favor of all those mentioned in canon 514, paragraph 1, and, therefore, can use his faculty, not only in favor of the professed members and the novices, but also on behalf of all those who live day and night in the religious house for the cause of service, education, hospitality, or health.

[89] St. Alphonsus, *Theologia Moralis,* lib. III, n. 255 sq.

[90] Genicot-Salsmans, *o. c.,* I, n. 329.

[91] St. Alphonsus, *o. c.,* lib. III, n. 255, who gives this view as "communissima."

[92] Cf. Genicot-Salsmans, *l. c.;* St. Alphonsus, *l. c.;* Cappello, *De Sacramentis,* III, n. 305, 2.

Both the Ordinary and religious Superior can dispense from the impediment either *ad matrimonium contrahendum* or *ad matrimonium convalidandum.* They can dispense either for the internal or external forum, but if the dispensation is granted in the internal (non-sacramental) forum only, notification of the same is to be made in the secret book kept in the Curial Archives.[93] Moreover, although possessing the power, they need not, and perhaps at times should not, dispense from the vow absolutely, but simply only for this particular marriage, so that the vow would again urge if this first marriage should be dissolved. Such a dispensation would effect a *removal* of the canonical impediment, but only a suspension of the vow for the time being.[94]

The power of Ordinaries and others over the two reserved vows in danger of death, and in other urgent cases, has already been treated, and does not need repetition here. It may be well, however, to repeat here one marked difference between his power in these extraordinary cases and his power in ordinary circumstances over the non-reserved vows. In the former case it seems he can dispense only from the canonical impediment *as such,* so that the vow remains only suspended during the time of marriage, and revives after its dissolution; while, in the latter instance, he can dispense from the vows themselves, and, therefore, from the impediment, even regarding all future marriages.[95]

Public Simple Vows:

Some doubt as to whether these vows are reserved to the Holy See or not, on the ground that canon 1313 speaks simply of *"vota non reservata,"* without drawing any dis-

---

[93] Canon 1047.

[94] Cf. Vermeersch-Creusen, *Epitome Juris Canonici,* II, n. 327, 3: "In circumstantiis ordinariis satis inutile est dispensare statim super voto castitatis in perpetuum, aut super voto suscipiendi ordines vel ingrediendi religionem."

[95] Cf. Feije, *De Impedimentis et Dispensationibus Matrimonialibus* (ed. III), n. 613.

tinction between public and private vows.[96] Whatever about the old law, in which it seems that ordinary power over temporary vows (not, however, over perpetual ones) in diocesan institutes was admitted in some cases,[97] in the present legislation there can be little doubt that no one, inferior to the Pope, has ordinary power to dispense *directly* from public vows.[98] Whatever about the vows themselves, it can be said, with certainty, that no one inferior to the Roman Pontiff can dispense from the impediments arising from public vows, as long as the vows themselves exist. If, however, the vow ceases in any way whatever, the impediment no longer exists. But all power over public vows is not to be denied local Ordinaries and others, for certain powers which they possess can effect a cessation of vows, so that indirect power over the vows of certain religious belongs to them under the present legislation.

A local Ordinary is empowered, by common law, to grant to religious of diocesan right, within his diocese, an indult of secularization.[99] As canon 640 makes no distinction, it is clear that an indult of secularization granted even by the local Ordinary has the effect of freeing those to whom it has been given from the obligation of their vows, even though they were perpetual.[100] Hence a local Ordinary can perform an act one of the effects of which is the relaxation of public vows taken in institutes of diocesan right. The cessation of the matrimonial impediment resulting from the vow is effected eo ipso with the cessation of

---

[96] Augustine, *A Commentary on the New Code of Canon Law* (ed. III), VI, p. 305: "It is certain that these vows must be considered reserved to the Holy See, *at least* on account of the *jus tertii*"; Kinane, *I. E. R.*, XXI, pp. 522, 523.

[97] *S. C. de Prop. Fide*, 24 August 1885: "Quoad vota ad tempus, in his institutis (Statuum Foed. Americae) dioecesanis . . . emissa, Episcopi facultate ordinaria (dispensare possunt)," *Coll. de Prop. Fide*, 1642.

[98] Cf. Cappello, *o. c.*, III, n. 305, 3, b; Cerato, *o. c.*, n. 52, 2, d; De Smet, *o. c.*, II, p. 220, nota 2; Cf. canon 251, par. 3.

[99] Canon 638.

[100] *Pont. Com. pro Interpt. Codicis*, 12 November 1922, *A. A. S.*, XIV, 662.

the vow itself, and to this extent it can be said that local Ordinaries are endowed with the power of dispensing *indirectly* from the impedient impediments which result from the public vows taken in religious institutes of diocesan right.

It may be well to add here that it is only the Ordinary of the place in which the religious house is situated who has this power. The Ordinary of the diocese in which the principal house is located has no power over the religious belonging to the filial houses situated in other dioceses, and, hence, can grant an indult of secularization (and consequently indirectly dispense from the impedient impediment) only to those religious belonging to the house which is in his diocese.[101]

The same is to be said of the *dismissal* of religious *with temporary vows.* In Orders and Congregations of pontifical right the Superior General, in monasteries, that are *sui-juris,* the Abbot, have the right of dismissing religious with temporary vows; but the Superior, as well as the Abbot, can proceed to act only with the consent of the counsellors, which consent is necessary for the validity of the act of dismissal.[102] If a nun with temporary vows is to be dismissed, the local Ordinary can dismiss her after the superioress, with her counsellors, has given a written attestation of the motives for the dismissal. If the convent is subject to regulars, the regular Superior may dismiss her after a similar attestation has been given. In congregations of diocesan right, the right of dismissing a sister belongs to the Ordinary in whose diocese the house is located, but he should not act without the knowledge of the Superioress, or against her just opposition.[103] A religious so dismissed is ipso facto freed from all her religious vows (there

---

[101] *S. C. Ep. et Reg.,* 21 April 1903, *Coll. de Prop. Fide,* 2167, *Fontes,* 2044.

[102] Canons 105, par. 1; 647, par. 1.

[103] Canon 647, par. 1.

is question only of those who have taken temporary vows) without prejudice to the obligations attaching to Major Orders in case a male religious has received such. Hence the dismissal causes a cessation of the impediments resulting from the vows, except, of course, the vow of celibacy for one who has received Major Orders.[104]

For the sake of clarity and brevity the relaxation of vows has been termed, throughout, *dispensation from vows.* This terminology, however, is not, strictly speaking, correct. The obligation of fulfilling a vow arises from the divine law. The obligations of the divine law are twofold. Some affect all men independently of any act of the human will, as, for instance, *Deus est honorandus.* Others affect only those who have voluntarily taken upon themselves such obligations, and, therefore, dependently on an act of the human will. In obligations of the first kind, all power of relaxation is denied even to the Roman Pontiff; he can simply infallibly interpret, and authentically declare, the divine law in this respect. Strictly speaking, not even the Roman Pontiff can *dispense* from obligations of the second kind, for he does not *relax* the obligation of the divine law. When a person makes a vow he voluntarily contracts an obligation towards God, and the act of the human will, by which this obligation is induced, cannot be changed *pro arbitrio,* but only with God's consent or permission. When the Roman Pontiff is said to *dispense* all he does is to *declare* that God consents to this changing, or retractation, of will, and that, thereby, the obligation, which arose in the divine law, ceases. A just cause must be present before the Pope can *validly* make even this *declaration,* for God's consent to such a change of will cannot be presumed except when there is a just cause for the change. God has wished the Pontiff to be endowed with this power, for the exercise of such power by the Supreme

[104] Canon 648.

Head of the Church is not only expedient at times, but also necessary, for, considering the frailty of human flesh, the imprudence and indiscretion of men, it happens, not unfrequently, that the fulfillment of many of the obligations voluntarily assumed by men is more injurious than beneficial.[105]

[105] Noldin, *Summa Theologiae Moralis,* I (ed. XIV), n. 117.

CHAPTER XI

Doubtful Impediments

Power of Dispensing

"Leges, etiam irritantes et inhabilitantes, in dubio juris non urgent; in dubio autem facti potest Ordinarius in eis dispensare, dummodo agatur de legibus in quibus Romanus Pontifex dispensare solet." (Canon 15.)

Doubt, in general, may be defined as *defectus judicii firmi.* Doubt, therefore, in its general acceptance, connotes the absence of a firm judgment. In its strict acceptance, doubt implies a total suspension of assent to either of two contradictory propositions, and may be defined as *"suspensio mentis assensus inter duas propositiones contradictorias."*[1] Any number of alternative propositions on the same subject may be in doubt at the same time; but, strictly speaking, the doubt is attached separately to each one, as between the proposition and its contradictory, that is, each proposition may or may not be true. The mind, when in a state of doubt in its strict sense, remains unsettled and undecided; it assents to neither proposition, it dissents from neither, since it does not possess a firm judgment.[2]

Doubt in the present context is not to be interpreted in this strict sense, but is to be understood of doubt in its wide sense. When the mind is in a state of doubt in this wide sense, the intellect actually assents either to the proposition or its contradictory, but *cum formidine errandi.*[3] Hence doubt, as used in canon 15, may be defined as: *"nu-*

[1] Cicognani, *Jus Canonicum,* II, p. 106.
[2] Cicognani, *o. c.,* p. 107.
[3] Noldin, *Summa Theologiae Moralis* (ed. XIV), I, n. 220, b.

tamen intellectus imperfecte adhaerentis uni de oppositis."[4] It does not exclude all adhesion to either proposition, but presupposes that assent is given to one part, but *cum formidine errandi.*[5] Such a doubt will be positive when there are grave reasons for and against the adhesion of the mind to the proposition. It will be negative when such grave reasons are absent. It is thus possible that a doubt may be positive on the one side, and negative on the other (Positivo-negative, or negativo-positive), that is, in cases where evidence on one side only is attainable and does not, of itself, amount to absolute demonstration.[6] Mere negative doubt is nothing more than ignorance.[7]

A doubt may be prudent or imprudent, according to the reasonableness or unreasonableness of the considerations on which the doubt is based. Finally, doubt may be either *dubium juris* or *dubium facti.* It is *dubium juris* when the object of the doubt is the existence or extension of a law; this doubt has to do immediately with the existence of the law itself, or its extension to a particular case:[8] strictly speaking it is a doubt as to the sense or extension of the law, while less strictly, but *proprie,* it is a doubt as to the existence of the law itself.[9] In a dubium facti the existence of the law and its extension to a particular fact are known with certainty, but there is not certainty as to the existence of that fact, or of all the circumstances required by law.[10]

Either of these two species of doubt may be objective, or merely subjective. It is objective when there is some-

[4] Marc, *Institutiones Morales Alphonsianae,* I, n. 38; Cf. St. Alphonsus, *Theologia Moralis,* lib. I, n. 67.

[5] Cf. Vermeersch-Creusen, *Epitome Juris Canonici,* II, n. 154.

[6] Cf. Marc, *o. c.,* n. 37; St. Alphonsus, *o. c.,* lib. I, n. 20.

[7] Genicot-Salsmans, *Institutiones Theologiae Moralis* (ed. X), I, n. 51; Noldin, *Summa Theologiae Moralis* (ed. XIV), I, n. 221; Marc, *l. c.*

[8] Cicognani, *Jus Canonicum,* II, p. 107; Noldin, *o. c.,* I, n. 221, 3.

[9] Vermeersch-Creusen, *o. c.,* I (ed. II), n. 86.

[10] Maroto, *Institutiones Juris Canonici* (ed. III), I, n. 230; Vermeersch-Creusen, *o. c.,* II, n. 154.

thing in the nature of things to respond to the doubt existing in the mind.[11] A doubt *per se* signifies something subjective, but if it resides in a mind possessed with due knowledge of the law it will be an objective doubt also; if the existence of the doubt is due *solely* to a defect of due knowledge it is merely a subjective doubt.[12] Objective doubt is required in the present context, while mere subjective doubt effects nothing juridically in the matter under discussion.

Applying canon 15 to the matter of matrimonial dispensations, it follows at once that when the existence of an impediment is doubtful by reason of a doubt of law, there is no need of a dispensation (*impedimentum non urget*), and the marriage can be celebrated once the doubt of law is established. If, however, the existence of an impediment, in a particular concrete case, is doubtful by reason of a doubt of fact only, there is need of a dispensation, which, however, the Ordinary can grant. If the doubt is a *dubium juris et facti simul*, it is clear that no dispensation is necessary.[13]

This doctrine of the New Law is practically in unison with that taught by canonists previous to the New Code. The power of Bishops over doubtful impediments was generally admitted. The present law is, however, the first written law on the matter. It has settled, once and for all, some controversies, and clarified some ambiguities, which were prominent in the writings of the older canonists. Under the old law many authors who extended the power of Bishops to doubts of fact, perhaps in deference to those who restricted it to doubts of law, spoke with caution, and were willing to withdraw their claim when there was a strong presumption in favor of the existence of the im-

[11] Cicognani, *o. c.*, II, p. 107.

[12] Blat, *Commentarium Textus Codicis Juris Canonici*, Lib. I, n. 72.

[13] Cerato, *Matrimonium* (ed. III), n. 22; Chelodi, *Jus Matrimoniale* (ed. III), n. 35, 4.

pediment.[14] But the New Code has given a radical solution. It is satisfied with the simple division of doubt into doubts of law and doubts of fact. In a doubt of fact, the Ordinary can dispense, independently of whether a presumption urges in favor of the impediment or not, provided there is a real solid dubium facti.

Canon 15 deals only with ecclesiastical laws, and, hence, in its application to marriage dispensations, only with impediments of the ecclesiastical law. Augustine [15] maintains that the term *leges* in canon 15 applies to all laws in general, but more especially to ecclesiastical laws. But this is not so. It can refer only to laws of ecclesiastical origin. This is clear from the inscription of the title in the Code, and, above all, from the whole context of the title.[16] Moreover, not even the Roman Pontiff can *dispense* from impediments of the natural or divine law, even when they are doubtful, for as long as there is not certainty as to the non-existence of an impediment of either of these two laws, it must be regarded as existing because of the certain danger that would otherwise be incurred.[17]

Dispensation From Doubtful Impediments

No dispensation is necessary where, in a particular case, the existence of an impediment of the ecclesiastical law is doubtful because of a doubt of law. There is question here of doctrinal doubt. The fact in the case may be certain, but there is not agreement among Theologians and Canonists as to whether an impediment to marriage results from that fact or not.[18] Strictly speaking, an impediment

[14] See Part I, chap. III, art. IV, of this work; Cf. Sanchez, *De Sancto Matrimonii Sacramento,* lib. VIII, dis. VI, n. 18; Gasparri, *De Matrimonio* (ed. III), I, n. 438; Wernz, *Jus Decretalium* (ed. 1904), IV, n. 620.

[15] *A Commentary on the New Code of Canon Law* (ed. III), I, p. 85.

[16] Cicognani, *o. c.,* II, p. 108; Blat, *o. c.,* lib. I, n. 72; Vlaming, *Praelectiones Juris Matrimonii* (ed. III), II, n. 401; Wernz-Vidal, *Jus Canonicum,* V, n. 413.

[17] Cappello, *De Sacramentis,* III, n. 202; Blat, *l. c.*

[18] Gasparri, *o. c.,* I, n. 261.

can be doubtful, by reason of a doubt of law, in two different ways. Theoretically it *could* be doubtful as to the existence of the law establishing an impediment in general. In practice, however, this is now inconceivable, for the number and species of marriage impediments now existing are clearly laid down in the New Code. But a doubt of law can, and does, arise in the second way, that is, where the doubt has to do, not with the existence, but with the extension of the law establishing an impediment. It is certain that priests and confessors can dispense, in urgent cases, only in "occult cases" of matrimonial impediments.[19] But it is disputed among canonists as to whether occult cases include impediments that are by nature public but occult in fact. The affirmative and negative opinions are defended by the various authors; each opinion is solidly probable, and, hence, there is a *dubium juris*. *Lex dubia non obligat* is a valid axiom in this respect, and hence, in practice, it is at present practically certain that priests and confessors can dispense, in urgent cases, from impediments that are public in nature, provided they are occult in fact.

Before an impediment can be considered doubtful, by reason of a doubt of law, it is necessary that the opinion favoring the non-existence of the impediment in the case be "*vere probabilis, communiter vel certe recepta tamquam probabilis a A. A.*"[20] Hence, it is not sufficient that there be merely a diversity of opinion among recognized authors. The arguments put forth by each division must enjoy internal probability, and the opinions themselves must be recognized as probable. But it is not necessary that the opinion in favor of the existence of the impediment be more probable than the contrary opinion, but it is sufficient that it be probable and accepted as such.[21] From this it is clear that there must be question of objective doubt. If one falsely thinks that there is a dubium juris, and de facto there

[19] Canon 1045, par. 3; Cf. Chap. IX of this work.
[20] Gasparri, *o. c.*, I, n. 262. Cf. Sanchez, *o. c.*, lib. VIII, dis. VI, n. 18.
[21] Gasparri, *l. c.*

is not, this does not militate against the existence of the impediment.

If marriage is contracted without a dispensation at a time when an impediment is doubtful, by reason of a doubt of law, and after the marriage it becomes certain, either through the accepted teaching of canonists, or through an official declaration of the Church, that an impediment does de facto exist in the circumstances, there is no need to become disquieted, or to obtain a *sanatio in radice,* for the marriage is *certainly* valid, provided there was a real dubium juris at the time it was contracted.[22]

While it is true that an impediment does not urge when there is a doubt of law, and that marriage can be contracted in the case without a dispensation, it does not pertain to the office of the parish priest, and, a fortiori, of the confessor, to *declare,* in a concrete case, that such a doubt exists. Hence, when there is question of contracting marriage, and there is no urgency in the case, the parish priest or confessor should not apply the solution of canon 15 on their own authority, but should, if time and convenience permit, have recourse to the Ordinary, who will not dispense, but declare that there is no impediment, and that the marriage can be celebrated at once. If the Ordinary himself should think it expedient, and should time permit, he is to recur to the Holy See itself. In a case of urgency, however, the parish priest and confessor are to form their own conscience, and acquire practical certainty, by utilizing the reflex principle (recognized by canon 15), "*Lex dubia* (dubio juris) *non obligat.*"[23]

When the existence of an impediment is doubtful, in a particular case, by reason of a doubt of fact, a similar course of procedure is not permissible, but a dispensation

---

[22] Gasparri, *l. c.;* Cerato, *o. c.*, n. 22, f; Chelodi, *Jus Matrimoniale,* n. 35.

[23] Gasparri, *o. c.*, I, n. 262; Cappello, *De Sacramentis,* III, n. 202; Wernz-Vidal, *Jus Canonicum,* V, n. 154; Vlaming, *Praelectiones Juris Matrimonii* (ed. III), II, n. 401; Chelodi, *o. c.*, n. 35; Cerato, *o. c.*, n. 22; Holy Office, 18 September 1852, Pollottini, *Collect. Omnium Conclus. et Res.*, VII, p. 528.

must be obtained before the marriage can be celebrated.[24] In a doubt of fact the existence and extension of the law itself are certain, but it is doubtful whether the fact which, if present, would certainly induce an impediment, is de facto present in a concrete case or not. It is certain that consanguinity in the third degree of the collateral line begets a diriment impediment to marriage,[25] but if it is really doubtful whether Titius and Sempronia are de facto related in this degree of consanguinity, there is a dubium facti, and a dispensation must be obtained.

Heiss[26] and De Smet[27] maintain that when a merely impedient impediment is doubtful by reason of a doubt of fact there is no need of a dispensation, and the marriage can be contracted at once, for, since there is question only of the liceity of an act, on the principles of Moral Theology the parties can pass from speculative doubt to practical certainty. However, it seems that a dispensation is also necessary in case of doubtful impedient impediments, even though the validity of the marriage is not involved. An impedient impediment is not *merely* a disposition necessary for the liceity of an act. It is a circumstance, as De Smet himself teaches,[28] which directly affects marriage *qua contractus est,* and is not, consequently, a disposition necessary merely for marriage *quo sacramentum est.* An impedient impediment, therefore, contains a positive element, a prohibition imposed by a positive act of the Church.[29] This element is just as positive in the impedient impediment as in the diriment, though not so strong or so extensive, and continues to exist, as a positive prohibition, until it is positively removed. Moreover, canon 15 clearly implies this. It includes all laws, but lays special stress on "leges irritantes et inhabilitantes." Hence, in its application to

---

[24] Canon 15.
[25] Canon 1076, par. 2.
[26] *De Matrimonio,* tract. I, sect. II, tit. 12, n. 1.
[27] *De Sponsalibus et Matrimonio* (ed. IV), II, n. 471.
[28] *O. c.,* II, n. 463.
[29] Canon 1036.

the question under discussion, it includes also impedient impediments, and clearly shows that a dispensation is necessary in a doubt of fact.[30]

If the existence, therefore, of any impediment of the ecclesiastical law becomes doubtful by reason of a doubt of fact, previous to the celebration of marriage, the first thing to do is to endeavor to settle the doubt one way or the other. If the doubt remains after diligent inquiry has been made, provided it is a "*dubium positivum, prudens, discretum, grave, et fundatum*,"[31] a dispensation *ad cautelam* is to be sought from the Ordinary.[32] If the doubt is, however, a merely negative one, or an indiscreet and unfounded doubt, it is to be disregarded after diligent examination has established it as such, and the marriage is to be proceeded with.[33]

All Ordinaries are competent to dispense from impediments that are doubtful by reason of a doubt of fact, provided the impediment in question, if it certainly existed, would be one from which the Holy See is accustomed to dispense.[34] It will be noted that all Ordinaries are endowed with this dispensatory power, and, therefore, that the major superiors of exempt clerical religions enjoy this faculty also.[35]

Ordinaries, however, can dispense only when the impediment in question (if it did exist with certainty) is one from which the Holy See is accustomed to dispense (*dispensare solet*). Hence, the first class of impediments which come under the category of those excluded by canon 15 consists of those impediments which, though doubtful, would, if they certainly existed, belong to the natural or

[30] Cf. Maroto, *Institutiones Juris Canonici* (ed. III), I, p. 243; Cicognani, *Jus Universum*, II, p. 109.

[31] Feije, *De Impedimentis et Dispensationibus Matrimonialibus* (ed. III), n. 636.

[32] Genicot-Salsmans, *Institutiones Theologiae Moralis* (ed. X), II, n. 481.

[33] Genicot-Salsmans, *l. c.*

[34] Canon 15.

[35] Canons 198, pars. 1, 2; 488, n. 8.

divine law, whether certainly or doubtfully. Hence, Ordinaries cannot dispense in doubtful cases from the impediment of *ligamen,*[36] or of consanguinity in any grade of the direct line,[37] or from *impotentia,* when the impotency in the case is certain,[38] for these impediments certainly belong to the natural or divine law. Neither can they dispense from consanguinity in the first degree of the collateral line, for this impediment *probably* belongs to the divine law.[39] If impotency, in a particular case, is, however, doubtful, either by reason of a doubt of law or doubt of fact, marriage is not to be impeded.[40]

The second class of impediments that are placed outside the ambit of the power conferred by canon 15 are those impediments of the ecclesiastical law from which the Roman Pontiff is not wont to dispense. It will be noted that the legislator uses the words *dispensare solet,* and not *dispensare potest,* or *dispenset.* The word *solet* conveys the idea of usualness, or of a more or less degree of frequency. Some authors interpret this phrase *dispensare solet* too extensively, and, consequently, attribute to Ordinaries more extensive powers than canon 15 guarantees or warrants. Of the ecclesiastical impediments, Cerato and Ferreres [41] would exclude only those two excluded by canon 1043, namely, the impediments resulting from the Priesthood, and from affinity in the direct line, matrimonio consummato. De Smet at first [42] likewise excluded only those two impediments, but later [43] extended the limits of exclusion in accordance with the more restrictive and true interpretation. The opinion of Cerato and Ferreres is unwarranted

---

[36] Canon 1069, par. 2.

[37] Canon 1076, par. 3.

[38] Canon 1068, par. 1.

[39] Canon 1076, par. 3; Vlaming, *o. c.*, II, n. 401.

[40] Canon 1068, par. 2; No dispensation is granted in such a case, but the Ordinary will simply *declare* that marriage is to be permitted.

[41] *Matrimonium* (ed. III), n. 148; *Compendium Theologiae Moralis* (ed. III), II, n. 952.

[42] *De Sponsalibus et Matrimonio* (ed. III), II, n. 755.

[43] *O. c., Supplementum,* I (ed. IV), n. 755.

by the Code, for if the legislator had intended to bestow such an extensive faculty he should have used the word "*dispenset*" in place of the phrase *dispensare solet*. Hence, in accordance with the interpretation given by most authors, and which is the only interpretation warranted by the words of the law, the faculty given by canon 15 extends to all impediments of ecclesiastical law except the following: (a) *Age;* (b) *Sacred Orders,* especially that of the Priesthood; (c) *Solemn vow;* (d) *Raptus;* (e) *Public crime of conjugicide;* (f) *Affinity in the direct line,* especially when the marriage which occasioned the affinity had been consummated.[44] Noldin [45] adds to this list the impediments of consanguinity in the collateral line *tangente primum gradum,* and spiritual relationship *inter levatum et levantem.* De Smet [46] does not seem to be correct when he claims that the law on the form of marriage falls under the dispensatory power conferred by canon 15, for it can scarcely be said that the Roman Pontiff is accustomed to dispense (*dispensare solet*) from the form of marriage.

The faculty of dispensing from doubtful impediments is valid only in favor of the subjects of the dispenser.[47] Canon 15 inserts no extensive qualification as do canons 1043 and 1313. Hence, a bishop can dispense in favor of those who have a domicile or quasi-domicile in his diocese, even though they are actually outside his diocese at the time of dispensing.[48] He can also dispense in favor of *vagi* who are *hic et nunc* within the confines of his diocese.[49] *Peregrini* do not come under this power of the Bishop *directly,* for they are not his subjects. Maroto [50] would also include *peregrini* among the Bishop's subjects in this

[44] Vlaming, *Praelectiones Juris Matrimonii* (ed. III), II, n. 393 bis; Cappello, *o. c.*, III, n. 202; Blat, *o. c.*, Lib. I, n. 72; De Smet, *l. c.*

[45] *De Jure Matrimoniali,* n. 121, a.

[46] *O. c.*, II, n. 755.

[47] Canon 201, par. 1.

[48] Canon 201, par. 3.

[49] Canons 94, par. 1; 198, par 1; De Smet, *o. c.*, n. 773; Maroto, *Institutiones Juris Canonici* (ed. III), I, n. 305.

[50] *L. c.*

respect, but this does not seem correct, especially in view of canon 1313, par. 1, which clearly distinguishes between *subjects* and *peregrini,* and expressly includes the latter among those capable of being dispensed by Ordinaries from non-reserved vows.[51] Canon 15 makes no such extension. *Pereregrini,* however, may come under the local Ordinary's power *indirectly,* as happens when a local Ordinary dispenses one of his subjects from a relative impediment, and thereby, as a consequence, dispenses a peregrinus who is bound by that relative impediment.[52]

Lastly, this faculty enjoyed by Ordinaries is operative both for public and occult impediments, and for the external and the internal forum,[53] and, consequently, the doubt which existed under the old law, regarding the extension of this power to the external forum and to public impediments, is now definitely settled.[54]

The faculty is valid both *ad matrimonium contrahendum,* and *ad matrimonium convalidandum.* If marriage is contracted by persons who are bound by an impediment that is doubtful by reason of a doubt of fact, the marriage is probably valid, and is to be presumed valid until such time as the invalidity is proven with certainty. But the marriage is also probably invalid, and, therefore, a dispensation should be obtained, at least *in ordine ad debitum petendum,* and to provide for the certain validity of the marriage.[55]

TRINO DEO ET UNI
PER QUEM LEGUM CONDITORES JUSTA DECERNUNT
HONOR ET GLORIA IN SAECULORUM SAECULA
AMEN

[51] De Smet, *o. c.*, II, n. 774, 3.

[52] De Smet, *o. c.*, II, n. 774, 2.

[53] Canon 202, par. 3.

[54] Cf. Giovino, *De Dispensationibus Matrimonialibus,* consult. CCCXXXVII, n. 2; Heiss, *o. c.*, p. 197; St. Alphonsus, *Theologia Moralis,* lib. VI, n. 902; Wernz, *Jus Decretalium* (1904), IV, n. 620, nota 93; Ojetti, *Synopsis Rerum Moralium et Juris Pontificii,* II, n. 2373; Gasparri, *De Matrimonio* (ed. III), I, n. 438.

[55] Cf. Feije, *o. c.*, n. 636; De Smet, *o. c.*, II, n. 427, nota 1.

BIBLIOGRAPHY

I

SOURCES

Acta Apostolicae Sedis, 19 vols., Romae, 1909–1927.

Acta Sanctae Sedis, 41 vols., Romae, 1865–1908.

Codicis Juris Canonici Fontes cura Emi Petri Card. Gasparri editi, vols. I–IV, Romae, 1923–1926.

Collectanea Sacrae Congregationis de Propaganda Fide, 2 vols., Romae, 1907.

Corpus Juris Canonici, ed. Richter-Friedberg, 2 vols., Lipsiae, 1922.

Jaffe, Philippus, *Regesta Pontificum Romanorum,* 2 vols., Berolini, 1851.

Mansi, Joannes Dominicus, *Sacrorum Conciliorum Nova et Amplissima Collectio,* ed. H. Welter, 51 vols., Paris & Leipzig, 1901–1924.

Martin, Conrad, *Omnium Concilii Vaticani Documentorum Collectio,* Paderbornae, 1873.

Pallottini, Salvatora, *Collectio Omnium Conclusionum et Resolutionum quae in Causis propositis apud Sacram Congregationem Cardinalium S. Concilii Tridentini Interpretum,* 17 vols., Romae, 1868–1893.

II

REFERENCE WORKS

Aichner, Simon, *Compendium Juris Ecclesiastici,* 2 ed., *Brixinae,* 1887.

Aertyns, Joseph C., C. SS. R., *Theologia Moralis,* 7 ed., Paderbornae, 1907.

Amat, Thaddeus, *A Treatise on Matrimony According to the Doctrine and Discipline of the Catholic Church,* San Francisco, 1864.

Arregui, Antonius M., *Summarium Theologiae Moralis ad recentem Codicem Juris Canonici Accomodatum,* 7 ed., Bilbao, 1922.

Augustine (Bachofen), Chas. P., *A Commentary on the New Code of Canon Law,* 3 ed., 8 vols., St. Louis, 1921–1924.

Ayrinhac, H. A., *Marriage Legislation in the New Code of Canon Law,* New York, 1918.

———. *General Legislation in the New Code of Canon Law,* New York, 1923.

Bangen, Joannes Henricus, *Instructio Practica de Sponsalibus et Matrimonio in Usum Sacerdotum Curatorum,* Monasterii, 1858.

Barbosa, Augustinus, *Tractatus Varii,* London, 1660.

Bargilliat, M., *Praelectiones Juris Canonici,* 37 ed., 2 vols., Parisiis, 1923–1924.

Bellarminus, Robertus, *Opera Omnia,* 8 vols., Neapoli, 1872.

Benedict XIV, *De Synodo Dioecesana,* 2 vols., Romae, 1806.

———. *Institutiones Ecclesiasticae,* 3 vols., Romae, 1784.

Billot, Ludovicus, *De Ecclesiae Sacramentis Commentarius in Tertiam Partem S. Thomae,* 2 vols., Romae, 1897.

Binterim, Anton J., *Die Vorzüglichsten Denkwürdigkeiten de Christ-Kathollischen Kirche,* 17 vols., Mainz, 1830.

Blat, Albertus, O. P., *Commentarium Textus Codicis Juris Canonici,* 8 ed., 5 vols., Romae, 1921–1924.

Brillaud, P. J., *Traite Pratique des Empêchements et des Dispenses de Mariage,* Paris, 1871.

Brys, J., *De Dispensatione in Jure Canonico praesertim apud Decretistas et Decretalistas usque ad medium Saeculum Decimum Quartum,* Brugis-Wetteren, 1925.

Busembaum, Hermann, S. J., *Medulla Theologiae Moralis,* 2 vols., Parisiis, 1863.

Caillaud, L'Abbe, *Manuel des Dispenses, à L'usuage du Curé, du Confesseur et de L'official,* 5 ed., Paris, 1882.

Cappello, Felix, S. J., *Tractatus Canonico-Moralis de Sacramentis juxta Codicem Juris Canonici,* 3 vols., Taurinorum Augustae, 1921–1926.

Cerato, Prosdocimi Sac., *Matrimonium a Codice Juris Canonici integre Desumptum,* 3 ed., Patavii, 1920.

Chelodi, Joannes, *Jus de Personis juxta Codicem Juris Canonici,* Tridenti, 1922.

———. *Jus Matrimoniale juxta Colicem Juris Canonici,* 3 ed., Tridenti, 1921.

Cicognani, Hamletus J., *Jus Canonicum,* vols. 1, 2, Romae, 1925.

Cocchi, Guidus, *Commentarium in Codicem Juris Canonici ad Usum Scholarum,* 3 ed., Vols. I, II, III, IV, V, VI, VIII, Taurinorum Augustae, 1925.

Collet, L'Abbe Pierre, *Institutiones Theologiae Moralis,* 5 vols., Lugduni, 1768.

———. *Traité des Dispenses,* 3 vols., Louvain, 1760.

Cronin, Charles J., *The New Matrimonial Legislation,* Romae, 1908.

D'Annibale, Josephus, *Summula Theologiae Moralis,* 3 vols., Romae, 1892.

De Becker, Joseph, *De Sponsalibus et Matrimonio Praelectiones Canonicae,* 2 ed., Lovanii-New York, 1903.

De Episcoporum in Dispensationibus super Matrimonii Impedimentis Potestate Dissertatio adversus Libellum A., Faventiae, 1789.

Degni, F., *Del Matrimonio,* Torino, 1926.

De Justis, Vincentius, *De Dispensationibus Matrimonialibus,* libri tres in 1 vol., Lucae, 1726.

De Lugo, Joannes, *De Sacramentis in Genere,* Venetiis, 1718.

———. *Disputationes Scholasticae et Morales,* 8 vols., Parisiis, 1868–1869.

Dens, P., *Tractatus de Sponsalibus et Matrimonio,* Mechliniae, 1861.

De Smet, Aloysius, *Commentarius in Decretum de Sponsalibus et Matrimonio,* Brugis, 1908.

———. *De Sponsalibus et Matrimonio,* 4 ed., 2 vols., Brugis, 1923.

———. *Praxis Matrimonialis ad usum Parochi et Confessarii,* Brugis, 1920.

Esmein, A., *Le Mariage et le Droit Canonique,* 2 vols., Paris, 1891.

Fagnanus, Prosperus, *Commentaria in Quinque Libros Decretalium,* 4 vols., Venetiis, 1696.

Fanfani, P., Ludovicus, I., *De Jure Parochorum ad Normam Codicis Juris Canonici,* Taurini-Romae, 1924.

Farrugia, Nicolaus, *De Matrimonio et Causis Matrimonialibus Tractatus Canonico-Moralis juxta Codicem Juris Canonici,* Taurini-Romae, 1924.

Feije, Henricus Joannes, *De Impedimentis et Dispensationibus Matrimonialibus,* 3 ed., Lovanii, 1885.

Ferraris, Lucius F., *Bibliothecae Prompta Canonica, Juridica, Moralis, Theologica,* 8 vols., Romae, 1885.

Ferreres, Joannes B., *Institutiones Canonicae,* 2 ed., 2 vols., Barcinone, 1920.

———. *Compendium Theologiae Moralis ad Normam Codicis Juris Canonici,* ed. sexta post Codicem, 3 vols., Barcinone, 1925.

Gasparri, Petrus, *Tractatus Canonicus de Matrimonio,* 3 ed., 2 vols., Parisiis, 1904.

Genicot-Salsmans, *Institutiones Theologiae Moralis,* ed. decima, tertia post Codicem Juris Canonici, 2 vols., Bruxellis, 1922.

———. *Casus Conscientiae,* 4 ed., Bruxellis, 1922.

Gennari, Casimirus Card., *Consultations de Morale, de droit Canonique, et de Liturgie,* 2 vols., Paris, 1908.

Giovine, Petrus, *De Dispensationibus Matrimonialibus Consultationes Canonicae,* 2 vols., Neapoli, 1863.

Heiner, Franz, *Grundriss des Katholischen Eherechts,* 6 ed., Münster, 1910.

Heiss, M., *De Matrimonio Tractatus Quinque Usui Venerabilis Cleri Americani Accomodati,* Monachii, 1861.

Hergenröther-Hollweck, *Lehrbuch des Katholischen Kirchenrechts,* Freiburgi Brisgoviae, 1905.

Hilling, N., *Das Eherecht des Codex Juris Canonici,* Freiburgi Brisgoviae, 1927.

King, James I., *The Administration of the Sacraments to Dying Non-Catholics,* Washington, D. C., 1924.

Knecht, Augustinus, *Grundriss des Eherechts,* Freiburgi Brisgoviae, 1918.

Konings-Putzer, *Commentarium in Facultates Apostolicas,* Ilchestriae, 1893.

Kubelbeck, William J., *The Sacred Penitentiaria and Its Relations to Faculties of Ordinaries and Priests,* Washington, D. C., 1918.

La Croix, Claudius, *Theologia Moralis,* 2 vols., Venetiis, 1766.

Laurin, Franciscus, *Introductio in Jus Matrimoniale,* Vindobonae, 1895.

Lehmkuhl, Augustinus, *Theologia Moralis,* 12 ed., 2 vols., Freiburgi Brisgoviae, 1914.

Leitner, Martin, *Lehrbuch des Katholischen Eherechts,* 3 ed., Paderborn, 1920.

Le Plat, Jud., *Dissertatio Canonica de Sponsalibus et Matrimoniorum Impedimentis,* Lovanii, 1784.

Ligouri, St. Alphonsus, *Theologia Moralis,* 10 vols., Ratisbonae, 1879.

Linneborn, Joannes, *Grundriss des Eherechts nach dem Codex Juris Canonici,* ed. secunda et tertia, Paderborn, 1922.

Lupus, Christianus, *Synodorum Generalium ac Provincialium Decreta et Canones,* 13 vols., Venetiis, 1724–1729.

Marc, Clement P., *Institutiones Morales Alphonsianae,* 2 vols., Romae, 1885.

Maroto, Philippus, *Institutiones Juris Canonici ad Normam Novi Codicis,* 3 ed., 2 vols., Romae, 1921.

Mastrius, Bartholomeus, *Theologia Moralis,* Venetiis, 1671.

Matharan, M. M., *Casus de Matrimonio,* Parisiis, 1893.

———. *Theologia Moralis,* 2 vols., Neapoli, 1910.

McNicholas, John T., *The New Legislation on Engagements and Marriage, Commentary on the Decree "Ne Temere,"* Philadelphia, 1908.

Michalicka, Wenceslas Cyrill, *Judicial Procedure in Dismissal of Clerical Exempt Religious,* Washington, D. C., 1923.

Migne, J. P., *Patrologia Graeca,* 161 vols., Parisiis, 1858–1864.

———. *Patrologia Latina,* 221 vols., Parisiis, 1847–1870.
Noldin, H., S. J., *De Jure Matrimoniali juxta Codicem Juris Canonici,* Lincii, 1919.
———. *Summa Theologiae Moralis juxta Codicem Juris Canonici,* 14 ed., 3 vols., Oeniponte, 1921–1922.
Oesterle-Brenninkmeyer, *Dispensatiebevoegdheden van Huwelijksbeletselen in Dringende Gevallen,* Leuven, 1921.
Ojetti, B., *In Jus Ante-Pianum et Pianum ex Decreto "Ne Temere,"* Romae, 1908.
———. *Synopsis Rerum Moralium et Juris Pontificii,* 3 ed., Romae, 1909–1914.
Palmieri, Dominicus, S. J., *Tractatus de Matrimonio Christiano,* Romae, 1880.
Perrone, Joannes, S. J., *De Matrimonio Christiano,* 3 vols., Leodii, 1861.
Petrovits, Joseph J. C., *The New Church Law on Matrimony,* 2 ed., Philadelphia, 1926.
Pighi, Jo. Bapta., *De Sacramento Matrimonii Tractatio Canonico-Moralis,* 2 ed., Veronae, 1921.
Pignatelli, Jacobus, *Consultationes Canonicae,* 11 vols. in 4, Coloniae Allobrogum, 1700.
Piontek, Cyrillus, O. F. M., *De Indulto Exclaustrationis necnon Saecularizationis,* Washington, D. C., 1925.
Pirhing, Ernricus, *Jus Canonicum Novo Methodo Explicatum,* ed. novissima, Dilingen, 1722.
Planchard, M. J., *Dispenses Matrimoniales Règles a Suivre pour les Demander, les Interpréter les Mettre a Execution,* Angouleme, 1882.
Pompen, J., *Tractatus de Dispensationibus et de Revalidatione Matrimonii,* Amstelodami, 1897.
Pontius, Basilius, *De Sacramento Matrimonii,* Bruxellis, 1627.
Prümmer, Dominicus M., O. P., *Manuale Theologiae Moralis,* 3 ed., 3 vols., Friburgi Brisgoviae, 1923.
———. *Manuale Juris Canonici,* 3 ed., Friburgi Brisgoviae, 1922.
Pyrrhus Corradus, *Praxis Dispensationum Apostolicarum,* Venetiis, 1735.
Reiffenstuel, Anacletus, *Jus Canonicum Universum,* 4 vols., Venetiis, 1735.
Reuter-Lehmkuhl-Umberg, *Neo Confessarius Practice Instructus,* Friburgi Brisgoviae, 1919.
Rigantius, Josephus B., *Commentaria in Regulas, Constitutiones, et Ordinationes Cancellariae Apostolicae,* 4 vols. in 2, Coloniae-Allobrogum, 1751.
Rosset, Michael, *De Sacramento Matrimonii Tractatus Dogmaticus, Moralis, Canonicus, Liturgicus, et Judiciarius,* Parisiis, 1895–1896.
Rossi, Josephus, *De Matrimonii Celebratione juxta Codicem Juris Canonici,* Romae, 1924.
Rohling, Augustinus, *Medulla Theologiae Moralis,* Sti. Ludovici, 1875.
Sanchez, Thomas, S. J., *Disputationum de Sancto Matrimonii Sacramento Libri Tres,* Antverpiae, 1626.
Santi, Franciscus, *Praelectiones Juris Canonici juxta Ordinem Decretalium,* 5 vols., in 2. Ratisbonae, 1886.
Sasse, Joannes, S. J., *Institutiones Theologicae de Sacramentis Ecclesiae,* 2 vols., Friburgi Brisgoviae, 1898.
Scavini, Petrus, *Theologia Moralis Universa ad Mentem S. Alphonsi M. de Ligouri, Pio IX Pontifici M. Dicata,* ed. undecima, 4 vols., Mediolani, 1869.

Scherer, Rudolph R. Von, *Handbuch des Kirchenrechts*, 2 vols., Graz und Leipzig, 1898.

Schmalzgrüeber, Franciscus, S. J., *Jus Ecclesiasticum Universum*, 12 vols., Romae, 1843–1845.

Schulte, Friedrich J., *Handbuch des Katholischen Eherechts*, Giessen, 1855.

Sebastiani, Nicholaus, *Summarium Theologiae Moralis ad Codicem Juris Canonici Accomodatum*, ed. Sexta minor, Taurinorum-Augustae—Romae, 1921.

Simon, J., O. S. M., *Faculties of Pastors and Confessors for Absolution and Dispensation According to the Code of Canon Law*, New York, 1922.

Slater, Thomas, *A Manual of Moral Theology*, 2 vols., New York, 1908.

Stiegler, Albert Maria, *Dispensation Dispensationswesen und Dispensationsrecht im Kirchenrecht*, Mainz, 1901.

Tanquerey, Adrian, *Synopsis Theologiae Moralis et Pastoralis*, 8 ed., 3 vols., Romae, 1921.

Thomassinus, Ludovicus, *Vetus et Nova Ecclesiae Disciplina*, 10 vols., Magontiaci, 1787.

Van de Burgt, F. P., *Tractatus de Dispensationibus Matrimonialibus*, Sylvae-Ducis, 1855.

Van Den Acker, *Decreti "Ne Temere" de Sponsalibus et Matrimonio Interpretatio*, Buscoduci, 1909.

Vecchiotti, S. M., *Tractatus Canonicus de Matrimonio ex Opere Card. J. Soglia*, Taurini, 1868.

Vermeersch, Arthurus, S. J., *De Forma Sponsalium et Matrimonii post Decretum "Ne Temere,"* Brugis, 1908.

———. *Theologiae Moralis Principia, Responsa, Consilia*, 3 vols., Parisiis-Romae, 1923.

Vermeersch-Creusen, *Epitome Juris Canonici cum Commentariis ad Scholas et ad Usum Privatum*, 2 ed., 3 vols., Mechliniae-Romae, 1925.

Villien, A., *L'Empêchement de Mariage. Sa Notion Juridique D'Apres L'Histoire*, apud *Le Canoniste Contemporain Discipline Actuelle de L'Eglise*, vol. XXVI (1903).

Vlaming, Th. M., *Praelectiones Juris Matrimonii ad Normam Codicis Juris Canonici*, 3 ed., 2 vols., Bussum in Hollandia, 1919–1921.

Watkins, Oscar D., *Holy Matrimony*, London, 1895.

Wernz, Franciscus Xav., *Jus Decretalium ad Usum Praelectionum in Scholis Textus Canonici sive Juris Decretalium*, 6 vols., Romae, 1904.

Wernz-Vidal, *Jus Canonicum, auctore P. Francisco Wernz, S. J. ad Codicis Normam Exactum opera P. Petri Vidal ejusdem Societatis Sacerdote*, vols. II, V, Romae, 1923–1925.

Wood, Charles W., *Marriage*, Manchester, 1887.

Wouters, Ludovicus, C., SS. R., *Commentarius in Decretum "Ne Temere" ad Usum Scholarum Compositus*, 2 ed., Amstelodami-Galopiae, 1909.

Woywod, Stanislaus, O. F. M., *A Practical Commentary on the Code of Canon Law*, 2 vols., New York, 1925.

Zitelli, Zephyrinus, *Apparatus Juris Ecclesiastici*, Romae, 1888.

———. *De Dispensationibus Matrimonialibus*, Romae, 1887.

III

PERIODICALS

American Ecclesiastical Review, The, Philadelphia, 1889—

Archiv für Katholisches Kirchenrecht, Mainz, 1857—

Irish Ecclesiastical Record, The, Dublin, 1864—
Gregorianum, Romae, 1920—
Homiletic and Pastoral Review, The, New York, 1900—
Il Monitore Ecclesiastico, Romae, 1888—
Jus Pontificium, Romae, 1920—
Le Canoniste Contemporain, Paris, 1877—
Nouvelle Revue Theologique, Paris, 1856—
Revue du Clergé Français, vols. 1-103, Paris, 1895-1920.
Theologisch-Praktische Quartalschrift (quoted in the footnotes as *Linzer Quartalschrift*), Linz, 1832—

IV

ABBREVIATIONS

A. S. S.—*Acta Apostolicae Sedis.*
A. K. K.—*Archiv für Katholisches Kirchenrecht.*
A. S. S.—*Acta Sanctae Sedis.*
E. R.—*American Ecclesiastical Review, The.*
Fontes—*Codicis Juris Canonici Fontes.*
H. P. R.—*Homiletic and Pastoral Review, The.*
I. E. R.—*Irish Ecclesiastical Record, The.*
L. Q. S.—*Linzer Quartalschrift.*
M. E.—*Il Monitore Ecclesiastico.*
Mansi—Mansi, J. D., *Sacrorum Conciliorum Nova et Amplissima Collectio.*
N. R. T.—*Nouvelle Revue Theologique.*

Universitas Catholica Americae

WASHINGTONII, D. C.

FACULTAS JURIS CANONICI

1926-1927

No. 45

DEUS LUX MEA

TITULI

QUOS

AD DOCTORATUS GRADUM

IN

JURE CANONICO

APUD UNIVERSITATEM CATHOLICAM AMERICAE

CONSEQUENDUM

PUBLICE PROPUGNABIT

GIRALDUS MICHAEL O'KEEFFE

SACERDOS DIOECESIS

ANGELORUM ET SANCTI DIDACI

JURIS CANONICI LICENTIATUS

HORA IX A. M. XXVII MAII MCMXXVII

TITULI

JUS CANONICUM

I.	De Historia Juris Canonici.	
II.	De Jure Publico Ecclesiae.	
III.	De Dissertatione.	
IV.	Canones 1–7	De Canonibus Introductoriis.
V.	Canones 8–24	De Legibus Ecclesiasticis.
VI.	Canones 25–30	De Consuetudine.
VII.	Canones 31–35	De Temporis Supputatione.
VIII.	Canones 36–62	De Rescriptis.
IX.	Canones 63–79	De Privilegiis.
X.	Canones 80–86	De Dispensationibus.
XI.	Canones 87–107	De Personis in Genere.
XII.	Canones 118–123	De Juribus et Privilegiis Clericorum.
XIII.	Canones 329–349	De Episcopis.
XIV.	Canones 445–450	De Vicariis Foraneis.
XV.	Canones 451–470	De Parochis.
XVI.	Canones 492–498	De Erectione et Suppressione Religionis, Provinciae et Domus Religiosae.
XVII.	Canones 499–517	De Superioribus et de Capitulis Religiosorum.
XVIII.	Canones 518–530	De Confessariis et Cappellanis Religiosorum.
XIX.	Canones 542–571	De Novitiatu.
XX.	Canones 572–586	De Professione Religiosa.
XXI.	Canones 592–612	De Obligationibus Religiosorum.
XXII.	Canones 738–744	De Ministro Baptismi.
XXIII.	Canones 1019–1034	De iis quae Matrimonii celebrationi praemitti debent.
XXIV.	Canones 1035–1080	De Impedimentis Matrimonialibus.
XXV.	Canones 1081–1093	De Consensu Matrimoniali.
XXVI.	Canones 1094–1103	De Forma Celebrationis Matrimonii.
XXVII.	Canones 1110–1117	De Matrimonii Effectibus.
XXVIII.	Canones 1118–1127	De Dissolutione Matrimonii.
XXIX.	Canones 1307–1315	De Votis.
XXX.	Canones 1960–1989	De Causis Matrimonialibus.
XXXI.	Canones 1990–1992	De Casibus Exceptis a Regulis traditis pro Causis Matrimonialibus.
XXXII.	Canones 1993–1998	De Causis Contra Sacram Ordinationem.
XXXIII.	Canones 2147–2156	De Modo Procedendi in Remotione Parochorum Inamovibilium.
XXXIV.	Canones 2157–2161	De Modo Procedendi in Remotione Parochorum Amovibilium.
XXXV.	Canones 2162–2167	De Modo Procedendi in Translatione Parochorum.
XXXVI.	Canones 2168–2181	De Modo Procedendi contra Clericos non residentes; contra Clericos concubinarios.

XXXVII.	Canones 2182–2185	De Modo Procedendi contra Parochum in adimplendis paroecialibus Officiis negligentem.
XXXVIII.	Canones 2186–2194	De Modo Procedendi in Suspensione ex Informata Conscientia infligenda.
XXXIX.	Canones 2215–2219	De Poenarum notione, speciebus, interpretatione atque applicatione.
XL.	Canones 2236–2240	De Poenarum Remissione.

ROMAN LAW

INSTITUTES OF GAIUS, INSTITUTES OF JUSTINIAN

LAW RELATING TO PERSONS

XLI. The Sources of Roman Law.
XLII. Personality, its nature and conditions.
XLIII. Liberty, its nature, origin, and end.
XLIV. Slavery, its origin, nature, and end.
XLV. Patria Potestas.
XLVI. Tutela et Cura.

LAW RELATING TO THINGS

XLVII. Distinction of Things.
XLVIII. Modes of acquiring res singulae ex Jure Gentium.
XLIX. Modes of acquiring res singulae ex Jure Civili.
L. The Acquisition of Things through others.
LI. Ownership in its relation to the Power of Alienation.
LII. Modes of acquiring things titulo universali.

INTERNATIONAL LAW

LIII. The Drago Doctrine.
LIV. The Monroe Doctrine.
LV. Immunities and Privileges of Diplomatic Agents.
LVI. Extradition.
LVII. The Jurisdiction of Rivers.
LVIII. The Jurisdiction of Vessels.
LIX. Intervention and non-Intervention.
LX. Enemy Property in time of War.

Vidit Facultas:

PHILIPPUS BERNARDINI, S.T.D., J.U.D., Decanus.
LUDOVICUS H. MOTRY, S.T.D., J.C.D., a Secretis.
VALENTINUS T. SCHAAF, O.F.M., J.C.D.
FRANCISCUS J. LARDONE, S.T.D., J.U.D.
MANOEL DE OLIVEIRA LIMA, L.H.B.

Vidit Rector Universitatis:

✠THOMAS J. SHAHAN, S.T.D., J.U.L., LL.D.

VITA

Gerald Michael O'Keeffe was born in Kilfinane, Co. Limerick, Ireland, on June 21, 1900. His primary education was received in the National Schools of that town. In September, 1916, he entered St. Colman's College, Fermoy, Co. Cork, Ireland, and, having matriculated as a student of the National University, he entered the Seminary of St. John, Waterford, Ireland, in September, 1919. He was ordained to the Priesthood on June 21, 1925, by the Rt. Rev. Bernard Hackett, D. D., Bishop of Waterford.

In October, 1925, he matriculated at the Catholic University of America, Washington, D. C., and registered in the School of Canon Law. At the end of the academic year 1925-26, the degrees of Bachelor and Licentiate in Canon Law were conferred upon him. In partial fulfillment of the requirements for the degree of Doctor in Canon Law, he wrote this dissertation.

The writer takes this opportunity to express his gratitude to the members of the Faculty of Canon Law for the kind assistance given him. He also wishes to thank the assistant librarians for the freedom accorded him in consulting the valuable works of the University Library.

www.ingramcontent.com/pod-product-compliance
Lightning Source LLC
LaVergne TN
LVHW050249080826
844660LV00012B/612
* 9 7 8 0 8 1 3 2 2 2 3 4 9 *